ALSO BY ANDREW BACEVICH

After the Apocalypse: America's Role in a World Transformed

American Conservatism: Reclaiming an Intellectual Tradition (editor)

The Age of Illusions: How America Squandered Its Cold War Victory

Twilight of the American Century

America's War for the Greater Middle East: A Military History

Breach of Trust: How Americans Failed Their Soldiers and Their Country

Washington Rules: America's Path to Permanent War

The Limits of Power: The End of American Exceptionalism

The Long War: A New History of U.S. National Security Policy Since World War II (editor)

The New American Militarism: How Americans Are Seduced by War

American Empire: The Realities and Consequences of U.S. Diplomacy

The Imperial Tense: Prospects and Problems of American Empire (editor)

ALSO BY DANIEL A. SJURSEN

Patriotic Dissent: America in the Age of Endless War

Ghost Riders of Baghdad: Soldiers, Civilians, and the Myth of the Surge

PATHS OF DISSENT

PATHS OF DISSENT

SOLDIERS SPEAK OUT AGAINST AMERICA'S MISGUIDED WARS

ANDREW BACEVICH AND
DANIEL A. SJURSEN, EDITORS

Metropolitan Books
Henry Holt and Company
New York

Metropolitan Books
Henry Holt and Company
Publishers since 1866
120 Broadway
New York, New York 10271
www.henryholt.com

Metropolitan Books® and m® are registered trademarks of
Macmillan Publishing Group, LLC.

Distributed in Canada by Raincoast Book Distribution Limited

Portions of Erik Edstrom's "As American as It Gets" previously appeared in his memoir *Un-American: A Soldier's Reckoning of Our Longest War* (New York: Bloomsbury, 2020).

The views expressed in Buddhika Jayamaha's "When Grunts Complain" are those of the author and do not necessarily reflect the official policy or position of the United States Air Force Academy, the Air Force, the Department of Defense, or the US government. PA# USAFA-DF-2022–26.

Library of Congress Cataloging-in-Publication data is available.

ISBN 9781250870179

First Edition 2022

Designed by Kelly S. Too

Printed in the United States of America

1 3 5 7 9 10 8 6 4 2

In memory of
Ian Fishback,
Major, US Army
1979–2021

CONTENTS

PATHS OF DISSENT

INTRODUCTION

REFLECTIONS ON MILITARY DISSENT

Andrew Bacevich

In response to the 9/11 attacks, the United States plunged willy-nilly into a war that political authorities explicitly characterized as global. Few observers at the time objected to the formulation. For a globally preeminent power, a war undertaken on a scale acknowledging no limits seemed eminently plausible.

To say that things haven't gone well since is to engage in considerable understatement. Interventions begun with high hopes of quick, decisive victories led instead to protracted, inconclusive, and exceedingly costly campaigns. The world's self-proclaimed greatest military found success elusive. In the case of Afghanistan, twenty years of exertions culminated in unambiguous "strategic failure," a judgment offered by none other than the chairman of the Joint Chiefs of Staff.

The American people have yet to reckon with the implications of military miscalculations and disappointments stretching back to the beginning of this century. Lest they be charged with failing to "support the troops," ordinary Americans shy away from inquiring too deeply into the cumulative errors of judgment and execution that have marred recent US military misadventures. And if mere citizens are disinclined to confront those failures, members of the nation's political and military elite are even less willing to do so.

A conviction that such a reckoning is both necessary and long overdue inspired this book. *Paths of Dissent* offers insights into how and why recent US military efforts have gone so badly astray. Flagrant malpractice by those at the top inflicted untold damage on the troops we ostensibly esteem, on populations US policymakers vowed to liberate, and ultimately on our own democracy. The adverse effects of war are by no means confined to the immediate arena in which fighting occurs.

By their very nature, wars are complex. Authoritative truth regarding any war is necessarily hard to establish. Arriving at even an approximation of the truth requires tapping into varied and perhaps even contradictory perspectives.

In practice, when it comes to staking out claims to truth about any war, those who wield power—presidents, cabinet secretaries, senior advisors, and top field commanders—occupy positions of privilege. They possess the biggest megaphones. Granted preferred access to the media and opportunities to publish widely reviewed and read memoirs, they disseminate their own inevitably self-exculpatory versions of the story. More often than not, they obscure rather than clarify.

Danny Sjursen and I conceived this book to give voice to a different group: veterans of our post-9/11 conflicts who in a time of war freely volunteered to serve and then developed second thoughts about the conflicts in which they participated. We invited these military dissenters to bear witness to what they saw, did, and learned. We asked them in particular to reflect on what had brought them to the military in the first place, and how the realities they encountered might have differed from their expectations. Given our nation's notable propensity for war, combined with a general aversion to actually donning the uniform—those who serve tend to come only from "military families" and the economically deprived—the candid firsthand testimonials contained in this book amount to an instructive exercise in civic education.

With just a single exception, everyone whose words appear in this book is a veteran of our nation's post-9/11 wars. Several completed multiple combat tours. In many respects, they are a diverse group. They are male and female, of varied ethnicities and upbringings, veterans of service in different branches of the armed forces. Some fought as foot soldiers; others served as artillerymen, combat engineers, intelligence specialists, and in assorted other capacities. Some were commissioned officers, others members of the rank and file. A few briefly tasted a simulacrum of victory, participating in the initial, hopeful stages of wars where actual success was destined to remain out of reach. Others arrived after stalemate had long since set in.

The one exception is myself. I am a veteran, but not of Iraq or Afghanistan. I participated in a different war, though one equally misguided, mismanaged, and wasteful: Vietnam. And I have come to appreciate the connecting tissue linking my own experience of a half century ago to that of these much younger veterans.

My tour of duty in Vietnam occurred during the war's later phases, after the turning point of the 1968 Tet Offensive, and after it had become abundantly clear (even to a green-as-grass lieutenant) that events were headed toward a less-than-satisfactory outcome. Subsequent decades, spent first on active duty and then as a teacher and writer, brought me to a deeper understanding of the Vietnam War and sharpened my appreciation of what it signified. With the passage of time, I concluded that classifying Vietnam as either a mistake or a tragedy amounts to little more than subterfuge. To use those terms is to evade a much deeper and more troubling truth. In fact, from its very earliest stages until its mortifying conclusion, America's war in Vietnam was a crime.

That realization played a large role in propelling me on my own belated path toward dissent, a role that has never come naturally to me. By upbringing and early education, I am inclined to defer to authority. Four years of intense socialization as a cadet at West Point reinforced this tendency. As a youth and young adult, even into middle age, I was inclined to give the benefit of the doubt to the official lines handed down from on high, whether by high-ranking government officials, senior military commanders, or cardinal archbishops of my church. Their ascent to positions atop the relevant hierarchy testified to their personal worthiness and to the basic integrity of the institutions over which they presided. Or so I believed, in the face of ever more abundant evidence to the contrary.

Some of us learn quickly, others less so. It has always been my lot to be a slow learner.

On that score, the wars in Afghanistan and Iraq served

for me as a final tipping point. The latter in particular, an illegitimate war of choice utterly divorced from US security interests and the well-being of the American people, played a decisive role in completing my education.

The invasion of Iraq in March 2003 and the debacle that ensued brought into sharp focus the disastrous implications of the interventionist turn in US policy that had followed the end of the Cold War. Midway through the first decade of the twenty-first century, with US forces bogged down in two unwinnable wars and various other lesser contingencies, it became evident that policymakers and generals alike had either forgotten the mistakes that doomed US efforts in Vietnam or were seemingly intent on repeating them.

Ignorance, incompetence, and mind-boggling hubris combined to produce the cataclysm of the Vietnam War. Those same qualities pervaded the planning and implementation of the several campaigns on which the United States embarked in the aftermath of 9/11. That the United States had resumed its march to military folly within my own lifetime was beyond distressing. It was cause for mourning.

My personal role in Vietnam had been utterly inconsequential. So, too, was my contribution to the post-Vietnam reforms implemented to purge the United States Army of toxins it had absorbed during that war. Informed by visions of war as primarily a technological undertaking, those reforms turned out to be wildly misconceived. Instead of restoring a badly abused institution to health, they instead introduced a different set of ills. Above all, by fostering delusions of military mastery, they set the stage for grotesque misjudgments.

In this way, America's wars in Iraq and Afghanistan are

stepchildren of Vietnam, as are the various other post-9/11 campaigns that have destroyed the US military's reputation for prowess and the nation's claim to global primacy. Many aspects of Vietnam remain contentious, but of this we can be certain: rarely has an excruciating experience yielded such a paltry harvest of learning.

The contributors to this collection experienced firsthand the consequences of this inability (or refusal) to learn. While leaders of governments and armies are well practiced at concealing folly beneath a veneer of purposefulness, the writers lending their talents to this book strip away that veneer, bearing witness to truths that politicians and generals would prefer to remain hidden. In doing so, they perform an invaluable service for their country.

* * *

WHILE MILITARY DISSENT may not be as American as apple pie, it is a motif that recurs throughout US history. Whether consciously or not, post-9/11 military dissenters are part of a long if underappreciated tradition.

Most Americans take it for granted that those serving in the armed forces of the United States are compliant, if not altogether politically inert. As a broad judgment, this is mostly correct. Both individually and collectively, US troops routinely demonstrate the discipline that is an essential predicate to even minimal military effectiveness. They obey orders and are reliably subservient to the chain of command.

But mostly is not entirely. And the exceptions can be illuminating.

That said, it is important to distinguish military dissent from other forms of protest. As used here, military dissent is not synonymous with opposition to war in general. For our purposes, military dissenters are *serving soldiers or combat veterans who actively oppose military policies that they deem ill advised, illegal, or morally unconscionable.*

Not every act of resistance by a current or former service member qualifies. Opposition stemming from bureaucratic rivalries—the 1949 "Revolt of the Admirals," for instance, in which leaders of the US Navy fought against budget reallocations that favored the Air Force—does not fit our definition. Genuine military dissent transcends parochial considerations. A similar judgment applies to unrest involving GIs stationed overseas following the end of World War II. In no mood to comply with War Department plans for an orderly demobilization, the troops wanted to go home immediately, and rioted on a massive scale. This was not dissent; it was a de facto mutiny, and it succeeded.

Genuine military dissent is patriotic. It expresses a determination to right wrongs, especially policies that victimize US troops without yielding any discernible benefit to the nation. Military dissenters are not self-seeking. Their commitment is to a cause larger than themselves.

So military dissent can't be a cause casually adopted and then quickly abandoned. It becomes an ongoing obligation or calling. It entails a sustained and inherently political commitment, whether carried out alone or as part of a collective.

Military dissent is not easy. While on active duty, military dissenters often annoy, exasperate, or provoke the chain of command. Some may face disciplinary action, including courts-martial. Others eventually resign in protest or are involuntarily separated from active duty. Upon returning to civilian life, military dissenters carry on their activism in myriad ways. They join antiwar organizations. They lobby elected officials and, if invited, testify before Congress. They may run for office themselves. They teach, bringing their first-hand experiences into the classroom. To reflect more deeply on their encounter with war, they write memoirs, compose novels and poetry, and make documentary films. In books, essays, and interviews, they take issue with US military policies, whether past or present. In short, they persist.

During the Vietnam War, military dissent was sustained and widespread, involving many thousands of soldiers, sailors, airmen, and marines. It took many forms, some of which intersected with an array of pathologies at odds with "good order and discipline." Military dissent did not cause but cannot be easily separated from those pathologies: pervasive indiscipline, widespread drug use, acute racial tension, and an epidemic of violence that often targeted superiors.

These maladies were not limited to a particular service or cohort, nor were they confined to the war zone itself. The effects were felt at home and abroad, on land and at sea, wherever US forces were to be found. And Vietnam-induced military dissent, even more broadly, transcended the boundaries separating service life from the civilian world. It both drew on and fed the unrest that was roiling American society during the 1960s and 1970s. In that sense, it was part of a larger social movement centered on the rejection of traditional norms and a loss of confidence in established authority.

Generals and admirals at the time struggled without noticeable success to suppress this contagion. Soon enough, it became evident that restoring good order and discipline would require a political solution. In 1973, President Richard Nixon and a compliant Congress provided that solution, scrapping the concept of the citizen-soldier that since the Revolution had formed the basis of the American military system and replacing it with what came to be called the "all-volunteer force."

* * *

THE ALL-VOLUNTEER FORCE (AVF) was a late-twentieth-century reincarnation of the "standing army" that America's founders in the late eighteenth century had decried as a threat to liberty. In the wake of the Vietnam War, a generation of political leaders desperate for an alternative to conscription disregarded the founders' concerns. To induce young men and women to serve, the new military system emphasized better pay and benefits, while reducing "chickenshit," the day-to-day hassles that made so much of military life for ordinary GIs something between a trial and a total waste of time. Henceforth, military service would take on the trappings of a profession, with even recruits treated less like disposable day laborers and more like valued employees. It was tacitly understood by all that there would be no more Vietnams.

The experiment got off to a rocky start, as attracting qualified volunteers in sufficient numbers to fill the force proved a challenge. By the 1990s, however, the AVF seemed to be working well enough, albeit without having undergone a test more serious than the Persian Gulf War of 1991.

That conflict, lasting only a handful of weeks, entailed only the barest amount of close combat, none of it sustained. Enemy resistance proved to be tepid at best. Even so, civilian and military leaders alike, not to mention a cheerleading media, chose to enshrine Operation Desert Storm as an unprecedented triumph that validated post-Vietnam military arrangements. With that, the AVF took its place alongside Social Security and Medicare as politically untouchable. Americans congratulated themselves on having devised a military system that was both extraordinarily effective and also nicely suited to a democratic republic with a limited appetite for sacrifice. Everyone in uniform and out could take satisfaction with the result.

Soon enough, however, events exposed such satisfaction as misplaced. The real test of the AVF came after 9/11. Responding to the attacks on New York and Washington, an administration confident of US military supremacy embarked upon an open-ended Global War on Terrorism. Centered initially in Afghanistan and Iraq, the GWOT thrust US troops into extensive combat against determined adversaries. The resulting campaigns dragged on for years.

Once it became clear that decisive victory was not in the offing, comparisons with Vietnam inevitably materialized. Most of those comparisons, though, were off target for a multitude of reasons. For our purposes, two differences in particular stand out.

The first has to do with the public response to wars gone awry. Americans had reacted with anger and dismay when the war in Vietnam went badly but proved remarkably tolerant of the disappointments encountered in Afghanistan and Iraq. In twenty-first-century America, to "support the troops" was a civic duty to which all citizens at least paid lip service. Yet this did not imply any requirement to attend to what the troops were actually called upon to do and with what results. Supporting the troops might entail striking a posture, but it imposed no substantive obligations.

So while many Americans disagreed with the course of post-9/11 military policies, especially as the wars dragged on with precious little to celebrate, nothing remotely comparable to the Vietnam-era antiwar movement developed. The nation might have been nominally "at war," but ordinary citizens tended to other priorities. That the absence of a draft might have contributed to this collective apathy regarding failed wars figures as at least a possibility.

The second important reason why comparisons with Vietnam do not hold up is that while US troops in Iraq and Afghanistan did not prevail, neither did they buckle. The AVF proved to be largely immune to the maladies that had virtually destroyed the armed forces of the United States during the late 1960s and early 1970s. Even as multiple combat tours took their toll on *individual* soldiers and marines, durability emerged as an *institutional* hallmark of the AVF. In other words, just as the American public did not revolt against manifestly defective post-9/11 military policies, neither did the rank-and-file troops called upon to implement those policies.

As the post-9/11 conflicts dragged on, phrases such as *endless wars* or *forever wars* found their way into the American lexicon. Politicians campaigning for high office vowed to terminate these wars. Once elected, however, they discovered other priorities. Rather than ending wars, they perpetuated them in modified form.

Through it all, the post-Vietnam military system remained sacrosanct. In effect, protecting the AVF from critical scrutiny took precedence over achieving success on the battlefield or holding policymakers accountable for persisting in futile military misadventures.

That the all-volunteer force meshes with US national security policy while also conforming to American democratic ideals became one of the Big Lies to which political, military, corporate, and media elites routinely paid tribute. While disagreement on this point might be permitted—sporadic calls for restoring the draft or enacting a program of national service were heard—such eccentric proposals gained no discernible traction beyond the occasional mention in op-eds. Out there in Afghanistan and Iraq, the AVF might not have been delivering the intended results, but at home it remained agreeably convenient.

That was the political and military environment in which the contributors to this volume volunteered to serve their country: a time of prolonged armed conflict that exacted a terrible toll while making at best a negligible contribution to international security or the well-being of the American people.

* * *

Ian Fishback, to whose memory this volume is dedicated, was one of those volunteers who subsequently saw through the Big Lie and confronted it. Over the course of his military career, Fishback exemplified all that is best in the American tradition of military dissent. Yet the arc of his life also testifies to the costs that principled dissent can exact. In November 2021, shortly before *Paths of Dissent* went into production, he died. He was just forty-two years of age.

Should a memorial honoring the US troops who lost

their lives in Iraq and Afghanistan one day grace the Washington Mall, Major Fishback's name will surely deserve to be included—this, despite the fact that he died years after leaving active duty. He sacrificed his life for this nation no less than did the several thousand who fell in battle.

For a brief moment in the early years of our post-9/11 wars, Fishback achieved a measure of fame (or, to some, notoriety) by calling attention to the torture and prisoner abuse practiced by US forces in the field. He was a uniformed whistleblower, who took seriously the values of "Duty, Honor, Country" he had learned at West Point. A classic straight arrow, Ian found intolerable even the slightest deviation from what the soldierly code of conduct required.

Encountering credible allegations of widespread misconduct by US troops, Fishback—as was his duty—brought those allegations to the attention of members of his chain of command. When they tried to brush him off or suggested that pursuing the matter might adversely affect his career, he refused to be silenced.

With very senior military officers thereby complicit (in Fishback's judgment) in a cover-up, he pressed on, bringing the matter to the attention of human rights organizations, members of the press, and eventually sympathetic legislators such as Senator John McCain (R-AZ). The eventual upshot was congressional passage of the Detainee Treatment Act of 2005, prohibiting the "cruel, inhuman, or degrading treatment or punishment" of any person detained by the US government. That December, President George W. Bush grudgingly signed the bill into law. It should rightly have been called the Ian Fishback Act.

The same year, *Time* magazine's annual list of the one hundred people most influential in transforming the world included then-captain Fishback and quoted a letter he had written to McCain: "I would rather die fighting than give up even the smallest part of the idea that is America."

Not long thereafter, however, Ian's personal and professional life began to unravel. An inability or refusal to compromise imposes burdens that can become unbearable.

Unaware of the demons that were afflicting him, Danny Sjursen and I invited him to contribute to this collection. He had demonstrated impressive moral courage at a moment when such courage had been in notably short supply: that's what we wanted him to write about.

Ian accepted our invitation and eventually submitted an essay. It differed radically from what we had expected. The piece charged US government agencies with subjecting him to ongoing and relentless persecution of the most vicious sort, naming several very senior general officers as his chief tormentors. Yet the essay lacked the kind of specific detail needed to make it credible. Dates, places, Ian's own actions in response—he provided none of these. Reluctantly, I deemed the piece unpublishable. When I notified Ian that we would not be using it, he did not reply.

I do not regret that decision. But with Ian's passing, and knowing more about the travails of his recent years, I find myself haunted by two particular portions of the essay. In the first, Ian recalls being told by a senior officer at Fort Bragg, North Carolina, that "nothing sticks to people in the Beltway." As that officer saw it, the military itself is innocent of blame: when bad things occur in distant war zones, it's the politicians who are getting away with murder. Ian wrote that he found this buck-passing statement "extraordinarily dishonorable."

Of course, the officer's words were not entirely off the mark. Civilian leaders do demonstrate a remarkable aptitude for dodging responsibility when things go wrong. Yet in our era of very long and futile wars, nothing much sticks to senior military commanders either. Even today, the accountability that Ian Fishback sought in 2005 remains missing in action, as the lamentable conclusion of the Afghanistan War reminds us. The generals who presided over this massive failure have gotten away scot-free. In effect, they have conspired with the politicians to evade responsibility.

The other remarkable passage was the harsh judgment with which Ian concluded his essay. "America is not free," he wrote, "and the Constitution is a model of American hypocrisy." The gap between the bitter note of despair in that indictment and Ian's prior professed willingness to sacrifice his life for the American idea brought me up short. To dismiss his charge as overwrought would be too simplistic. Ian has earned the right to be taken seriously.

In the modern era, all wars are alike in certain respects, but each has its own distinctive attributes. The terminology that recurs over and over again in America's post-9/11 wars—*improvised explosive devices*, *traumatic brain injuries*, *post-traumatic stress disorder*—hints at some of the qualities of those conflicts. So, too, does the epidemic of suicides among serving soldiers and recent veterans. But of greater significance still is the persistent indifference of the American people.

This volume pulls back the veil on that collective indifference, allowing a diverse group of participants in those wars to reflect on all that has been lost and at what cost. The testimony of these military dissenters is of inestimable value. Like Ian Fishback, they deserve to be heard.

AS AMERICAN AS IT GETS

Erik Edstrom

Four columns abreast, a platoon of cadets marched between the buildings at West Point. A centipede of dour skinheads.

"Smirk off, new cadets!" snapped the older ones in charge of our training. Smiles denoted insubordination. There were none. The most fearsome cadets wielded their voices like a whip. When they singled you out, "got in on your ass," it felt like an electric convulsion, or that squirmy feeling when the dentist drills a nerve.

It was a cheerless place.

The summer leading into the first cadet year at West Point is known as Beast Barracks—Beast for short. It marks the beginning of one's military indoctrination. For me, Beast took place in the summer of 2003. I was seventeen years old. My first year at the academy, as for most of my classmates, was characterized by fear, intimidation, exhaustion, and infantilizing rituals.

Early on, we were sent to Robinson Auditorium—Rob Aud, in cadet vernacular—for a "motivational spirit briefing."

On the way, our cadet platoon sergeant—two years older than us—marched us to cadence:

> Left right, left right, left right *kill*!
> Left right, left right, you know I will.
> I went to the mosque, where all the terrorists pray,
> I set up my claymore, *and blew 'em all away*!
>
> Left right, left right, left right *kill*!
> Left right, left right, you know I will.
> I went to the store where all the women shop,
> Pulled out my machete, *and I began to chop*!
>
> Left right, left right, left right *kill*!
> Left right, left right, you know I will.
> I went to the playground where all the kiddies play,
> I pulled out my Uzi, *and I began to spray*!

I didn't know what to make of it. Was it badass? Was I some kind of tough guy now? Across the path of stone pavers, we reached Thayer Hall, a peculiar, near-windowless building once used for equestrian practice, back when *cavalry* meant horses, not helicopters and armored vehicles. We were led inside and took seats in the auditorium.

Severe-looking officers took turns mounting the stage. We didn't know who they were or what they did, but they radiated gravity. Authoritative presence. I wanted that.

"All of you who graduate from here will almost certainly be sent to war in Iraq or Afghanistan," said a lieutenant colonel, doing what appeared to be a rendition of the famous opening scene in *Patton*—the one where General Patton galvanizes his troops with a speech about going through "the Hun" like "shit through a goose." The lieutenant colonel continued, "I want you to look within and ask yourself if you are willing to lead men and women in combat. It's not for everyone and if you want to quit, do everyone a favor—just stand up and walk out of this auditorium right now."

No one budged.

"Your class, the West Point Class of 2007, has the auspicious honor of being the first class to apply to West Point after 9/11. That moment was a call to action. You, the men and women sitting in this auditorium, answered that call."

Hoots and hooahs from the new cadets.

"That is true patriotism—the essence of what it is to be American. Now it's time to share a motivational video so you can see what some of our forward-deployed troops are doing to win this war. Are you *motivated*?"

To this we responded with our well-rehearsed chant:

"M-ma-ma-ma-mo-motivated."

"New cadets, are you *dedicated*?"

"D-de-de-de-de-dedicated."

The lights dimmed. We heard the recognizable opening chords of "Bodies" by Drowning Pool, basically the theme song for the "War on Terror."

Let the bodies hit the floor.
Let the bodies hit the floor.

The auditorium went wild. Ravenous screams. My skin turned to gooseflesh. The hairs on my arms stood erect. The anticipation and adrenaline were amplified: this was what we had come here for. The video began.

A highlight reel of death and destruction. Supernova nighttime explosions in an Iraqi city. M1 Abrams tanks rolling through Baghdad. Dismounted infantrymen patrolling dusty, rubble-strewn streets, communicating with hand and arm signals.

An AC-130 Spectre gunship is flying a large orbit around its objective: a couple of sedans and a beat-up pickup. A small assemblage of people stand jaw-jacking around them. So *killable*. Unbeknown to them, they are seconds from death. The crosshairs are on them, center mass. The Bofors 40 mm antiaircraft gun begins pounding them, literally to pieces. Through the thermal lens, a yard sale of body parts. The heat signature shows streaks of white—splashes of blood and chunks of still-warm flesh scattered around the engagement area.

We cheered, practically frothing at the mouth.

A man flees the scene—a "squirter." He starts running. The gunner switches to the 25 mm Gatling gun and hoses him down. A snail trail of blood. A video game, but not. The camera pans out, revealing a Jackson Pollock painting made of gore.

Where was the popcorn? We were loving it. Finish him!

Different scene. First-person shooter. A .50-cal machine gunner cranks hot, saltshaker-sized shells at a building. Anti-tank missiles explode. Now the screen is pixelated and green. Night-vision goggles. Soldiers on a night raid. Stack formation beside a mud shanty. Flash-bang grenades are tossed inside. Bright lights and deafening sounds. The soldiers flow through the "fatal funnel" into a room, surprising what appears to be a family. Their faces reveal what can only be called a pants-shitting expression.

My classmates and I reached a fever pitch of feral screams. Hoots. Applause. Glee.

At a place like West Point, you couldn't help but get excited at the prospect of shooting, bombing, and invading. It was presented as a borderline pornographic affair. Maybe we cheered because everyone was doing it. Maybe because we didn't want to be seen as "unmotivated"—a term slung around with the intensity of a slur. Or maybe we had already developed a taste for bloodshed.

Whatever sorcery drove us to mania, we accepted it. We embraced it. After all, this was West Point, the world's most celebrated military academy. It's hard to find an institution more iconically American than West Point, and it's hard to find Americans "more American" than West Point cadets. A book by journalist David Lipsky about West Point cadets is titled *Absolutely American*. We certainly didn't want to be anything less than absolute in our ideological devotion to the cause.

Whatever was happening in this auditorium was as "American" as it gets. And I wanted to belong. I wanted to make friends. I wanted my future soldiers to respect me. I wanted to be a winner. I would never quit.

I screamed until it hurt.

You're welcome, Middle East. Tell us, how would you like your freedom: large, extra-large, or supersize?

* * *

THERE ARE A handful of moments in life—inflection points, inciting incidents, liminal thresholds, event horizons, whatever you want to call them—that are so powerful they shift our entire frame of reference, forcing us to see the world, and perhaps ourselves, differently. They shatter the old truths, revealing that the compass we had trusted to direct us was broken all along.

There, in that West Point auditorium, I experienced one of those moments. The profession of political violence—my chosen career path—was no longer a romantic abstraction held at arm's length. It was messy, violent, and required near-absolute devotion to a pair of beliefs: that the people our country was killing *deserved it*; and that the costs—the attendant horrors of military occupation—were, somehow, *worth it*. The moment I cheered for contextless Kill TV was the moment I became capable of celebrating ignorance and glorifying barbarity.

I had a motivational quote sticky-tacked to the faux-wood bookshelf in my room:

> Somewhere a true believer is training to kill you. He is training with minimum food and water, in austere conditions, day and night. The only thing clean on him is his weapon. He doesn't worry about what workout to do—his rucksack weighs what it weighs, and he runs until the enemy stops chasing him. The true believer doesn't care how hard it is; he knows that he either wins or dies. He doesn't go home at 1700; he is home. He only knows the cause. Now. Who wants to quit?

Now I, too, was becoming a true believer. A fanatic. An American supremacist.

My classmates and I arrived young, most of us still teenagers. Like blank paper, we were ready to receive whatever the military wanted to imprint upon us. And even though I was, in a legal sense, a minor, the topics we dealt with were major—and complex. Devilishly more complex than the boilerplate *we are good, they are bad* absolutist messages used by the military to recruit clueless, trusting children. At my core, I trusted the institution. I trusted that my classmates and I would be used as a force for good, even if that didn't fully square with killing people who had nothing to do with 9/11, living in countries our government had not formally declared war against, for reasons that even the academy had trouble explaining.

As was true for many of my classmates, my reasons for joining the military were a conflated mix of economic necessity and idealistic do-goodery. It wasn't necessary to pore over Census Bureau data or read books about income inequality written by Nobel Prize–winning economists to see that the socioeconomic cracks in American society were plentiful and widening. In a world where college is a form of mandatory certification for many desirable vocations, I wanted a degree and the social mobility that it enabled. But no matter how invested my parents were in my future, the family college fund was empty. Not a single dollar. Meanwhile, two years of stocking shelves on the weekend at the local grocery store for $7.40 an hour wouldn't cover even two months of tuition.

The fear of joining America's ever-growing precariat has been motivation enough for two-thirds of college students to leverage themselves in debt, sometimes for decades. But there are other ways to pay for college. One such option is the military. Only later would I realize that this is a perverse carrot to dangle before you: trade college funding for the formative years of your life. In the richest country on earth, you may literally have to kill, or die, for a decent education.

And yet, a stint in the military also felt like a good idea on its own merits. Serving in the American military provides a new identity and, with it, a special higher class of citizenship. I took the cue from Pa, my step-grandfather, a World War II veteran who was sometimes treated like Audie Murphy by appreciative churchgoers after Sunday service.

Pa wasn't some decorated war hero or eminent general. He had no war wounds. He'd spent the war as an administrator at a station hospital in the United Kingdom. But that was enough. Enough to be respected—maybe even revered—for the rest of his life. All this just for doing his job half a century earlier. I liked the idea of being on the receiving end of such veteran worship. A recipient of the hefty social subsidies heaped upon America's military service members.

The extreme psychosocial dynamics of America's military fetish do not translate to other public service professions. Imagine an alternate universe where the stories we tell one another are different and it's the IRS agents who get to board the plane first. Maybe it's they who get to ask, as if entitled, for "IRS discounts" at chain restaurants and theme parks. People stop tax collectors in the street to thank them for their service. "Just part of the job, ma'am," says one taxman, smug as hell. There are IRS Appreciation Day truck sales. SUPPORT THE IRS bumper stickers. TAXES: THE PRICE WE PAY FOR CIVILIZATION, proclaims a T-shirt sporting an American flag with one money-green horizontal stripe, a version of the Blue Lives Matter iconography. Just before kickoff at the IRS Bowl, tax collectors step up to the fifty-yard line, pyrotechnics exploding in the background, as sixty thousand proud Americans rise to their feet and sing the national anthem. And when honest, salt-of-the-earth tax collectors pass away after a lifetime of faithful service to our country, they receive a twenty-one-gun salute and are buried with a copy of this year's federal budget, perfectly balanced.

If serving as an IRS agent were the status job—if it received the same social perks as being in the US military—maybe America would be better at collecting taxes. Maybe we would have more funds for development, infrastructure, education, health care, climate change mitigation. But we don't. Instead, the military is prioritized, and as a result, we have more shiny military toys and more unnecessary, counterproductive wars.

* * *

THE 9/11 ATTACKS, too, were a compelling factor in my decision. Like nearly everyone, I was swept up in the hysteria of the times. Seeing the towers collapse on TV during my high school chemistry class forced me to ask myself a hard question: Would I do anything about it? Who would I be if, at this moment of national need, I refused to answer the call?

Of course, the same line of questioning could be applied toward any complex and urgent problem. There are countless causes worthy of people's time and devotion. It is a uniquely American answer to look at the problems that face our country—the climate crisis, systemic racism, a broken health-care system, extreme income and wealth inequality, a public education system befitting a developing country, cringeworthy public services and infrastructure—and conclude that what really requires our time, attention, and trillions of taxpayer dollars is a series of wars unbound by time or geography.

Despite having never visited West Point, I applied nowhere else. And when I arrived, my indoctrination began.

Military indoctrination is the voluntary surrender of one's own identity to join a profession that often takes away the human dignity of others by force. Through repetition, service members have their values, behaviors, and identity recalibrated with the ultimate aim of making them willing to kill or be killed in political violence without thinking about it too much. It is the construction of blind faith in the state and the deconstruction of any critical thinking that could stand in opposition to the state's aims.

The academy gave careful treatment to facts that were likely to make cadets feel embarrassed by or skeptical about the state, especially the military adventurism that we were about to partake in. Instead, we were trained to believe that we should be concerned only with things we could immediately influence—our conduct, and the conduct of those around us. The message was: keep your head down and focus on your warrior tasks and drills. Also: soldiers are made to win wars, not think about them.

A famous 1962 address from General Douglas MacArthur illustrates this point well. "Others will debate the controversial issues, national and international, which divide men's minds," he told cadets at West Point. "These great national problems are not for your professional participation or military solution. Your guidepost stands out like a tenfold beacon in the night: Duty, Honor, Country."

There it is. Our job was to focus on *proximate outputs*—a uniform prepared for inspection, a faster two-mile run—rather than judging what really mattered, the ultimate outcomes, like whether our collective actions were statistically "moving the needle" on safety for Americans at home, and whether, if deployed, the military could do it in an ethical, legal, and cost-effective way. Burdened by seventeen-hour days of exercise, classwork, military rituals, and study, we scarcely had time for reflection. We did not take our responsibilities lightly, and we trained with vigilance. Without any understanding of the world outside West Point or what I'd ultimately be serving after graduation, I redoubled my efforts, devoting myself to the task at hand.

I derived a good amount of satisfaction from the process. Hiking the ski slope in winter with ninety pounds on my back to prepare for summer military training was a good way to make great friends. These shared burdens brought people together. I felt deeply loyal to my classmates—to the corps of cadets. I felt like I was part of something bigger than myself.

Even now, I still think fondly of rowing on the Hudson River in the predawn darkness with the self-proclaimed "fastest eight in Army crew history." Golden light would stream across the hilltops and saddles of the Hudson River valley, dispelling stubborn pockets of shade as our team shouldered the boat at the end of a hard morning practice, panting, exhausted. It felt as though we were beating the day before it even had the chance to start.

I received coaching from older cadets, like Sam. A year ahead of me, Sam wasn't the strongest on the team, but he was determined and consistent, eventually ending up as the stroke of the heavyweight varsity eight. He taught me to honor the work, always strive to beat my average, and prioritize technique over dumb, brute force. These were good lessons to learn.

Our team spent racing season in threadbare Econovans, driving up and down the Eastern Seaboard along I-95: Pennsylvania, Massachusetts, Virginia, Delaware, with spring training often in Florida. Our hands were bloodied and bandaged. We lived on Nutella-and-banana sandwiches, and were bound together by the common pursuit of "better." A remarkable sense of brotherhood was built in unremarkable places.

Most alumni speak positively of growth during their four years at West Point. So it was for me: In this span of time, I transitioned from self-doubt to self-confidence, from insecurity and mediocrity to grit and conviction. I had grown as a leader and was now capable of issuing clear instructions to a company of 120 new cadets. I was proving myself physically strong, capable, and resilient. I had passed some of the most demanding Army courses, including Special Forces Assessment and Selection at the age of nineteen. The more success I had, the more devoted I became.

One decision led to the next, often more extreme one almost effortlessly. *Why go to West Point unless you want to lead troops in combat? If you wanted to push papers, you could have done so for more pay, with a better lifestyle, elsewhere.* The logic extended in the same direction. *If you're going to go infantry, why not join the Rangers or Special Forces, and work with better-trained troops?* Knowing there was something more to strive for was seduction enough to pursue it. In those moments, everything made sense.

Aim high. Train. Achieve. Repeat.

With the greatest conviction, I channeled all my energy onto a course toward direct combat.

* * *

On graduation day, I received my diploma from Dick Cheney, the soft-handed architect of the War on Terror. It was clear that those flabby hands would never carry out the rough deeds ordered by his administration. He was leaving that dirty work for us. I pinned on my infantry branch insignia, swore my oath, and drove away, putting West Point in the rearview mirror with a sense of both excitement and sadness. Castle Grayskull wasn't all bad, and I had made some incredible friends. But it was not long before the illusion fell apart. Bearing witness to the human costs of America's War on Terror started almost immediately, and it hasn't stopped in the fourteen years since.

At my first duty station in Fort Carson, Colorado, while serving as the staff duty officer, I got a call in the middle of the night. A soldier had slit his wrists with a razor blade.

His mutilated arms looked like a grid of bloody squares. Lines going both vertically and horizontally, six inches up his wrist. He had not cut himself deep enough to end his life. When the military medics arrived, they expressed what I can only describe as mild irritation for getting the call. "Come on, why would you play tic-tac-toe on your wrists with a razor?" They acted as if they had dealt with this before.

After the wrist-slitting event, the Army briefly put the troubled soldier in an inpatient mental health ward and gave him medications that, his father said, made him seem "dangerously stoned." Eventually he was sent back to the unit.

Missing from formation one morning, he was found dead in his barracks room. He had overdosed on the prescription drugs the Army gave him, plus a couple of his own.

Not long thereafter, I received a call informing me that Sam, my close friend from the crew team, had been seriously injured by an IED in Afghanistan. Arriving at the intensive care burn unit in San Antonio, I saw him lying in bed. His lithe six-foot-four-inch frame was mummified in gauze; only the portions of his body needed for intravenous tubes were exposed. He was nearly unrecognizable. Parts of his face were raw and marbled, as if a psychopath had flayed him with a cheese slicer and then worked him over with a blowtorch. His ears and nose were charred black; a stiff breeze would've made them crumble to dust. His lips were split, oozing a putrid brownish wax. He was covered in greasy ointment. Although his hands were bandaged like oven mitts, I noticed a missing finger. His resting heart rate was in the 130s—a constant jog just to survive. Sam was a living revenant.

Foolishly, I had packed up my Xbox 360 and *Call of Duty*, hoping it would provide Sam with some entertainment and distraction during what I'd assumed would be a dull recovery process. In my mind he'd be on a sofa somewhere, sipping milkshakes and being chastised for pushing the limits of his rehab, complaining that his run times were slipping. I felt like an idiot when it dawned on me that I had brought a video game console for a man whose fingers had been literally burned off and who lacked the strength to speak.

As cadets, we were never exposed to wounded veterans, never encouraged to consider whether their suffering was at all connected to the security of America, thousands of miles away. Seeing Sam in that bed, I felt as though I had been asleep all my life. There was no greater cause—just tens of thousands of American troops fumbling around in countries we should never have been in.

From that point, I witnessed a veritable funeral procession. In the decade following graduation, the number of my friends injured or killed crossed into the double digits and kept going. Some were shot to death. Others were blown up. One died in a helicopter crash. A couple committed suicide. Many more were maimed and horrifically disfigured. Nearly all of us harbored internal demons.

I started to see how the War on Terror was breaking the people I cared about. Adam Snyder, a senior at West Point when I was a freshman there, was killed in Iraq. The *New York Times* mentioned Snyder's death in an article dishearteningly titled "Veterans Watch as Gains Their Friends Died for Are Erased by Insurgents." Snyder "idealized the Middle East," according to a fellow platoon leader. "In Hawija, though, the idealism 'fell apart for him, the reality of trying to effect change through force.' By the time they had deployed to Baiji, 'he had become disillusioned over the whole thing.'" To hear that he was disillusioned with the war at the hour of his death only exacerbated my own disillusionment.

Dan Hyde, a classmate of mine, was one of the four regimental commanders at West Point. He possessed exceptional talent and at the age of twenty-one was responsible for one thousand cadets. After the two of us graduated from Ranger School, he was deployed to Iraq. Soon he went back home to California—in a government-issue coffin. A grenade had penetrated the roof of his vehicle.

Whenever good people are killed, the natural reaction is to retrofit their death with some higher meaning or purpose.

It is easier to invent a noble military fable than it is to confront the reality that a loved one's death may have served no one. Not the American people. Not the Afghan people. Not an abstract moral arc toward justice. But soldiers dying in inglorious ways for no coherent reason wouldn't provide much solace to grieving families and friends. For the sake of our sanity, we had to push these thoughts out of our mind and remain resolute.

* * *

About a month after I heard about Hyde's death, I was deployed to Kandahar as a platoon leader. By the time I stood on the tarmac in southern Afghanistan, it was very clear that this was not going to be some *Lawrence of Arabia*–type epic filled with horses and camels and curved *pulwar* swords. Yet I tried to cling to the fantasy that we'd drink black tea with too much sugar and sit cross-legged on hand-tufted carpets. Afghan elders would praise us for offering our help. In a great climax, we would outwit the black-clad Taliban in a skirmish. The schools would be reopened, and the villages would rejoice in celebration. We would return home dusty, tan, and more interesting—our war experience a rough-and-tumble ornament that we could place upon the mantel of a well-rounded, adventure-filled life.

It took less than a week before my platoon started getting ripped apart. There was no romantic daybreak assault on our position. No action-packed shoot-out. Instead, as we drove down a dusty road in Maywand District, my squad leader's vehicle hit an antipersonnel mine linked to 250 pounds of homemade explosives.

Maybe it was the ketamine talking. Or maybe A. J. Nelson, an eighteen-year-old private, possessed a type of bravery that I did not. Whatever it was, lying on his back, bones broken, blood pouring from his lacerated lips, he said something that I can't forget.

"I want to come back." Flecks of blood sprayed in the air with each word, speckling his uniform. "I want to come back to the platoon, sir."

Nelson was one of four soldiers injured in the blast. The desert around us was a jumble of twisted metal and vehicle parts. The wreck of their vehicle—its engine block completely sheared off—looked as if it had been stripped at a junkyard. As the Black Hawk helicopter hovered to land, we attempted to shield the wounded men from the sandblasting rotor wash. At that moment, I knelt, looked at A.J., and proceeded to lie directly to his face.

"You're going to be okay."

I had no idea what *okay* might even mean in that situation. Did *okay* mean quadruple amputee with a pulse? Did it mean years of horrific facial reconstruction surgeries? Or the loss of only one eye? Paralyzed just from the waist down? Or maybe *okay* meant being really lucky—merely a single-leg amputation below the knee, what my wounded friends from Walter Reed Hospital would later call a "paper cut." I would have a lot of time to figure this out. Before our tour was over, eleven months later, 25 percent of my men would become casualties.

One soldier had his face and torso torn up by shrapnel after a pressure cooker filled with homemade explosives, bicycle chains, and nails blew up nearby. Another was shot from six feet away by a member of the Afghan National Police who was high on drugs, a negligent discharge. A squad leader, transferred to a different platoon because of the number of casualties in our unit, received a traumatic brain injury after getting blown up in his vehicle. One of my best friends, serving in our sister battalion, was shot to death; later, as part of the honor guard, I buried him in Section 60 of Arlington National Cemetery, handing the folded American flag to his crying mother. Trauma was everywhere.

My former team leader stepped on an antipersonnel mine, losing both legs above the knee. He was evacuated to Walter Reed, where he died about ten days later. What made matters worse was that battalion headquarters had known where the mine was. On a video feed, they had observed the insurgents emplace the IED on our patrol route the previous night. They just didn't bother to tell us. I learned that this sort of stuff happens in combat all the time.

One of my soldiers, who was eighteen years old when he deployed to Afghanistan, killed himself not long after returning home, a reminder that suicide has been deadlier than combat for the military. There have been over thirty thousand suicides among US service members and veterans of the post-9/11 wars, significantly more than the roughly seven thousand service members killed in post-9/11 war operations.

Another soldier from my platoon has been in and out of rehab for years. Hard drugs. Alcohol. Depression. The works. Whenever we speak on the phone, it seems like he is nursing a buzz. At his best, he's getting by; at his worst—we don't need to talk about his worst.

As for A. J. Nelson, the soldier injured by a roadside bomb during our first week of deployment—the one who had wanted so badly to return to the platoon—he got his wish: the military patched him up and sent him back to us seven months later. He may have recovered from his physical wounds, but still, I was wrong. He was not "going to be okay." In 2012, he and an accomplice kidnapped a stranger and rammed a crossbow bolt through his ear; when this failed to kill him, they choked him to death with a chain. After they chopped up his body in a bathtub, they used his car to rob a bank. Nelson is now serving life in prison without parole.

It makes you wonder: Were these accumulated traumas of the War in Afghanistan necessary to protect the national territory of the United States?

No. No, they were not.

* * *

But it was not the harm inflicted on US soldiers alone that fed my disillusion. That came with the moral injury of realizing that the War on Terror—the thing I had spent years of my life preparing for—was illegal, immoral, self-perpetuating, and counterproductive.

I remember the moment of this realization: it was Halloween 2009.

We were supporting a mission that the soldiers had nicknamed Operation Highway Babysitter. It worked like this: the infantry secured the road, allowing logistics convoys to resupply the infantry—all so that the infantry could secure the road, so that the logistics convoys could resupply the infantry. For several months, we did this with no greater follow-on objective. A complete waste.

Worse, whenever a stretch of road was blown up—since protecting all the roads, all the time, was impossible—American forces would grant exorbitant cost-plus contracts to Afghan construction companies to rebuild it. It was common knowledge that many of these companies were owned by Afghan warlords guilty of human rights abuses. The construction companies, in turn, would pay a protection tribute to the Taliban. Then the Taliban would buy more bomb-making materials to destroy more roads—and US vehicles. We were, indirectly but also quite literally, paying the Taliban to kill us.

Nicholas Kristof described this dynamic in the *New York Times*: "Afghan contractors in Kabul who supplied U.S. forces told me that for every $1,000 America paid them, they gave $600 to the Taliban in bribes to pass through checkpoints." That's 60 percent. Sixty percent of US taxpayer dollars were estimated to be going to the Taliban!

Meanwhile, our patrols were not only mind-numbing but dangerous. On Halloween 2009, our stakeout was interrupted by the sound of gunfire a couple of kilometers down the road. We buttoned up our trucks and set course toward the commotion. By the time we arrived at the reported location—a large grape field—the shooting had stopped. Just a little skirmish. No biggie. Probably just a few insurgents taking potshots at a convoy before bugging out.

To investigate, about ten of us dismounted and started off toward the field in a V-shaped wedge formation. Fifteen seconds later, our world erupted in gunfire. We had walked into an ambush.

Thankfully, my soldiers performed a spectacular "react to ambush," field-manual perfect. We returned fire, found cover, called out suspected enemy locations, maneuvered ourselves into more defensible positions, radioed our trucks to provide support by fire, and, lastly, called in a pair of Kiowa helicopters for close air support.

The insurgents had fled and we could not tell where they had gone, as we explicitly told the Kiowa pilots when they arrived. But they must have positively identified the armed fighters because they released a salvo of rockets on the nearby village. The gun runs were punishing. The Kiowas took turns flying nose up until they were right over the target, at which point, almost birdlike, they swooped downward, launching 2.75-inch rockets one after another into the fields and buildings.

The *whooosh* and impact of each incoming rocket could be felt by every soldier in the grape field. Then the Kiowas strafed the entire area with their .50-caliber machine guns. They continued their attacks on the buildings until they expended all their ammunition.

My soldiers erupted in cheers. We had survived. Eventually, the sweat on our faces began to dry. The adrenaline wore off. I had just experienced my first real firefight. My NCOs seemed to have more respect for me. For a moment it felt as if it might become one of the proudest moments of my life: our small group of dismounts had performed admirably. We finished the mission, our heads held high.

It was only later in the evening, after we had returned to FOB Wilson—after our fifteen-hour patrol—that I learned the truth.

The helicopters hadn't had positive identification on any insurgents. They'd fired their rockets at the village blindly, leaving it in fiery shambles. The US military had the entire thing on film. Above the helicopters was an unarmed drone, which provided a direct-to-battalion live video feed. By the end, it showed three dead civilians, including a woman in a blue burka lying in a pool of blood.

I dropped my equipment in a heap inside my tent and walked to the company headquarters to fill out the debrief paperwork. I looked at the SIGACT (significant activity) whiteboard to see how the Army had described the engagement. The report was vague: small arms fire, grid location, call for helicopter air support. The final column—the punch line—was BDA, battle damage assessment. Here, in bold capital letters, was written UNKNOWN.

There was no mention of the civilian casualties in the reporting. I felt urgently sick. Was this a war crime being covered up and intentionally misreported? Where were the "Army values" that I had been taught at West Point?

* * *

OVER TIME, I realized that the people who were trying to kill me weren't international terrorists. They weren't attacking me because "they hate our freedoms" or some other bullshit Bush-era line. They were mostly angry farmers and teenagers with legitimate grievances. Their loved ones, breathing and laughing minutes before, had been transformed before their eyes into little more than stringy sinew and bloody flesh. Like someone hit a piñata full of raw hamburger meat. That's what rockets fired from helicopters do to human beings. It's always a mistake, always the result of extenuating circumstances, and always excused. The paperwork is easier if the corpses rest as "enemy" or "unknown."

I started to realize that if the birth lottery had allocated me to Afghanistan, I probably would have joined the insurgency too.

"We have shot an amazing number of people, but to my knowledge, none has ever proven to be a threat," said General Stanley McChrystal, the senior American and NATO commander in Afghanistan at the time. A couple of weeks later, as if to prove his point, just a few hundred meters from our platoon outpost, the Arkansas National Guard hosed down a passenger bus with an M240B machine gun, killing five and injuring eighteen innocent Afghans. It had all the trappings of yet another unforced error, reported as justifiable. Another "whoopsies" mass shooting of innocents—gunned down by US soldiers and excused by the US military propaganda ministry.

I saw the systematic dehumanization and devaluation of Afghan lives on a regular basis. We searched homes, people, and cars unilaterally and without warning. By and large, we never sought the consent of the Afghan people for anything. We regularly violated Karzai's Twelve, a series of rules intended to protect civilian lives and safeguard Afghan citizens against the deep indignities of a foreign military occupation. What the Afghan people wanted was completely immaterial to our own on-the-ground military operations.

Not once during deployment did our military leadership say any of the following phrases in relation to the people of Afghanistan:

"What do they want?"

"Are we putting their interests above our own?"

"Are we respecting their habits and culture?"

"If we were in their shoes, how would we see America's occupation?"

The truth is, the US military would never treat Americans the way it treated Afghans. I saw the hypocrisy of US military actions abroad as cutting to the bone of America's own identity.

If America is truly a country based on justice and racial equity, it should not be willing to tolerate innocent civilians being killed in foreign countries by the US military any more than it should tolerate innocent civilians being killed in America by the police. It's not just citizens of this country who have a right not to be killed by uniform-wearing, gun-wielding Americans who habitually use excessive force.

And if Afghans and Iraqis know they'll never be treated with equal dignity, doesn't it seem ridiculous to be expecting *their cooperation* with *our vision* for *their country* during *our war*?

I couldn't justify the way we were treating our Afghan and Iraqi brothers and sisters. So when I received an email from the Army stating that I had been chosen for the Special Forces Qualification Course, to begin after deployment, I knew what I had to do.

Had I received this offer one year earlier, I would have accepted without hesitation. Now, war-rattled and disillusioned, in five minutes I respectfully wiped away five years of work and ambition. It was the first time I said no to what others in the military kept telling me was "a great opportunity."

The War on Terror strip-mined my soul. My time in Afghanistan, from May 2009 to June 2010, was defined by the horror of watching good people getting mutilated and dying terrible deaths. It was filled with intense moral anguish, gnawing fear, butt-puckering anxiety, boredom, aggression, envy, and hatred. It strained my relationships, destroyed my notion of patriotism, eroded my support for American foreign policy, dissolved whatever faith I may once have had in religion, and made me deeply sad.

The decision to leave the military, on the other hand,

filled me with joy, hope, and anticipation. I would have the agency to pick a career that wasn't actively making the world worse off. A "good day" would no longer be measured by the absence of tragedy.

* * *

It's one of America's darkest ironies: in efforts to "prevent terrorism" in our country, we commit far larger acts of terrorism elsewhere. Terrorism—and the images that come with it: targeted assassinations, bombings, drone strikes, secret black site prisons, torture, and wanton civilian murder—is precisely what we inflict on others. Particularly galling is America's arrogance in expecting that this won't come back to haunt us, even when we've historically proved that we ourselves will destroy far more for far less.

We Americans are truly raised to believe that terrorism isn't a crime—when America does it.

Fed up with the war and the lobotomized patriotism that perpetuated it, I left the country as soon as my contractual obligation was over. I went on to earn a dual degree from the University of Oxford, then moved to Australia for five years, working primarily in management consulting. But all along I found my mind wandering, always returning to the place I tried to forget.

I kept tabs on my friends still in uniform and on the war itself. I was disappointed, and sometimes aghast, at what I found.

In 2016, four years after I had left the military, I learned that one of my friends, Andy—Captain Andrew Byers—had been killed in Kunduz, Afghanistan. The place where he died was not far from where the United States had bombed a Médecins sans Frontières (Doctors Without Borders) hospital roughly a year earlier, killing at least forty-two people, including numerous patients and staff.

Andy was an exceptional and talented guy, a Green Beret detachment commander in the Special Forces. Reading about his death, I found two very different accounts of the facts.

An article from the US Central Command titled "Until Dawn: Surviving the Battle of Boz Qandahari"—a dramatic and romantic-sounding name—provided a rah-rah account of the mission and contained many interviews with soldiers from Andy's team. Andy and a fellow Green Beret were said to have been killed in a mission to "target known enemy safe havens and disrupt the refit operations of several high-level Taliban leaders." The article said that the US Special Forces had inflicted "catastrophic damage on multiple enemies."

One Air Force combat controller attached to the unit was "recommended for the Air Force Cross Medal for his actions, [having] spent the night calling in precision air strikes on enemy positions." The mission that killed my friend was described as "a bittersweet victory," and one Green Beret from Andy's team "felt content with the effects that we had on the enemy that night." For their actions that night, members of the team were awarded "three Silver Star Medals, three Bronze Star Medals (two with Valor), four Army Commendation Medals with Valor, and six Purple Heart Medals."

Articles in the *New York Times* and *Al Jazeera* told a very different story. The *Al Jazeera* article was titled "US Forces Admit Killing 33 Civilians in Taliban Clash." One Afghan resident whose family was killed by the air strikes said the attack "only killed innocent people," whose houses were targeted based on "speculation." Afterward, "residents carried more than a dozen bodies, including children, towards a local governor's office in a show of anger."

As deeply tragic as the death of American soldiers is, it's remarkable how the official Army account completely omits any mention of the thirty-three civilians killed by US air strikes during the battle—more than fifteen times the number of Americans killed. To avoid moral dissonance, the military does not like to publish accounts that mix "medals with valor" and dead children. But the collateral damage made the circumstances of Andy's death all the more tragic.

The methods America uses to achieve "peace," presumably the ultimate goal of warfare, assure that it will never happen. If General McChrystal's "insurgent math"—for every innocent person you kill, you create ten new enemies—is correct, the raid that killed Andy created another 330 insurgents. This 10:1 ratio means that just to keep an insurgency from growing, the American military needs to kill more than ten insurgents without a single civilian death, a seemingly impossible task in modern warfare. Grégoire Chamayou's book *Drone Theory* puts it well: "Caught up in an endless spiral, the eradication strategy is, paradoxically, destined never to eradicate."

As a kid, I'd wanted the kind of adoration my step-grandfather got for his military service. But now I was tired of the brainless veteran worship and shallow praise. I was tired of never-ending, counterproductive war. I was tired of witnessing the hypocrisy of America, its failure to adhere to its stated values. Andy's death inspired me to take a stand

and speak my mind. This, for me, was the inciting incident that shifted me from disillusion to dissent.

I took a break from the private sector and devoted myself to writing. About two years later, I had completed *Un-American: A Soldier's Reckoning of Our Longest War*. I hope I was successful in getting my point across. From the letters I've received, I knew that the book had a deep impact on some people's lives—even if that number was smaller than the number of Americans who need to hear this message.

But the military-industrial complex is a force of nature. Neither my efforts nor the efforts of all the other contributors to this book have been successful in getting our country to confront its permanent war posture and profligate military spending. (The price tag for the post-9/11 wars is over $8 trillion.) Like the climate crisis, America's military fetish needs a million voices—voices like yours, reader—to demand change. Without more pressure, our country and our troops will be condemned to more of the same.

Individuals—young men and women looking to prove their worth to society—must not be misled by the Disneyfication of military service. At the first sniff of adulthood, the military bamboozles children into one of the largest commitments ever conceived: to leave your life, be issued a new identity, and be sent across the world to inflict violence on people you don't know, for political reasons you're not meant to understand. I believe in informed consent, and I'm no longer sure that's what happens when a military commitment is pitched to teenagers too young even to be allowed to drink alcohol or buy a ticket for an R-rated movie depicting gory military combat.

Society, for its part, must not overlook the incalculable costs of acquiescing to these aimless wars—to civilians overseas, to American soldiers who are wounded or killed, and also to the ones who finish their service intact in body but not in spirit. I have seen how those long-term effects—divorce, alcohol and drug abuse, depression, violence, suicide—have seeped into every corner of our country.

The American public has been complicit in allowing our troops to be sent into a series of wars that everyone knew to be costly and self-defeating, while simultaneously maintaining the audacious idea that, in doing so, we "support the troops." That is not patriotism; that is betrayal.

* * *

WHEN I WAS sixteen years old, reflecting on the War on Terror and how I could be a good American, I asked myself a question: What will I do about it?

My answer then was to join the military. My answer now is different: dissent.

Given that the military is uniquely unlike everything else government runs—because of its expense, because of its ability to destroy the fabric of society—the costs are too high not to question the military. Rather, it is your civic duty to *always* question the military.

Without a legitimate and worthy purpose, death in war is merely a tragic and absurd loss. It is our duty as patriots to ensure that our country maintains nobility of purpose. And therefore, it is our civic duty to dissent—and loudly—whenever our country loses its way.

Military service is not an absolute good, but only as good

as the purpose for which it is being used. Likewise, dissent is patriotic only insofar as it aims to redress society's entrenched wrongs. For at least the past twenty years, the US government has misused the military in a way that runs counter to American ideals and undermines our country's security.

In times like these, dissent is nothing short of a moral obligation.

HOW I GOT MY HUMANITY BACK FROM THE ARMY

Joy Damiani

"Have you heard of Iraq veterans against the war?"

The wineglass nearly fell from my hand. The pleasant face attached to the friendly voice smiled, not knowing it had just shorted my circuits.

"I mean . . . I am one of those." It was nearly a year since I'd returned from my final deployment, and I had yet to meet any Iraq veterans against the war who were not my friends or me. Was this a trap?

"Yes, but the group—Iraq Veterans Against the War. Have you heard of them?"

Invisible sparks burst as my neurons exploded. "There's a group?"

This was not a conversation I'd expected to be having backstage. I glanced up at my new boyfriend, whose California jam band was the reason I was standing in this greenroom in Falls Church, Virginia. He had just introduced me to a friend of his yet again as "an Iraq veteran." Before I could prepare to mask my annoyance at the inevitable "Oh . . . ooh?" accompanied by a look of panicked confusion, this new acquaintance had changed the script as casually as she'd told me her name. Sonia. Had Sonia just said there was a whole group of Iraq veterans who were against the war?

A broad grin filled her petite face. "I can bring you some literature if you want! Will you be at the show on Thursday?"

Thursday night in a Bethesda guest room, as the band after-partied with our hosts, I stared at a pile of papers spread out before me on the bed. Words jumped off the printed pages—*illegal . . . unjust . . . occupation*—that I'd rarely heard other soldiers say out loud.

The War on Terror had come along as my young brain was still forming. I was barely nineteen when I enlisted, a few short months after 9/11. I wanted to be a journalist, so I became a soldier. My recruiter, like all good recruiters, made it make sense.

"Look, you want to go to journalism school, right?"

"Right." I'd been getting myself ready for morning classes at Onondaga Community College, hastily applying makeup, when my mom had handed me the phone. I cradled the receiver between my ear and shoulder. The voice introduced itself as Sergeant Brown. He said he'd gotten my number from the college, and asked what I was studying. Reflexively, I told him. Nobody at home had shown much interest in my plans for the future. Sergeant Brown was interested, though—and he had a plan.

"But you can't pay for journalism school, right?"

"Right."

"Well, what if I told you I could get you a journalism job in the Army?"

I allowed his words to flutter around my mind for a moment before letting out what I thought was an uninterested "Oh?"

He couldn't see my raised eyebrow over the phone, or my smirk. But he could spot an open door a mile away, and in he strode.

"Not only can I get you a journalism job in the Army, and all the training, but I'll also guarantee you can still go to journalism school after you're done—for free. You only have to sign up for five years!"

By now I'm not too proud to admit I heard only what he wanted me to hear. I was a reform school dropout who had enrolled in community college with a GED and a distant journalistic dream. I wanted a way out of my parents' house, a way to live my own life and get job training for something resembling a respectable writing career. Instead of taking my parents' orders for free, I could take the government's for pay. I thought I'd be fighting terrorists, if anyone. I had no idea I'd be sent to Iraq even once, let alone twice. I took the offer I was given, signed on the dotted line, and prepared for five years of active-duty adventure.

War to me was only a concept, a heading to be memorized in history class. It meant olden days and long-ago people. My grandfathers had been in the Army, but not in any wars. They never talked about it. *War is brutal and bad,* my conscious mind would say, before interrupting itself. *I mean, the Vietnam War was bad. World War II was good . . . except the nuclear bombs were bad . . . and the Revolutionary*

War was good . . . but the Civil War was bad . . . except the slavery side lost, so that's good. . . . Wait, when was World War I? What was that one about again? I decided I'd have to wait and see for myself. *Isn't that what journalists do? Look around and find things out?*

My recruiter never brought up the war. I didn't notice. My mind was busy entertaining me with visions of myself as an intrepid reporter. The only thing I tuned out more effectively than the questions I should have asked was the irony of never having asked them.

Six years later, I was released from that "five-year contract," and I no longer wanted to be a journalist. Neither soldiering nor war reporting had turned out to be anything like what my teenage brain had been led to believe as I rushed to my community college US history class. That morning felt like a lifetime ago, and in many ways it did belong to another life. I'd stepped into a camouflage skin and learned to blend in, to stay alert and alive, to watch my six and keep my head down. I'd been trained to fight in a war—to die in one, even—but not to live through one. Now, Sergeant Brown nowhere to be found, my admittedly damaged but at last fully formed adult brain had to somehow make it make sense.

The only thing that made sense to me as a newly minted civilian was to get in my car and drive as far away from the military as I could, so that's what I did. Crossing the country from east to west and back again, I celebrated my hard-won survival by making new friends, drinking away painful memories, taking every less-traveled path and earnestly offered drug, embracing all that glittered. I never suspected the road I was on would send me careening toward the past.

* * *

In November 2002, I was walking across the Student Company barracks at Fort Meade, Maryland, when my senior drill sergeant barked "*Soldier!*" at me from across the company's common area. I was still a new recruit—only a couple of months into wearing rank on my collar, a week or two before my graduation from the Defense Information School. I stopped in my tracks and snapped to parade rest.

"Hooah, Drill Sergeant!" The Army's ubiquitous grunt-word that meant everything except no was the only safe reply.

"Soldier! What do you think about going to Kuwait?"

Drill Sergeant Waltman sneered down at me. I tried to determine whether his tone was sarcastic or sincere, but his beady eyes and creepily curved upper lip were set in that time-honored drill sergeant jeer face that could indicate pleasure or rage or both. Like most authority figures who take their roles very seriously, Drill Sergeant Waltman seemed to enjoy reminding me who was in charge in this relationship, almost as much as I enjoyed knowing I'd be leaving his custody in a matter of weeks.

"R-r-roger, Drill Sergeant?" I had not, in any practical sense, thought about going to Kuwait. Even if I'd had the inclination, I wouldn't have had the time—I was too busy learning how to write "the Army's Story" about the places where we were already at war. I had read enough news about Saddam Hussein and his undiscovered weapons of mass destruction to know that all signs pointed to Don't Invade Iraq. I had read enough to know that invading Iraq would be a historically grievous error. I thought I had read everything, until I realized I'd somehow skimmed over the writing on the wall: whether it was justifiable or not, we were going to invade Iraq.

Looking back now, I understand that when he signed the paperwork that month assigning me to the imminently deploying 3rd Infantry Division, Drill Sergeant Waltman thought he was sending me directly into a brand-new combat zone. If he'd had his way, I would have spent my next birthday in Baghdad. But when I arrived at Fort Stewart, Georgia, I was told the unit already had enough personnel for its deployment. Instead of finding out quite quickly what I thought about Kuwait, I spent the next two years in the division's public affairs offices, dutifully distributing news of the Army's version of the war to soldiers who were either on their way to it or finally returning home. Waiting my turn, listening to friends who'd made it back, soaking up all the gritty details, I had plenty of time to take in the variety of accounts.

According to the Army's official narrative, the war was always in the process of being won. There were never any mistakes, never any defeats, and certainly never any failures—a semantic lesson I learned from my boss after I'd made that faux pas while interviewing the division's chief of staff for the base newspaper.

"We do not ever refer to failures," the public affairs officer, Lieutenant Colonel Martin, chastised me in his thin, uncertain voice, nervous eyes darting around the room as if he were looking for hidden cameras. "That is not appropriate terminology for addressing the division chief of staff." He twitched when he saw the corner of my mouth flicker upward. "This is not funny, Specialist."

"Roger, sir." It was hard to keep from cracking a smile as I imagined his encounter with full-bird colonel McKnight. The chief of staff resembled Dr. Evil in every way except fictionality and stood at least a foot taller than my boss, who had, I assumed, spent the entire conversation trembling in fear. It was his ass on the line, after all. I was a mere specialist: a lowly enlistee, junior-grade nothingsauce. It was his duty to stomp out my don't-give-a-fuck attitude when it came to what I subsequently started calling "the other F-word."

Failure, though, was the only word I could think of to adequately describe what was going on. Long after our commander in chief had stood on the deck of the USS *Abraham Lincoln* and given his "Mission Accomplished" speech, my friends were still dying in the war and I was still expected to participate in it. Even in my most idealistic moments, I could no longer bring myself to give any benefit of the doubt to our ever-changing mission in Iraq or to our never-changing narrative that the terrorists were definitely being defeated. I could cover only so many memorial services, interview so many grieving mothers, photograph the dog tags dangling from so many pairs of empty boots—boots that had recently been on the feet of wide-eyed recruits just like me—without asking myself after every polished article the one question I could never ask in any official interview: Why?

When the time came around for me to go to war, I had already been casually calling it an "occupation" for nearly a year. Saddam was gone. There were no weapons of mass destruction. There had been no Iraqi attacks on US soil, or that of any other nation. We were staying in Iraq, said both the journalists and the generals, to "bring democracy" to . . . the cradle of civilization? We were there to "liberate"

Iraq . . . by taking over? The longer it dragged on, the more the knowledge that my job was to tell a story I couldn't believe in incessantly nagged. I couldn't help knowing I was one of the bad guys before I'd even set foot in Baghdad. A more conscientious person would have refused to go, but my conscience couldn't convince me to break my contract.

They say if you end up in quicksand, struggling to free yourself will only make you sink faster. Joining the military to be a journalist had given me a job making PR look like news and an unwinnable war look like a victory. The Army was sucking me down into its moral void, and it seemed the only way to eventually extricate myself was to make peace with being stuck in it for a long while.

When I was seven, my favorite movie was Disney's *Little Mermaid*—the story of a teenager who signs a contract that requires her to give up her voice in exchange for a chance to escape her frustratingly constricting world. It was one of the few films my homeschooling evangelical Christian parents would allow in the house, so I watched it at least twenty times as an impressionable child, memorizing the songs and singing them passionately to any unfortunate soul who happened to be in the room. By the time I reached the age of the eponymous heroine, I hadn't watched it in nearly a decade, but I related to the misunderstood sixteen-year-old even more—desperate to escape my surroundings and unaware of how much I was willing to give up to do so.

As it turned out, I was willing to give up not only my voice but all the rest of my autonomy too. In basic training they'd sat us through hours of classroom lectures about what we were and were not allowed to say and do, now that we had volunteered to "defend freedom." There were rules and red-tape mazes for every aspect of our lives in the military—body, mind, word, and deed. With every violation of those regulations came a broad swath of potential consequences ranging from symbolic to severe. Even the mildest wrist slap could mean lost pay, but at the furthest end of the spectrum were dishonorable discharges and jail time. Our health care, college money, and veterans' benefits hung in the balance between the ability to play the game and the ability to resist being played. At the end of training, every new baby soldier could see in high definition what all our recruiters had handily glossed over: we were now government property.

Offered an escape hatch from my constricting world, I'd taken a cursory look before eagerly leaping, only to hear the door lock behind me as my recruiter disappeared with a nearly audible cackle. His lies had been a tiny taste of the military's version of truth, the version I'd soon be hard at work telling. It truly was a world of new possibilities—but then, once you've leaped from the frying pan, so is the fire. And unlike a Disney movie, there was no guarantee of anything remotely resembling a happy ending.

* * *

By the time the Army got around to sending me to Iraq, I was more than ready to go see for myself what the real story was. For two years I'd waited my turn as nearly every other soldier I knew left and, if they were lucky, returned to tell me their tales. The ones who hadn't come home took up residency in my head, their voices quietly nagging me: *pay attention*. As challenging as it was to keep from being swallowed by the monstrous job of crafting morale-boosting marketing for my fellow soldiers and calling it news, it was easy to stay skeptical when I could feel the emptiness of the spaces where my friends used to be.

The first day my boots were on the ground in Baghdad—February 23, 2005—I slept through a mortar attack on our base, the optimistically named Camp Victory. It became such a regular occurrence that I promptly forgot about that initial incident until reviewing my journal years later, recalling all the ways one could be hunted down by death while keeping calm and carrying on in a combat zone. Over the course of that year, as all the sidewalks and concrete slabs around our base were shattered and pockmarked by incoming explosives and scattering shrapnel, it became discomfortingly clear that if I got out of the war alive, it would be due just as much to luck as to skill. My life was government property, and I'd been a soldier long enough to know that the government is notoriously bad at taking care of its property.

The longer I settled into my role as one of thousands of disgruntled little cogs in identical camouflage, all doing our damnedest to avoid death together, the smokier the constantly exploding skies became, and the clearer it became that a significant number of Iraqis wanted us in their country even less than most of us wanted to be there. My job was to create a newspaper filled with the news of our victories, but on the last page of every issue, I typed a list of deaths. The official term, *casualties*, never felt sufficient to do justice to the growing number of names that had so recently belonged to so many living faces. The font size shrank in every issue, the list stretching into two and then three columns as the months heaved on.

As directed, our public affairs team never used the word *failure* in print, never hinted at the possibility that every victory was actually a loss, and never, ever technically lied. Military public affairs is a propaganda of omission. We, the government's very own uniformed "journalists," didn't overtly fabricate. We just diligently told only the news deemed appropriate for team spirit. We painted only the pictures the generals wanted the troops to see. Resistance was not entirely futile, but it was swiftly punishable. Any attempt at sketching even a minimally accurate portrait of the daily chaos that we observed would be censored, at best. Instead, we adeptly performed the moral contortions required to maintain a semblance of sanity while spinning the yarns of winning we wrapped around our battle buddies' eyes, at times not even noticing we'd gotten ourselves tangled up in them too.

As instructed, anyone we detained became, in print, *a detained insurgent*. Our ever-expanding presence in Iraq was officially *the theater of operations*. Our actions: *combat operations*. Our mission: *Iraqi freedom*. We never used the word *war*—at least not outside the safe confines of its bookends, *Global* and *on Terror*—because we had already won the war. What we were now engaging in was *reconstruction*. It would last as long as the commander in chief deemed necessary, we were told, and as long as it did, our team's task was to tell the story of victory.

I wasn't often permitted to venture outside the base. This was due partly to my admittedly lacking tactical prowess but also, according to every single one of my superiors, my inability to keep from letting a little too much truth make its way onto the printed page. Although I knew better than to try to print photos of children playing in sewage thanks to our destruction of Baghdad's infrastructure—or to run images of lines of unnamed detainees sitting cross-legged in the desert sun, their hands bound and eyes covered—the articles I wrote did more than dance around my increasingly hard-to-disguise dissent with the mission.

"Watch for Low-Flying Sheep over Latifya" read the headline of what I considered to be a sufficiently positive news story I'd written after returning from one of my infrequent trips outside the wire. My mission: accompany one of the generals to a combat outpost south of Baghdad in the so-called Triangle of Death, fully cover the momentous occasion of his visit, and "see if you can get a light human-interest story while you're out there."

My story had come from an enlisted soldier on a rare off-day from regular patrols, who'd chuckled when I asked him if anything funny ever happened in such a dangerous part of the war.

"Yeah," he said, and grinned. "The other day I saw a sheep fly."

I sat down on one of the cots in the dank, cramped structure that served as living quarters for some soldiers, with others sleeping outside under camouflage netting. "Oh?"

A couple of weeks earlier, he told me, his team was out on what was an abnormally quiet patrol, compared with the area's usual volatility. The most action they saw that day was an unexploded bomb they'd found on a bridge, so all they had to do was radio the explosive ordnance disposal team and wait. They even had interpreters with them to warn any Iraqis who happened by that they should keep their distance. For a while the danger seemed to have been dodged.

That was when the sheep showed up.

"It was a whole herd!" His voice grew more animated as

he described the animals slowly moseying their way down the road, no shepherd in sight. The soldiers had looked on dumbfounded as the sheep moved toward the bridge . . . and then up to it . . . and then onto it . . . and then . . .

"What could we do?" He shook his head. "You can't tell sheep to back up! We just had to let it happen. Then I heard this *BOOM*—and all of a sudden I see this fluffy, legless thing flying over my head!" The soldier emitted the kind of guffaw that seemed to say he couldn't believe he was laughing either. "I don't know if that's funny. But it's the funniest thing that's happened here. After the weeks we've had out here, we're just glad nobody died."

My boss just shook his head when I handed him my article back at the headquarters building. "No. Really? No. Why would you even—?"

"It's good news, Sergeant! Nobody died!"

He'd already turned back to his computer. "I'm not even going to show this to the colonel. Get back to work on the layout."

My full-time mission became the production of a biweekly newspaper full of the troops' winningest accomplishments, distributed to them for the sole purpose of keeping their heads in the game. Their heads, of course, were fully in it already, being concerned with saving their asses. My head, on the other hand, was a mess. No matter how many pictures of smiling Iraqi children I printed in the newspaper, the images I saw in my mind were of their harsh reality: their homes and communities bombed and ravaged, regularly raided, surrounded by barbed wire and blast walls. Children using trash as toys. Children living in an abandoned theater with a hole in the stage for a bathroom, with a seven-foot pile of feces and garbage nearly reaching the top. But every story I printed was one of unquestionable success.

It was a daily feat of psychological strength to wake up to the sound of small arms fire mingled with intermittent largish explosions nearby, then spend the day dutifully producing publications cheerily trumpeting all the winning we were doing here in the reconstruction. As my first year in Baghdad stretched on, my job description as an Army journalist broadened to include teaching soldiers on our base how to speak to actual journalists. All the reporters who had access to the troops were embedded in regular units, and those units contained soldiers who had to be briefed that they weren't supposed to tell the media any sensitive information, such as what they were really thinking. Now I was tasked not only with twisting the truth with a spoonful of sugar for my fellow soldiers themselves but also with contributing to whatever fresh narrative the powers that be had dreamed up for our families and friends back home.

I responded to the stress in the best way I knew how: by going unquestionably, obnoxiously insane. It wasn't the kind of insanity you're probably picturing—I did not Rambo my way around the headquarters, spraying rounds left and right in a fit of howls and shrieks, at least not unless you count my daydreams. My slow drift into madness manifested in a way that not even I could have predicted. Yes, there was the sporadic, compulsive rage that would bubble up without warning, and the steady stream of self-destructive tendencies, and the suicidal ideations, but beyond those surface-level responses, my craziness took shape as the terrifying drive to . . . deeply, helplessly care about the quality of my work.

My newly obsessive passion for technical scrupulosity

became the bane of all my fellow public affairs peons' existence. I had joined the Army to be a journalist, dammit, and if I couldn't control the content I was producing, I would make its presentation as close to perfect as I damn well could. There was no point in botching the one part of the job that didn't make me feel like one of the bad guys—even if it did turn me into the Editrix from Hell, Emotional Slayer of Sloppy Propagandists, Indomitable Fighter of Errorists. Once my integrity and morals had been thrown to the wind, all I could do was cling to the rules that remained: those of the *Associated Press Stylebook*. It was the only stable ground my feet could find. And it was there I planted myself, unable to accept, for the sake of my remaining sanity, that I was the only one who gave even the tip of the tail from a rat's ass whether the propaganda we produced looked "professional."

All I was expected to care about, of course, was getting home alive and staying there. But by the time I'd made it back, staying home was not an option. Instead, there was stop-loss.

* * *

IF THE ARMY had let me out at what I'd been led to believe would be the end of my active-duty contract, it's entirely possible I would've hightailed it to the nearest Rainbow Gathering and remained there until I felt my internal balance ease its way back toward human. But six months before my terminal leave days were set to begin, the 3rd Infantry Division received orders to return to Iraq three months earlier than we'd all been told. Everyone's active-duty contract was abruptly extended using a policy known officially as *stop-loss* but unofficially by its street name: *the backdoor draft*. Our go-getter commanding general had volunteered the 3rd ID to be part of the massive troop "surge" that would flood Iraq with thousands of additional soldiers, ostensibly rooting out the "insurgents" and making the nation much safer for us to continue occupying it. Unlike the previous deployment, which we had known would last a year, this time we were told we would be in Iraq for "twelve to eighteen months," the precise duration to be determined sometime in the future.

I'd begun my first deployment with plenty of severe doubts about our mission and leadership but still with a degree of anticipation for the adventure to come. The second time around—returning to the same place, with essentially the same job, holding the knowledge of all I already had seen for myself the first time—my outlook started dark and descended into despair. The surge initially seemed to work, as our military's finest minds had finally hit on the idea of simply paying or policing Iraqis so they would do what they were told—like join their national security forces, or not intentionally kill us. But it soon took a turn for the catastrophic.

Proving myself an abject failure as an aspiring journalist, I wasn't well versed in the surge strategy, nor did I know just how careless the commanders were being with our lives. But all I had to do was look around—as incoming rounds peppered every corner of Camp Victory, from headquarters to living quarters to gym to parking lots—to know for certain that no matter how many success stories I printed in our now-daily morale-boosting publication, all of us soldiers were getting screwed together in one big nonconsensual gang bang. What's more, we were certainly still not winning the war. I watched the Democratic primary debates that year on my work laptop, my ears perking up as the smooth-talking, polished young senator from Illinois campaigned on ending the Iraq War, and I counted down the days till I could stop trying to convince myself that we were not the terrorists.

Thirteen months into what we were eventually told would be a fifteen-month deployment, the Department of Defense passed a policy that awarded two and a half days of leave per extra active-duty month to stop-lossed soldiers. Having already accumulated a full month in anticipation of my previously scheduled exit, I suddenly discovered I'd either need to get back to the States quick-fast or start my end-of-contract leave—along with a migraine-sized pile of paperwork—while still in Baghdad. The Army chose to avoid the paperwork and send me on my way. A few weeks later, on a sunny day in May 2008, I walked out of the administration offices at Fort Stewart, Georgia, with an honorable discharge, a guilty conscience, and no clue how to be a civilian. I knew I had to write about what I'd seen, and that I had to write it my way, not under the shadow of someone else's bias . . . but first I needed to run away from it.

After ping-ponging my way around the country in my car from the beginning of that summer into the dark part of the fall, I let myself get swept up in a romance with a musician. He whisked me away to festivals and shows and kept me distracted from my war stories, supplying me with a life of parties, sparkly people, and plentiful psychedelics. When he invited me to join him for an East Coast tour, I hopped on a plane and met him in the Mid-Atlantic. There, almost exactly a year after my hasty return from the Middle East, awaited my first introduction to Sonia, her envelope full of literature, and Iraq Veterans Against the War (IVAW). That meeting started a chain of events that's been unfolding for nearly a dozen years and shows no sign of stopping.

Finding IVAW and other dissenting veterans' groups, like Veterans for Peace and Vietnam Veterans Against the War, was like being introduced to a team I hadn't known I was already on. With their guidance and encouragement, I learned more and more of the truth whose surface I'd barely scratched as a miserable, demoralized soldier, and I finally allowed that truth to infuse my whole life. I used my GI Bill funds for a bachelor's degree in Near Eastern studies at UC Berkeley; after years of helplessly observing the War on Terror, I was at last able to dive deep into its history and context, and to learn Arabic, a language I'd unconsciously associated with the conflict.

It was fellow dissenting vets who drew my attention to the Occupy movement in the Bay Area. Once I saw connections between Wall Street, the police state, and what I learned to call the military-industrial complex, I couldn't unsee them. It felt achingly obvious that it was time to use my "journalism" training to actually inform. I would dedicate myself to seeking out truth wherever it lurks, and to staying brave enough to speak, write, and even sing it; once I learned some chords on the ukulele, I was delighted to find that if I could make my opinions about the war into catchy, rhyming lyrics, people would not only listen to me but sing along too.

Over the following years, the world of new possibilities I'd been looking for as a naïve recruit rolled out beneath my feet, bringing with it countless ways to voice my ever-deepening discontent with a status quo that convinces well-meaning teenagers to die and kill other teenagers they don't know, on the orders of generals who will never even remember their names, for the sake of paying for an education that their taxes ought to buy—or worse, for the sake of being an upstanding patriot.

Throughout the last decade and more, I've written these thoughts into stories, songs, poems, prose, performance pieces, and tattoos prominently displayed on my body. I've told them to high school students, fellow veterans, paying audiences, angry mobs, random strangers, brutal police officers in several states, my own unaccepting grandmother, and so many more. My words have been applauded by plenty of my peers, but they've also been heckled, booed, silenced, and ignored. My path has been rocky, but I'm at last able to stand freely in the reality I see. Not only is it the firmest ground I've ever stood on, but others are always joining me, sometimes even thanking me for helping them feel seen and heard for the first time.

I can't speak to the value of dissent in general, or even of my own, other than to compare it to the value of clean air or water. When we keep our heads down, follow orders, and allow ourselves to be killers or be killed, we lose our humanity. When we refuse—by raising our heads, looking each other in the eyes, lifting one another up, and bellowing in one voice a resounding FUCK THIS!—that's when we reclaim it.

A FRESH PURPOSE

Dan Berschinski

The yellow jug, emptied of its cooking oil and refilled with crudely made yet highly effective ammonium nitrate explosive, was waiting to fulfill its purpose. Exactly how long it had been hidden in the footpath, buried slightly to the right of center, is impossible to know. In all likelihood, it had been placed there days or even weeks earlier. An insulated copper wire snaked through the dirt and undoubtedly emerged someplace out of sight a few yards away—probably on the other side of one of the seven-foot-tall adobe walls that flanked the trail. The wire would have been left alone until just before American troops appeared in the town. Then a Taliban soldier, or an angry farmer, or the widow of a man killed by American bombing, or some young kid paid or coerced into service would have run out ahead of our advance and plugged the wire into a nine-volt battery. Now the bomb was primed, armed, and ready to do its damage.

Walking down the dirt trail through a collection of mud-brick buildings in a remote, unnamed area of Kandahar,

Afghanistan, I was fulfilling *my* purpose. Nearly eight years after 9/11, I was one of roughly seventy thousand American soldiers sent to occupy and fight in Afghanistan for the ostensible mission of bringing security and stability to the country. I was a twenty-five-year-old first lieutenant—more specifically, a US Army infantry platoon leader, responsible for the actions and the lives of thirty-five soldiers. I loved my job, I loved my soldiers, and yet I fully believed that the war I had volunteered to participate in was unnecessary and unwinnable. So why was I on that dirt trail, 7,534 miles from home, my feet taking their last steps on this earth? Let me explain. . . .

When the terrorist attacks of September 11 occurred, I was a senior at a public high school in an idyllic suburb on the outskirts of Atlanta, Georgia. In considering my next step after high school, it was a foregone conclusion that I would be attending college. But while I was smart enough to be enrolled in a few Advanced Placement classes, I wasn't driven enough to take them very seriously. So I knew I wouldn't be able to follow in my older brother's footsteps by attending an Ivy League school. I did think, however, that I could put together an application that would give me a shot at getting into a different kind of prestigious college: one of our nation's military academies.

Veterans, including graduates of the United States Air Force and Naval Academies, were not at all unusual in my hometown—Atlanta is the main hub for Delta Air Lines—and my high school typically sent three or four kids off to the Air Force Academy every year. It was less typical for my high school to send a graduate to West Point, which piqued my interest.

By the end of the day on September 11, 2001, my mind was made up. It's not that the terrorist attack ignited any particular sense of patriotism: I had already been thinking of West Point as my first-choice school. Rather, I realized that the military, an institution that I had not thought about very deeply, was probably going to be involved in something significant in the near future. Teetering on the edge of adulthood, I was mature enough to glimpse the implications for our nation, yet also young enough to miss what these would mean for those charged with carrying out the nation's orders.

My application to West Point received a "soft rejection": the admissions team wouldn't take me right out of high school, instead suggesting that I spend a year at Marion Military Institute, a small military junior college in Marion, Alabama. At Marion, I received my first taste of military training, and I loved it. I loved the physical challenges, I loved learning infantry skills in the woods, I loved learning about weapons and how they are best employed, I loved leading teams and being a part of a team. It all just made sense to my eighteen-year-old self.

Two-thirds of the way through my year at Marion, I reapplied to West Point and was accepted. I entered West Point's class of 2007, a freshman once again, and began a four-year journey of rigorous academic study and military training.

By the time I was a junior, our military had successfully invaded and then transitioned into an occupation of Afghanistan, and we were one year into our invasion and subsequent occupation of Iraq as well. The ongoing events of the two wars, which to most Americans might have been interesting but not at all related to their daily lives, were front and center for me as both a cadet and a student majoring in

International Relations. Many of my classes—Constitutional Law, National Security Policy, Just War Theory, Politics and Government of the Middle East, and so on—took on a new urgency. My professors, military and civilian alike, pulled no punches when bringing the wars' realities into the classroom.

I left West Point with a conflicted mindset. I was excited to graduate and even more excited at the prospect of leading soldiers in combat. But I had also become convinced that both our ongoing wars were ill advised and structurally incapable of concluding in anything resembling success. I felt that America's initial invasion of Afghanistan, aimed at degrading al-Qaeda's ability to conduct more terrorist attacks in the aftermath of 9/11, was justified and reasonably prudent, but the mission creep toward nation-building and the ever-increasing footprint of our forces were not in the best interests of our country. As for Iraq, I did not think our initiating that war was justified in the first place, and I believed that our continued presence there was similarly ill advised and contrary to our national interests.

If the seeds of my dissent were planted during my studies in college, they germinated during my first year in the Army. While moving through the standard pipeline of infantry officer training—parachuting out of planes at Airborne School, advanced patrolling tactics at Ranger School, mounted operations in the Mechanized Leader Course—I met soldiers who had recently returned from deployments to Iraq or Afghanistan. A few had even served in both. I had tremendous respect for their firsthand experience; the individuals at the tactical and operational levels, it seemed to me, were handling difficult situations to the best of their abilities. At the same time, I began to see that the Army was like a running machine with no visible off switch. It was training and deploying its soldiers to wars whose goals were never even clearly stated, let alone achievable. The leaders at the strategic level—the generals and senior civilian leadership alike—were either unwilling to acknowledge the hard truths about these wars or, even worse, blind to those truths.

As a kid, I had always gone to my parents for advice when I needed it, and this time, early in my Army career, was no different. My father, despite never having served in the military himself, actually had quite a bit of experience in dealing with his own ill-advised war. In 1968, at the height of Vietnam, he was kicked out of his home—his father was a naval officer—and out of his high school because of his work as a full-time antiwar organizer for the Southern Student Organizing Committee. Growing up in New Orleans, he had loved watching mighty ships move up and down the Mississippi River. A precocious history nerd, he read military history and even thought that one day he might apply to the Naval Academy for college. But increasingly appalled by his still-segregated city and by America's folly in Vietnam, my dad decided that the most patriotic thing he could do was to oppose America's involvement in that war.

My father wasn't anti-military, he wasn't anti-America, he wasn't even antiwar in the broad sense. He just didn't think that America should be spending its resources—blood and treasure alike—in a conflict on the other side of the world when it had its own problems at home that needed work. Needless to say, I saw plenty of parallels to the current day.

When my dad was summoned before his local draft board at the age of eighteen, he told them that he wouldn't avoid service, but that if drafted he would continue speaking out against the war while in uniform. His number was never called. So instead of serving, my dad organized with those who had. His best friend during those years was a former Green Beret who had served two tours in Vietnam before returning home and becoming active in the antiwar movement. The two of them traveled around the Southeast organizing students against the war. Just as I felt now about Iraq and Afghanistan, their quarrel wasn't with the individual soldiers who participated in the Vietnam War—not with those who volunteered and certainly not with those who were drafted—but with the top military brass, and the national political leaders who had started the war but didn't seem capable of finding any reasonable way to end it. The more my dad and I talked, the more comfortable I became with my service—and the more I began to see the glimmer of a purpose that might extend beyond my profession.

I arrived at my unit—Bravo Company of the 1st Battalion, 17th Infantry Regiment, in the 5th Brigade of the 2nd Infantry Division—in the fall of 2008. I took command of Bravo Company's second platoon. After one year of prep school, four years at West Point, and a year of training at Fort Benning, I was finally doing my job.

My platoon was about a half-and-half mix of brand-new privates on one hand, specialists and NCOs with combat experience on the other. Many of them had been to Iraq and a few to Afghanistan. Demographically, my platoon was pretty much what I had expected it to be: mostly white guys with a handful of Black, Latino, and Pacific Islander soldiers mixed in. Some hailed from big cities, some from small towns; most, including myself, had grown up in the suburbs.

The Army had officially slated the 5th Brigade for deployment to Iraq, but sometime in January or February 2009 we were told that in July we would be deploying to Afghanistan instead. This wasn't quite a surprise; rumors to that effect had been circulating for many months. (Indeed, I had deliberately arranged to be assigned to the unit based on those rumors: I preferred to serve in Afghanistan, where the war had at least been initially justifiable, rather than in Iraq, which had been bullshit from the very start.) At the same time, though, the switch was more than a little disconcerting. All of the prior year's preparation had focused on Iraq. Our "language-enabled" soldiers, infantrymen given a crash course in a foreign language, had been taught Arabic—useful in Iraq but far less so in primarily Dari- and Pashto-speaking Afghanistan. Our unit was outfitted with Stryker eight-wheeled armored personnel carriers, and our training had heavily emphasized mounted operations—but Afghanistan was known to be an almost exclusively dismounted fight. By this point, the military had been fighting in Afghanistan for eight years. So how and why in the world were Army planners making a substantial mission change for a brigade-sized combat unit—four or five thousand soldiers—so close to our deployment date? It was yet another sign that our strategy for these wars lacked any semblance of coherence.

A few weeks after arriving in Afghanistan, my company moved into a newly established combat outpost located in an expansive patch of desert about fifteen kilometers west of the city of Kandahar. On our very first patrol, my platoon and I were providing flank security to a team of engineers sweeping a dirt road for IEDs when their vehicles unintentionally triggered a string of three hidden bombs, causing minor casualties. Later that same day, a fellow platoon leader and I led two of our squads (each numbering seven to nine infantrymen) into a nearby town. Shortly after entering the town center, our column nearly walked headfirst into an ambush. The town's tight quarters limited our ability to maneuver, but thankfully also limited the enemy's effectiveness. The local Taliban fighters let off a belt of machine gun fire and immediately retreated. One of our soldiers took a round straight into his armored chest plate; fortunately, that was the worst of the damage. We had been incredibly naïve and got incredibly lucky.

Over the following days, I led my platoon on numerous patrols within our new area of operations. Some patrols included Afghan soldiers. Many did not. We never received guidance in much more detail than just "get a lay of the land," and we were never issued the metal detectors or given access to the bomb-sniffing dogs that were so essential given the enemy's tactics.

On August 18, a little over a month into the deployment, I was given an order to take my platoon into a new part of our area of operations. There wasn't much logic or reason for the mission other than for us to see what was out there. The mission that had originally been planned for that day entailed partnering with a local Afghan National Army unit and checking out a few locations that were to be used as polling sites in the upcoming national election. But when my men and I woke up that morning, we learned that our Afghan partners had left the base during the night, fearing an uptick in Taliban attacks in our area as the voting approached. Eight years into our collaboration with the Afghan government, we could not rely on their army to secure their own national election. And so, the plan was changed. The new mission called for my platoon and another platoon from a sister company to move roughly in parallel for two or three kilometers through a few small villages and into some orchards. We'd then link up in the middle and depart together.

Little more than an hour into the patrol, with the other platoon about a kilometer away, we heard an explosion followed by machine gun fire. It was clear that the other platoon was in a fight. I halted my platoon, consulted the map, and chose a path that would take us to their location as quickly as possible. A quick radio message to the other platoon let them know we were en route to reinforce their position. Within minutes we had reached the edge of the town and were steadily moving toward a large orchard with our weapons at the low ready. One of my squad leaders jogged over to me and said, "Sir, this place is too quiet. Something is going to happen. You need to be ready." I nodded, and he jogged back into position.

Now our path funneled us toward a handmade footbridge stretching over an irrigation canal. I ordered one squad across the bridge to secure the far side. Then I crossed the bridge, followed by my forward observer, Jonathan Yanney, and my radio telephone operator, Roger Garcia—for calling in artillery and air strikes. I took a couple of steps on the far side of the bridge, and the world went dark. A bomb had gone off within yards of where I stood. My ears were ringing with a muffled yet high-pitched tone. I could hear rifle fire in front of me but could see only a couple of feet in any direction: there was a cloud of dust all around.

I knew that Garcia and Yanney were the soldiers closest to me, and thus probably also closest to the blast. I crawled on my hands and knees through the dust until I bumped into Garcia, who was lying on the ground. Getting my face close to his, I began speaking to him. It was clear that he was deafened and couldn't hear me. I patted him down to check for injuries, and he seemed to be in one piece. His face had some superficial cuts, which wasn't much of a problem, but I also noticed blood dripping out of his ears, which was a sign of more serious injury.

I then turned my attention back down the trail to the bridge. To where the bridge used to be, that is. As the dust settled, it became apparent that the bridge was now gone, replaced by a large and oddly dry crater. The blast had dammed up the canal to the left and the right. While all of this unfolded, my squad leaders were doing a head count. Within a minute we had accounted for everyone except Yanney. Yelling from the other side of the canal, one of my squad leaders said that Yanney had been on the bridge when it blew.

Time froze. We weren't being engaged by enemy fire, so there was no fight to direct. The men were automatically forming a security perimeter. My brain began to operate on autopilot. Get on the company radio net and submit a report? Find Yanney and treat him? Call in a medevac helicopter request? But we don't know where Yanney is—what's the medevac request procedure for that? With these thoughts racing through my mind, I slid down into the crater and clambered across.

My squad leaders moved toward me. Silently, we looked down at our feet, and that's when we all came to the same realization. Yanney was dead, and very small pieces of his remains were all around us. We could keep searching the area—and we would do that—but we all understood that Yanney was literally gone. And that's when something remarkable began to take place, in the midst of this horror. A squad leader simply said, "Sir, what do you need us to do?" There was no chatter, no swearing, not a single unnecessary word. It was all on me. I gave my orders and everyone got to work.

The platoon pulled back into a tighter perimeter. We breached every building nearby, hoping to find more of our friend's remains. Once a reinforcement unit arrived, I asked their platoon leader, one of my best friends, to assume security so my guys and I could continue the search. Having cleared the structures around us, we needed to push forward into the orchard, all the while aware that the trails and bridges—and who knew what else—were potentially booby-trapped. My soldiers formed a line, shoulder to shoulder. No metal detectors. No bomb-sniffing dogs. No explosives experts. Despite the obvious risk, no one complained and no one hesitated. It was a demonstration of professionalism, competence, and brotherhood in the obscenest of situations. It was the proudest moment of my life.

And later that night, in a nameless hamlet of adobe buildings about a kilometer away from the site of Yanney's death, my right foot stepped on the trigger of that yellow jug lying in wait for me—filled with homemade explosives, hidden in the dirt. My legs were instantly ripped off above my knees, my left hand and arm were mangled, my jaw was broken, and both eardrums were blown out. My time in Afghanistan was over. My men would continue on with eleven more months of their deployment. America would continue to pour tens of thousands more soldiers and hundreds of billions more dollars into an unwinnable war for eleven more *years*.

Since then I have endured countless surgeries and years of

physical therapy, and I have attempted, as best as possible, to reinvent myself and move on with a new career and a fresh purpose. In the Army, my purpose was to lead soldiers in an ethical and effective manner. Out of the Army, my purpose has been to bring what attention I can to the wastefulness and ineptitude that these last twenty years of war have revealed. I have written opinion pieces and spoken candidly to students, church groups, Rotary Clubs, Kiwanis Clubs, and retirement communities. I have delivered remarks at Veterans Day events, Memorial Day observances, and even once at a Christmastime service for a small town's first responders.

In 2019, I was invited to give the keynote speech to the graduating class of the Army's Infantry Officer Basic Course at Fort Benning—which I myself had attended a dozen years earlier. In that speech, I told the newly minted infantry officers that their job was to be the best and most trustworthy platoon leaders that they could be, and that the soldiers they were privileged to lead deserved their finest efforts. I also told them that they were entering an Army whose leadership had failed the nation. If and when they reached positions of higher rank and responsibility, our nation needed them to be better than their predecessors. I told them that the war that I had fought in, and that they were likely to fight in as well, was wasteful, unnecessary, and unwinnable. The lieutenant colonel who'd welcomed me onto the stage at the beginning of my speech refused to shake my hand when I finished. But more than a few of the lieutenants, and a lot of their family members, did come up and shake my hand. And they thanked me for what I had said.

America is a country with many faults, and our military, likewise, is far from perfect. But for better or for worse, as it stands, it is the only institution we have that brings Americans from all walks of life together for a single nation-sized purpose. It is also the single best way we have for an underprivileged American to advance their socioeconomic status. I wish there were another option. I wish there were another form of national service that we could offer as an alternative to the military. But until the day when that alternative is available, young Americans will continue to serve in uniform—and our national leaders, I fear, will continue to frivolously spend that precious resource.

I dissent because I have seen the wastefulness firsthand. I am a dissenter because I am an American, and I need our country to change.

GOING PUBLIC WITH THE TRUTH

Daniel L. Davis

Serving officers don't publicly dissent. It simply isn't done. The Army value of "loyalty" is supposed to mean that soldiers are loyal to the Army itself and to their fellow troopers. In practice, however, loyalty tends to require subordinates to endorse what "the boss" says, regardless of whether the boss is right or wrong. Those willing to adhere to the first definition while bucking the second tend to be few in number.

On February 5, 2012, the *Armed Forces Journal* and the *New York Times* simultaneously published two articles involving me. The first was a piece I wrote describing my just-completed deployment to Afghanistan, where I found that rosy official statements by US military leaders bore no resemblance to the abysmal conditions on the ground. The second, written by *New York Times* reporter Scott Shane, addressed the unusual nature of what I was doing: a high-ranking officer on active duty taking public his criticism of an ongoing war.

My journey from being an enthusiastic young soldier who loved the Army and believed in its leaders to one who was willing to publicly challenge the institution's top officials in a time of war was a long and painful one. Even now, years after retirement, I still love the Army, value the more than two decades I spent in it, and cherish the men and women who wear the Army fatigues. But I have been thoroughly purged of the naïveté that characterized my initial enlistment.

The truth, as Jesus said, will set you free. It can also hurt deeply.

I began my career in the US Army at the bottom, enlisting as a private in 1985. I had always planned on serving at least one tour of duty before entering the civilian workforce. I felt it was my moral obligation as a patriot to serve the country prior to pursuing my own career. My original plan was to spend two to four years in the military, then become a high school basketball and football coach. It didn't take long, however, for me to realize that I really liked the Army life—and even had a knack for it.

I served only two years of my initial four-year enlistment before realizing that I wanted to become an officer. So I went back to Texas Tech University to complete my college degree and earn a commission through the Reserve Officers' Training Corps (ROTC) as an Army second lieutenant. I reentered active duty in the summer of 1989 and attended the Field Artillery Officer Basic Course to learn the ins and outs of my assigned specialty. Upon graduation I joined my first combat unit: the highly respected 2nd Squadron, 2nd Armored Cavalry Regiment, known as 2/2 ACR.

Prior to my arrival, I had never heard of the cavalry outside of movies about America's frontier days. I quickly learned what being a modern cavalryman was all about: the 2/2 ACR was a firepower-heavy mix of tanks, armored infantry carriers, and mobile cannon. I loved it! I also loved that one of the primary mantras of the cavalry is: "When in doubt, move to the sound of the guns." In other words, when orders are unclear, you drive toward the fighting and engage the enemy wherever you find him.

As a young lieutenant serving in Germany at the tail end of the Cold War, I found that mentality greatly appealing. And it suited my personality. Though never a star athlete, I played point guard on several US Army basketball teams, matching up against other Army posts and semipro club teams in Germany. I enjoyed directing the offense and found more pleasure in getting the ball to a teammate for an easy score than in racking up high point totals myself. But when the game was on the line, I always wanted the ball in my hands to take the shot.

In early 1990, my unit took part in sophisticated war games at the German training center of Hohenfels. During the exercise, Eagle Troop, my subunit of 2/2 ACR, performed brilliantly and crushed the enemy. Our commander, then-captain H. R. McMaster—who would later rise to the rank of lieutenant general and serve as President Trump's national security advisor—was an exceptional tactician. He had prepared us so well, and provided field leadership so effectively, that we would all follow him anywhere in real combat.

Barely nine months later, we got our chance to do so. When Saddam Hussein invaded Kuwait in August 1990, President George H. W. Bush immediately sent US troops to block Saddam's presumed path to Saudi Arabia. By early 1991, my unit had been sent to the Middle East as part of the main counterattack force, and 2/2 ACR fought a pitched tank battle against the Iraqi Tawakalna Division. Eagle Troop performed under fire just as successfully as we had in training the year before.

I'll admit that I did not hate the war. I found combat to be an intense emotional rush. I was so thrilled with tank warfare, in fact, that I would eventually change my branch from Field Artillery to Armor so that I could spend my career with these rolling behemoths.

In 1991, I did not question the need for the war I fought. As a young lieutenant, I mainly focused on performing my duties. I knew that Iraq had invaded another country, and that our president had said that fighting Saddam's troops was necessary for America's security. That was enough for me; I didn't question it further.

That began to change after 9/11—though not right away. In the immediate aftermath of the terrorist attacks, I still wasn't asking any questions. Along with most of the rest of the country, I "knew" what had happened and what needed to be done: obey President George W. Bush's orders to punish the Taliban and destroy al-Qaeda. I did not have the slightest doubt that Bush sending the military to Afghanistan in October 2001 was the right thing to do.

By now a mid-level major, a staff officer assigned to the Pentagon, I soon realized that we were also about to initiate another war, targeting Iraq. Like many who fought in the 1991 war, I felt that we shouldn't have stopped our advance short of Baghdad, that we left too early, and that it was a mistake to allow Saddam to remain in power. I had always believed we would be going back someday to "finish the job." So when Bush told the American people that Saddam was a threat to our national security and that he had weapons of mass destruction (WMD) that he could use against us, I didn't hesitate to believe him.

I remember that many in Congress at the time were against the war. Still, in October 2002, the House of Representatives and the Senate both voted to authorize the use of military force against Iraq. The resolution passed comfortably, although there were still 133 votes against it in the House and 23 votes against in the Senate.

Almost all those nay votes were cast by Democrats, and at the time I dismissed them as mere partisan politics. There was far more opposition beyond our borders, however, especially from Germany and France. I remember thinking that once the invasion was complete and all those WMD found, the naysayers would realize how wrong they all had been. *They'll all be eating crow!* I thought to myself. But as the dust cleared after the fall of Baghdad in April 2003, and the days of occupation turned into weeks, there were still no WMD to be seen. That's when I began to worry.

After several months of intensive searching throughout Iraq produced nothing, it finally became clear that there had never been any WMD at all. I remember thinking in early summer 2003, *Oh my God. All those who voted against this war, all our allies who had been so adamant that there weren't any WMD, they are all going to turn on us—because we just invaded and destroyed a country without justification!* If the invasion had not been an act of self-defense, it violated the United Nations charter that the US government had signed at the end of World War II.

It was what happened next, though, that really shocked me. When the ostensible reason for invading Iraq vanished, most Americans just shrugged. Many devised an alternative rationale: "Saddam was a bad guy who deserved what he got." The president simply ignored the glaring absence of WMD. That's when things started changing for me. From that point forward, when it came to justifying war, I began to take almost nothing at face value. I would no longer merely take any leader at their word. Thenceforth, I would have to see independent evidence.

I continued working at the Pentagon until early 2005, when I was sent to my second combat deployment, this time in Afghanistan. Though many would later claim that the insurgency emerged in Afghanistan because Bush "took his eye off the ball" and diverted the war effort to Iraq in 2003, I saw firsthand that such views were inaccurate. In fact, by the summer of 2002, the Taliban had been eradicated as a viable military force; at that point, there was no need for US troops to be in Afghanistan at all. We could and should have ended the war right there and redeployed our soldiers. There was no longer an enemy to fight.

Instead, the number of US troops in the country swelled to about twenty thousand, and an insurgency began to fester. But even during my 2005 deployment, insurgents managed only sporadic, small-scale attacks, more a nuisance than anything else. In fact, I was able to drive safely to the northern city of Mazar-e-Sharif in an ordinary unarmored pickup truck, without wearing body armor. Even the then-nascent Afghan security forces would have been able to keep the remnant of the Taliban at bay without a US presence. *Why are we still in Afghanistan?* I wondered.

* * *

After my Afghanistan deployment and an eighteen-month tour in Germany, I was assigned to Future Combat Systems (FCS), the Army's premier modernization program at the time. My confidence and trust in the Army's senior leadership took another hit during this assignment.

Having already acquired a decent amount of combat experience, I identified serious flaws with FCS. I shared my concerns with senior leadership in the program and published a detailed assessment in the January 2008 edition of *Armed Forces Journal*, cataloging the problems and making recommendations for how to fix them. It didn't surprise me that the people in charge did not listen to the concerns of a relatively obscure Army major. What worried me deeply, however, was the senior leadership's willingness to obfuscate publicly and deceive Congress regarding the results of FCS testing and computer simulations.

In one particular war game simulation, for example, I played the role of the commander of a combat company equipped with FCS. A computer simulation will calculate results based only on the data programmed into it, of course. Upload the wrong parameters or inaccurate data, and the results will be equally inaccurate. In this case, without even knowing how the software had been written, I could tell immediately that it bore no resemblance to what would happen in actual combat. The simulation assumed, for instance, that every phone line, every satellite communications device, and every radio unit would be working perfectly throughout the battle, making no allowance either for interference from terrain and atmospheric conditions or for damage from enemy action. At the same time, further stacking the odds unrealistically in our favor, the enemy was scripted to be docile and unimaginative—something completely contrary to what I observed from enemy forces during my four combat deployments.

I wrote a detailed memorandum for my direct supervisor, a full colonel—and himself a combat vet—that laid out how inaccurate the simulation had been. It wasn't merely an academic question. I feared the results of this simulation would be presented as evidence that the new weapons systems worked as designed, and Congress would then be asked to fund and implement the program based on this alleged success.

As it turned out, my fears were fully realized. I was sitting in the back row of the briefing room when the civilian contracting company running the simulation presented the results of the war game to the FCS director (then a one-star general), claiming it had proved that the weapons would work in real combat. The general congratulated everyone on their fine work and then dutifully conveyed to higher headquarters that the simulation had proved FCS to be effective.

And that wasn't the worst of it. Shortly after the computer simulation, I saw the results of a field test of new equipment. It was a complete flop: almost nothing worked as expected. Upcoming in six months was a major milestone test that was critical to getting the next round of funding for FCS. By law, the results of that milestone test—good or bad—had to be reported to Congress.

FCS leaders realized that six months would not be nearly enough time to correct the equipment flaws. So they brazenly pretended that instead of failing to meet deadlines, the program was doing *better* than expected. The testing schedule had to be revised, senior leaders told Congress, because the technology was advancing more rapidly than anticipated and they were "accelerating" the program.

None of that was true, but they knew that Congress wasn't going to ask detailed questions or look carefully at the data. The falsified reports succeeded in deceiving the lawmakers. Only in mid-2009, after six years and $20 billion had been squandered, did the secretary of defense finally cancel the program. No general was ever held to account for the failure.

* * *

IT WOULDN'T BE long, unfortunately, before I would again see this seedy side of the Army's senior leadership.

In September 2009, famed *Washington Post* reporter Bob Woodward published a blockbuster article on Afghanistan. It featured a leaked report by the recently appointed commander of US forces in Afghanistan, General Stanley McChrystal, which concluded that the war was in grave danger of "mission failure." Success was "still achievable," McChrystal argued—but only if he got forty thousand more troops, on top of the sixty-eight thousand already authorized for Afghanistan.

Having already spent one combat tour in and around Afghanistan, I was very skeptical that adding yet more troops would accomplish what the previous decade of fighting had not. In an unclassified report I wrote while assigned to the Defense Intelligence Agency, I argued that the fundamentals at play in Afghanistan—standard principles of war, geography, culture, and history—were not in our favor. I listed a number of likely outcomes if President Obama chose to listen to McChrystal. Sending in forty thousand more troops,

I said, would probably exacerbate the anti-American feelings among the local population, while still not allowing us to completely eradicate the Taliban. It would produce inadequately trained Afghan National Security Forces while doing little to improve the weak and corrupt Afghan government. And it would put a major strain on our armed forces, which would suffer considerable casualties and be distracted from training their core warfighting skills.

Nearly all these predictions would turn out to be right. It bears noting that I am neither a visionary nor a prophet: the realities on the ground, the nature of the enemy, and the shortfalls of the proposed strategy should have made it obvious to anyone that McChrystal's proposal was deeply flawed. Nevertheless, in December 2009, the president largely acquiesced to McChrystal's request and ordered thirty thousand more US troops into Afghanistan (with NATO members contributing a further seven thousand).

A mere six months later, General David H. Petraeus, then commander of US Central Command, testified before Congress that US forces were moving "toward accomplishment of our important objectives in Afghanistan and we are seeing early progress as we get the inputs right in that country." I admit I was surprised that things were turning around so fast, but this was one case where I would have been delighted to be proved wrong. I was all for anything that would end the war faster, eliminate the need for US troops to be killed, and allow the Afghan people to finally live again in peace.

Around the same time, I received orders to deploy to Afghanistan as a member of the Rapid Equipping Force, a new organization created to streamline the acquisition process for deployed units. As part of the job, I traveled more than nine thousand miles during my yearlong deployment and met with well over two hundred soldiers of every rank, from privates to division commanders. To see their needs firsthand, I accompanied troops on foot patrols and vehicle patrols, attended their meetings with Afghan village leaders and military commanders, and even took part in a few special operations missions.

There probably wasn't anyone in Afghanistan at the time who witnessed as much of the fighting, at every level and region, as I did. As a result, I got to see in great detail just how dysfunctional America's war really was—and how dishonest some of our military leaders had become. The progress Petraeus and others had claimed was nonexistent.

It wasn't long before my aggravation started turning to anger. In March 2011, I read about a fairly large battle that had taken place in the mountains of eastern Afghanistan, near the Pakistan border and not far from where I had patrolled the previous month. It was known as Operation Strong Eagle III. Public reports indicated it was one of the more intense battles in recent Afghan history, with the US side suffering an uncharacteristically high casualty count: six dead and fifteen or more wounded.

The division commander, Major General John F. Campbell, told reporters that there had been large Taliban weapon caches near the site of the battle. Campbell said he "knew this area had a number of insurgents in there," and "that's why we were targeting this area." The 101st Airborne troops were saddened by the loss of their fellow troopers, Campbell said, but "they fight valiantly . . . they want to make sure their battle buddy didn't die in vain."

Anyone who has seen American combat troops in action

would not doubt the general's depiction of the troopers as fighting valiantly. The more research I did, however, the more I realized that contrary to Campbell's words, those lives had indeed been thrown away in vain.

A mere nine months before Operation Strong Eagle III, I discovered, another unit from the 101st Airborne had fought against the Taliban in almost exactly the same location, with two American soldiers killed during the battle. In that earlier engagement, the Afghan army and police ran away almost as soon as the shooting started, leaving the fight to the United States alone. We defeated the Taliban fighters, built the Afghan security forces an armored command post, and set them up to successfully hold the terrain after our departure. And yet, within weeks after we'd left, the Afghan forces abandoned the defensive positions we'd purchased with the lives of two Americans—because of rumors that the Taliban *might* return.

By the time of Operation Strong Eagle III, in other words, we knew that Afghan troops wouldn't hold the area after we attacked. So why in God's name did we go back in, throwing the lives of six more American soldiers into the dirt less than three weeks before their battalion was set to begin flying home? And as for the claims that the new mission was a serious setback for the Taliban, that our troops had found "several large, large caches," those were hogwash: we had actually found surprisingly little.

I was so furious I began contemplating a course of action that would dwarf anything I had ever done before: publicly taking on Petraeus and other generals to stand up for the truth. It wasn't just that they were deceiving Congress and the American people—though they certainly were—

but that men were dead, and more would die, to enable the perpetuation of these lies.

As months passed and my visits to forward areas piled up, I saw nothing to change my mind. Every troop unit I visited in the field reinforced the same truth: the war on the ground was going badly, we were not winning, the Afghan troops were minimally effective. And all along, senior US leaders continued selling the fiction of a war "on the right path."

If I still had any doubts about going public with my observations, they were destroyed in August 2011. I was at the forward headquarters of an infantry company in Kandahar Province, southern Afghanistan. The company commander said that despite what higher headquarters might have told me, the tactical situation for his men was dire. They had lost many lives and limbs to IED blasts, all their efforts to win the "hearts and minds" of the local population had uniformly failed, and the Afghan military was of little help. "This is becoming an all too familiar entry," I wrote in my journal, "but I am seething at the absurdity and unconcern for the lives of my fellow soldiers displayed by so many" of the senior Army leaders in Afghanistan.

I asked the company's first sergeant—the highest-ranking enlisted soldier—about his men's morale. He had been on the job for only a month, he told me; his predecessor was killed after stepping on a buried IED. (Another member of the company said that the previous first sergeant had been blown "into five pieces" by the blast.) In answer to my question, he said his men were basically "resigned to their fate. Guys are saying, 'I hope I can at least have some R & R leave before I get it,' or 'I hope I only lose a foot.' Sometimes they'll even say which limb it might be: 'Maybe it'll only be my *left* foot.'"

Though they had killed many Taliban fighters, the company commander told me, the situation was perpetually the same: the insurgents were immediately replaced, often with fighters better than the ones they'd killed. The Afghan military remained minimally capable, and the villagers still didn't trust the United States. "How do I look my men in the eye," the commander rhetorically asked me, "and ask them to go out day after day on these missions? What's harder, how do I look my first sergeant's wife in the eye when I get back and tell her that her husband died for something meaningful? How do I do that?"

To these questions I had to add one of my own: How could I go back to the United States and keep my mouth shut, doing nothing to counter the egregious lies that were getting so many Americans like these killed and dismembered?

* * *

By the time my deployment ended in October 2011, my spirit was deeply grieved and in turmoil. Many good friends were already telling me that while they sympathized with what I had observed, it would be career suicide to go public. "Why should you throw everything away and put your personal life in such trouble," one friend asked, "when you know it's not going to make any difference?"

The thing is, I knew he was almost certainly right. In all probability, I would bring considerable grief on my own head if I told the truth in public. There was active opposition to soldiers who bucked the system. And I wasn't so naïve as to believe that President Obama was going to change his war policy just because a single Army lieutenant colonel said things weren't going as advertised.

Ultimately, though, my conscience would not permit me to remain silent. I don't even think that I displayed any profound courage in what I did. I went public with the truth of the Afghan War because I *had* to; because the spirit within me would not allow me to do otherwise. Regardless of whether my words would help end the war, I felt morally obligated to report what I had seen.

If nothing else, America needed to know what was really happening on the ground in Afghanistan. The soldiers who had died there for no gain to our country were forever silenced: they could never again speak for themselves. Thousands of other troopers who knew the truth only too well also had no voice, because they had no access to publications and no reason to believe anyone would listen. The only messages that America did hear were the perpetually optimistic—and frequently outright false—reports from the senior leaders.

I had simply seen too much. I could no longer sleep at night knowing what I knew and yet not doing anything about it. The question was, how should I go about telling my story? Approach a reporter? Write something of my own? Going public in any form was sure to anger my superiors and get me in no small amount of hot water. What I didn't want to do was to make a peep that few would ever hear, and still suffer the consequences that would come from publicly rebuking the Pentagon's senior leaders. I needed to find the most "bang for the buck" so that the risk would have the maximum impact.

I enlisted the aid of three friends who would prove invaluable in helping me make the most of the situation: Matthew Hoh, Gareth Porter, and Tony Shaffer. Each played a crucial role in getting my story widely distributed. Hoh, who had gained national notoriety in 2009 when he resigned from a senior State Department job in Afghanistan in protest over the US strategies, put me in touch with Congressman Walter Jones, Republican of North Carolina. Shaffer, who took on the Pentagon when he published his 2010 book about "black ops" in Afghanistan, *Operation Dark Heart*, connected me with Scott Shane, a reporter from the *New York Times*. And Porter, author of a critically acclaimed book about the origins of the Vietnam War, *Perils of Dominance*, helped me refine my storytelling methods.

Congressman Jones eventually connected me to quite a few other members of the House and Senate, whom I met privately before anything was published. That proved enormously useful: more than one senator and representative told me that if I were to suffer retaliation from the Army, they would have my back.

The involvement of the *New York Times* was perhaps the most crucial: without it, few would ever have heard what I had to say about our military leaders' deception. The *Times* is inundated with great story ideas on a daily basis, and I am most fortunate that Shane chose to elevate mine. Shane also coordinated with the *Armed Forces Journal* to synchronize the publication of his article and the *AFJ* publishing my personal narrative.

After the *New York Times* piece ran, CNN and *PBS NewsHour* briefly covered the story and gave it further national exposure. But within weeks, the news cycle moved on and no one gave a second thought to what I had revealed. I did take quite a bit of heat from my immediate commanders, while the generals in the Pentagon—where I was working as a liaison officer at the time—did little to hide their contempt for me when we were in the same room. But compared with what other whistleblowers have suffered, my treatment was rather tame.

I have never at any point regretted my decision to go public. I knew then that it was the right thing to do, and nothing that has happened over the decade since has made me question it. I must confess, however, to some pretty significant discouragement—because the lies I illuminated in my public statements continued on, relentlessly, throughout the rest of the war. The Taliban kept getting stronger and stronger, while the Afghan government, mired in internal divisions, remained one of the most corrupt regimes in the world. Yet for years, US commanders continued to spread the fiction that we were succeeding—most infamously in late 2013, when General John Allen, outgoing commander of US forces in Afghanistan, said: "This is victory, this is what winning looks like, and we should not shrink from using these words."

The ignominious end to the Afghan War in August 2021 finally showed the whole world that twenty years of optimistic claims by a parade of generals and presidents had all been fiction. And thanks to the *Washington Post*'s Afghanistan Papers, the world got to see that it wasn't merely a matter of bad advice or "errors in judgment" but often a case of conscious, deliberate falsehoods. I and other whistleblowers knew more than a decade ago that the war would end in defeat, but the lies of our leaders ensured that this end would not come until America suffered *thousands more* unnecessary casualties.

My heart still mourns for them all.

WHAT GOOD IS DISSENT?

Roy Scranton

Socrates was a soldier. In Plato's *Symposium*, Alcibiades testifies to his courage and describes how during the Peloponnesian War Socrates disregarded physical discomfort to the point that "the men began to look at him with some suspicion and actually took his toughness as a personal insult." For Alcibiades, Socrates's wartime service spoke to his exemplary qualities as a citizen. Decades later, when Socrates was put on trial for impiety and corrupting the youth, the philosopher himself asserted that martial virtues, civic virtues, and philosophical virtues are one and the same. Courage, he contended, is foundational to the civic virtue of dissent, which is vital to the health of the nation.

His fellow citizens were not swayed, and condemned him to death.

So Socrates was a soldier. So what?

* * *

In spite of frequent invocations of war's eternal verities, the truth is that war has been experienced in different ways by different participants in different times. War is and always has been a cultural activity, and occurs in a specific cultural context. Indeed, war *produces* cultural meaning. Not only does your average grunt experience war in a given cultural context, but that grunt's particular culture derives its meaning—manifest, remembered, or imagined—from episodes of war. In this sense, war is like law or architecture, a human activity where ideas become meaningful through being embodied—in the case of war, through physical sacrifice. A dead soldier makes the imagined community of the nation real.

In contemporary American culture, war remains nationalistic and to some degree sensationalistic, focused on what I call the myth of the trauma hero: the story of a noble young man, usually white, psychologically wounded by his encounter with violence. Being a veteran marks one as having served one's country, but also as having been initiated into a select spiritual fraternity defined by a shared encounter with trauma. Soldiers, that is, embody not only the "imagined community" of the nation but a distinctive caste within it.

The historian David Bell, among others, argues that the particular constellation of meaning through which we now understand the experience of war emerged in the late eighteenth and early nineteenth centuries, along with the modern nation-state, the professional national army, and the cult of sensibility. This understanding of war as a spiritual experience, in which the veil of civilized life is pulled aside and the truth of existence is revealed—in Chris Hedges's words, "war is a force that gives us meaning"—took shape in writing by authors as different as Stendhal and Carl von Clausewitz, and achieved its most resonant articulations in twentieth-century war literature, particularly among writers responding to World War I and what Americans call the Vietnam War.

Today the trauma hero narrative is alive and well, and counterintuitively offers one of the great contemporary appeals of soldiering. War promises not only psychological wounding but also wisdom acquired through a violent encounter with the Real. But the wisdom of war is a double-edged sword. In films such as *The Hurt Locker* and *American Sniper*, novels such as Ben Fountain's *Billy Lynn's Long Halftime Walk* and my own *War Porn*, and short story collections such as Tim O'Brien's *The Things They Carried* and Phil Klay's *Redeployment*, the traumatic wounding, hardening, and socialization that characterize military training and the experience of war are depicted as being contrary to civic culture. The skills required to survive on the modern battlefield are at odds with life as a consumer-citizen in mass society. The resulting sense of alienation combines with the image of membership in a self-selecting elite to deepen the caste identity of the contemporary soldier or veteran.

War as an imagined and remembered act remains central to American national identity. Yet the actual experience of war affects a much narrower range of the population. As a practical matter, military service these days tends to be a family affair. According to the *New York Times*, "More and more, new recruits are the children of old recruits. In 2019, 79 percent of Army recruits reported having a family member who served. For nearly 30 percent, it was a parent—a striking point in a nation where less than 1 percent of the population serves in the military."

For Socrates, his war service was in many ways coextensive with his participation as a full citizen of Athens. Most of the other citizens of Athens—all men, of course—had been soldiers too. But these days, even during wartime, only a small minority of citizens serve. During the Civil War, slightly more than 10 percent of the population on both sides served in uniform. In World War II, the percentage of Americans in uniform was about the same. Today, less than one-half of 1 percent of the US population is serving on active duty, and a mere 7 percent of the population qualify as veterans.

Being part of the military caste means being part of a subset of American culture that stands in ambiguous relation to the rest of the body politic. The moral authority conferred by the experience of traumatic wounding both valorizes and alienates: embodying national identity positions the veteran as a living critique of our collective failure to maintain that identity. Like Captain America in Marvel's *Avengers*, the veteran is at once an avatar of traditional American values and the enemy of a decadent culture that has fallen away from or abandoned those values.

Today, wartime service and dissent have a curious and complex relationship. The former act creates collective identity; the latter strains it. When the two combine, they challenge the metaphysical foundation of the state, its monopoly on violence. Yet having participated in war grants dissent a moral authority.

A soldier, within the military, may dissent against the military; a veteran may dissent against civic society. In the first case, the dissenting soldier betrays their caste and fraternity for a higher ideal. In the second, they play a scripted role, imbued with moral authority but, since the Vietnam War, more or less empty of content. What is another Winter Soldier going to tell us that we don't already know? And what difference does it make? If we're winning, such dissent is irrelevant. If we're losing, it's unpatriotic. Either way, it serves mostly to remind civilians of how privileged they are to have such stalwart guardians doing their dirty work.

Whether war has ever truly served the American people or has always been just "a racket" (in the words of Major General Smedley Butler, US Marine Corps) may be an open question. What seems undeniable is that the transformation of physical sacrifice into trauma, the professionalization of the military (especially since the end of the draft), and the astonishing cynicism and failure of the American wars in Iraq and Afghanistan have attenuated whatever collective bonds might once have tied the military and citizenry together.

Some people say this military–civilian divide is a "failure of imagination" that endangers American democracy. I hold another view. The truth is, most Americans have a clear idea of what our soldiers are doing in distant theaters of war: they are defending US political and economic interests, hunting down our enemies, and wreaking vengeance on those who have done us harm. There is no divide here. The US military has a job to do, and most citizens understand exactly what that job is. "Our troops" are agents of American state power. Even in dissent, they are fiduciaries of national identity.

* * *

I WAS RAISED in a military family. My father, a grandfather, and an uncle all served in the Navy; another uncle served in the National Guard; my other grandfather served in both the Navy and the Coast Guard. Indeed, no other institution cast as large a shadow over my childhood as did the military, despite the fact that my father was discharged when I was only two years old. A squat Buddha my grandpa brought back from Southeast Asia sat near the door of my grandparents' home, and a mysterious framed award on the wall of their basement attested to his becoming a "Trusted Shellback" and servant of King Neptune after crossing the equator. My father's old white sailor cap was a beloved fetish, as were the various patches and insignia I began to collect. Military service, and particularly the adventure of fighting overseas, seemed a defining feature of masculine identity. I dreamed of growing up to become a grizzled, tattooed sailor with salty stories of danger, storms, foreign ports, and war.

The Vietnam War, though long over, seemed omnipresent. My grandfather had worked as a machinist's mate on a river patrol boat, an experience he never discussed. My father's closest brush with Vietnam was pulling duty on a destroyer tender that once anchored in Da Nang harbor, but even that slight connection to the war kept it alive in a concrete if dreamy way. All this was powerfully supported by pop culture representations of the war, as well as more literary and historical work. From the Rambo trilogy to action films such as *Missing in Action* and *Behind Enemy Lines* (a.k.a. *P.O.W. the Escape*), through memoirs such as Robert Mason's *Chickenhawk*, comic books like *G.I. Combat*, the magazine *Soldier of Fortune*, the cartoon *G.I. Joe*, and the TV show *M*A*S*H*, to say nothing of much more prestigious and well-known films such as *Apocalypse Now*, *Platoon*, and *Full Metal Jacket*, I absorbed the Vietnam War as an ongoing historical event whose meaning was still being fought over—a fight in which my family had a stake greater than others, because our men had served there.

My childhood was a mélange of Vietnam, World War II, and the Cold War, with its background threat of nuclear apocalypse. I spent hours playing "guns" with my friends in the neighborhood, digging trenches for my G.I. Joe figures, and poring over old military manuals and *Jane's Fighting Ships*. At the height of my obsession, I would sometimes go to school bedecked entirely in camouflage, and once got in trouble for bringing a hollowed-out Mk 2 hand grenade to class.

In junior high and high school, my interests changed, as did the culture. The Persian Gulf War, while presented in the media as a morally virtuous spectacle of American power, proved something of a disappointment. After the end of the Cold War, the US military's imperial mission seemed diminished. The armed forces looked less like a noble calling, and meanwhile I was getting interested in other things: role-playing games like *Dungeons & Dragons*, computers, girls, theater. I began to define myself more and more in opposition to my family, or so I thought, seeking my own sense of meaning and selfhood. By the time I graduated high school, the idea of going into the military seemed like a joke.

Fast-forward several years and I was in Moab, Utah, working as a breakfast cook and bookshop clerk. By that point I had few prospects. I'd dropped out of two different colleges, bounced through a series of soul-numbing service jobs, and quit the one job I'd ever had that meant something to me, working as a grassroots campaign organizer for a nonprofit research organization, because I had become disillusioned by the gap I perceived between their values and their practices.

I considered myself a writer, but I'd published only a couple of short pieces in tiny journals. Still, I'd found a community in the desert, and spent most of my time reading and writing. A quiet, quasi-hermetic life among the red rocks seemed an acceptable fate. But in the weeks after my twenty-fifth birthday, three things happened in violent succession that changed my perspective: a friend died; I broke my front tooth in a bicycle accident and couldn't afford to get it fixed; and nineteen dedicated soldiers of Islam gave their lives to strike a blow to the heart of American empire.

When people ask me why I joined the Army at the ripe old age of twenty-five, I tell them that I came from a military family, and that I wanted to see what war was like, go back to college, and understand how the world had changed after 9/11. I also needed health care and a new tooth. I enlisted neither innocently nor cynically but intentionally and curiously, even searchingly. I hoped to learn from the military and take advantage of the social mobility it promised. I also hoped that a term of service might shape me in meaningful ways without leaving me too warped or damaged to carry on toward my goal of becoming a writer.

I suppose it worked.

* * *

THE REALITY OF modern war is that it's not magic, not a spiritual encounter with truth, not a sacred duty, but a dirty, dangerous, mostly boring job.

Maybe that's just my perspective. I served four years in

the Army and spent fourteen months in Iraq, mainly driving a Humvee around Baghdad. I entered as a private and left as a sergeant. I sustained no combat injuries, though I was given a minor VA disability as compensation for what was essentially wear and tear. No PTSD, no crushing war guilt, and just enough of a taste of combat to know that I don't like shooting at people or being shot at.

I never experienced the thrill of leading an assassination squad to murder a suspected insurgent, nor did I ever have to fight my way out of a mountain ambush, nor was I responsible for the kinds of administrative and moral decisions faced by four-star generals. I was just another soldier, competent enough and grudgingly determined—first to do my job, then to get the hell out. I still remember my first sergeant trying to bully me into reenlisting, telling me that my idea of going back to school was a farce and that I'd wind up working at McDonald's. "That dog don't hunt, Sergeant Scranton," he kept saying. "That dog don't hunt."

The period from when I left the Army in 2006 to when I entered the PhD program in English at Princeton four years later was a complicated and challenging time for me. My efforts to make sense of the ongoing war in Iraq were tied up with my service there, my inherited identity as a member of the military caste, my working-class background, my aspirations to become a scholar and novelist, and my tumultuous personal life at the time, which revolved around a group of veteran writers who came together through the NYU Veterans Writing Workshop.

My thinking in those years was certainly critical, but hardly iconoclastic. There seemed to be widespread popular agreement that the invasion of Iraq was a mistake, a sentiment Barack Obama would leverage against both Hillary Clinton and former Vietnam POW John McCain to win the presidency. There was nothing special at that point in being against the war: it was part and parcel of being against George W. Bush, who had gone from having the highest presidential approval rating ever, in the aftermath of 9/11, to having the lowest rating ever, by early 2008 (an honor he still holds, even after Trump).

If I dissented from anything, it was from the simplistic and reductive ways that contemporary American society viewed military life, the experience of war, and the occupation of Iraq. I dissented especially from the trauma hero narrative, which not only obscured the reality of Iraq but was even forced on me at one point by a professor who seemed compelled to "save" me. I dissented from the idea that there was nothing valuable in military service or that anyone who served was a chump—that, as Chris Hedges put it, "war is a story of elites preying on the weak, the gullible, the marginal, the poor." The truth was more complex. The war in Iraq was indeed a disaster, but my service there meant something to me, however difficult that was to explain to my fellow New Yorkers.

The alienation and dissent I felt in relation toward the broader culture were more than made up for by the sense of belonging I felt among my veteran friends. Over time, though, that, too, began to change. The US occupation of Iraq came to an end. I started grad school and stopped going to the vets workshop as often. Several of us began to find some success as "veteran writers." And perhaps most important, with my experience as a soldier in Iraq fading into the past, I began to build a new identity as a literary scholar and writer, connected to and fed by but ultimately independent of my identity as a veteran. Or so I hoped.

I often recalled a line that J. Glenn Gray had written in 1973: "Building a life on solid accomplishment is more difficult than being an antiwar veteran and confessing one's guilt in public." The observation stung because Gray was himself a veteran. He'd served as an intelligence officer in Europe during World War II, then went on to a career in philosophy. He'd written about his war experience with power and subtlety in *The Warriors: Reflections on Men in Battle*, but only years after the fact. Like other soldier-scholars such as Paul Fussell, Samuel Hynes, and Frank Kermode, Gray built a new life after the war on work unrelated to his service, rather than trading on his experience to become a kind of "professional veteran." His example both shamed and inspired me.

* * *

In 2014, while finishing my dissertation, I got the chance to go back to Baghdad for *Rolling Stone* magazine, to write about the legacy of the American occupation there, ten years after my tour. Iraq was gearing up for its first post-occupation election, ISIS had just taken Fallujah, the violence was as bad as it had been during the war, and Americans seemed intent on forgetting the whole thing, as if electing Obama had absolved the nation of any responsibility for what happened in Iraq after US troops had left.

I was in Baghdad for almost two weeks. Most of that time I spent interviewing Iraqis: listening to stories of family members disappeared and children murdered in the sectarian civil war nurtured by the US occupation, learning about the legacy of the Iran–Iraq War (another conflict fostered by the United States), listening to weary Baghdadis tell me things had actually been better under Saddam because even tyranny is preferable to chaos. Confronting the irreparable human damage caused by the American occupation of Iraq was a powerful and painful experience, but even more painful was seeing how abruptly and completely the United States had abandoned the people of Iraq after 2011. There were American oil companies in Baghdad, of course, and the flacks at the embassy, a few investors comfortable with high risk, and some journalists visiting for the election—but very little sustained effort on the US side toward cultural exchange, civic investment, or even mere engagement. I was astonished and baffled that we could batter a country for decades, spill American blood to free it from tyranny, and then just walk away.

It was bad enough that the Iraq War was a horrific fiasco, a gruesomely cynical racket, and—in light of the Syrian civil war and the rise of ISIS—a dangerous political error. But that we thought we could wash our bloody hands and not even offer the pretense of humanitarian aid in the aftermath of our recklessness was so ghastly it turned my stomach. My piece for *Rolling Stone*, "Back to Baghdad: Life in the City of Doom," was one of the most difficult things I've ever had to write. Trying to wrap the article up in a conclusion was physically painful. By the end of the process, as I wrote then, "I could feel nothing but disgust and shame for having been an American soldier."

I feel the same today. I wish I could say that "Back to Baghdad" was the last thing I wrote about "my war," or being a veteran, or the problem of how to make sense of the relationship between military service, American empire, democratic ethics, and capitalism. But though the article felt (to me, at least) like a turn away from the ambiguous role of professional veteran I'd been playing, it was followed by the publication of the war novel I'd first drafted several years earlier; by a dissertation focused on war literature; by several other articles and book reviews on related topics; and by a collection of essays that featured a longer version of the *Rolling Stone* piece. To paraphrase Marx, we may make our careers, but we do not make them just as we please.

I marched against the Iraq War in 2007. I've publicly denounced our invasion and occupation of Iraq, American empire, and the American culture of violence from platforms as prominent as the *New York Times* and *Rolling Stone*. I've written a well-reviewed book of fiction that is both an anti-war novel and an anti-war-novel novel: it not only highlights the depravity of the war but implicates the reader's desire for war stories besides. I've studied war literature from the ancient Greeks to Elizabethan England to the present, and written a scholarly book about how the changing production and reception of American literature of World War II provides evidence of a transformation in how American culture thinks about war.

In other words, I've both "confessed my guilt in public" and tried to "build a life on solid accomplishment." I've dissented against American culture and politics as a veteran, and I've dissented against veteran culture and politics too. But unlike Socrates, I haven't been sentenced to death. Rather, it was precisely through my military service, the GI Bill, and my writing as a professional veteran that I've been able to climb

from a working-class military family to an Ivy League PhD, and now to a tenured job at the University of Notre Dame.

So it is no wonder to me that my nephew recently joined the Army, despite my warning him against it. My admonitions were undermined by my own example, and by the fact that the military is one of the few possibilities left in American society for upward social mobility. I couldn't deny that I was better off, physically, psychologically, and materially, because of my military service. And I'm certain that, among whatever other ideas might have motivated my nephew, he could see that. Indeed, it may be that the military was the best option he had, just as it had been my best option when I enlisted.

Perhaps I should have worked harder to impress on him that I was one of the lucky ones, and there was no guarantee he would be. Perhaps I should have worked harder to make myself more an example of dissent, and shown more moral courage, and taken more risks to speak out against the moral emptiness of twenty-first-century American imperialism. Because if I couldn't convince my own nephew that doing what George Orwell called "the dirty work of empire" was morally corrupting, how could I convince my fellow citizens that the moral costs of American empire outweigh the benefits of the "American way of life"?

* * *

When I think about what kind of dissent might really mean something in America today, I find myself increasingly skeptical of the Socratic example, the martyr for truth. Unlike in Socrates's time, when the dissenter philosophized in the marketplace and faced his critics in person, today voice is inseparable from platform, and platform inseparable from privilege. Dissent is thoroughly institutionalized, which means thoroughly tamed, whether that institution is a university, the *Washington Post*, or Twitter.

More and more, I am drawn instead to the quiet dissent of those who refuse the intoxications of social media and the seductions of "having a voice" altogether. I look to those who abjure self-aggrandizing fantasies of changing the world, reject the cynicism of rhetoric and the degradations of politics, and devote themselves to the humble reparative work of staffing homeless shelters, teaching in prisons, organizing the poor, building community gardens, caring for the sick, and volunteering for worthy causes—especially those who, in the words of Pope Francis, "tirelessly seek to resolve the tragic effects of environmental degradation on the lives of the world's poorest."

Socrates was a soldier and a dissenter, but so was Francis of Assisi, the current pope's namesake. As a youth, the man who would become Saint Francis fought in a campaign against Perugia, where he was captured and held prisoner for more than a year. After his return to Assisi, he joined another military expedition but was stopped on the way by a vision and turned from a life of wealth and ambition to a life of poverty, charity, and devotion. Today, as we confront a global ecological crisis with no easy or simple answers, while at the same time being faced with an interlocking proliferation of social crises that range from rising inequality to the failure of democracy to the deeply disturbing effects of social media, we would be wise to ask ourselves what lies behind our dissent, what goals we hope to achieve, and whether our means are consonant with our ends.

Speaking out may no longer be enough. In our time of flood and fire, much like the calamitous thirteenth century in which Saint Francis founded his order, dissent may need to take form not in words but in deeds: not as yet another public profession of critique but as the solid accomplishment of repair.

WHEN GRUNTS COMPLAIN

Buddhika Jayamaha

Not always, but sometimes, grunts can live in perfect harmony with war. The command environment, the caliber of soldiers, and the nature of the mission all play a role. Under good leaders, with good comrades, grunts will take extreme risks because they trust one another and their commanders. Along the way, they will also speak their minds with no sense of self-censorship. As the Army saying goes, it's a good day when grunts complain: it means they care.

In August 2007, at the tail end of back-to-back deployments to Iraq, a bunch of us in the 82nd Airborne Division were in just that frame of mind. It was the height of what came to be known as "the surge" in Iraq, a last-ditch attempt by US military officers to turn the tide of war and make the country into something resembling a functional state. Back in America, the already divisive political discourse was reaching new heights of acrimony. But it mostly focused on the superficial and the banal, with little attention to the realities on the ground that soldiers witnessed and Iraqis lived through. So as enlisted airborne infantrymen, we deemed it only appropriate to offer our assessment of the ongoing conflict to the august pages of the *New York Times*. After all, who had a better sense of how the war was really going in the streets of Iraq?

Paratroopers say, only partly in jest, that nicotine, caffeine, and unmitigated rage add up to a pretty effective formula. It was this formula, plus irreverent confidence, that motivated us to take aim at the commentariat and the pundits at home. We were not thinking in grand terms, nor were we driven by specific political predilections. But we were dead serious about highlighting some of the gritty realities soldiers face when fighting other people's wars.

Our presence may have released Iraqis from the grip of a tyrant, we wrote, but it also robbed them of their self-respect. The best way to regain that dignity would be for them to call us what we were—an army of occupation—and force our withdrawal. Until then, the best approach required increasingly letting them take center stage, assisting them from the margins while allowing them to resolve their differences as they saw fit. Ultimately, winning had to be their business.

The sentiment we expressed was by no means original, and eventually in the war against ISIS, something similar would be formalized into a strategy: "By, With, and Through." The notion of letting Iraqis take center stage in their own country seems self-evident in retrospect. Retrospect, though, always confers a false sense of clarity. Events leading up to our decision to share our irreverent confidence with the *New York Times* were a bit more complicated.

* * *

When I watched the Twin Towers come down on 9/11, I was a father, a husband, a bank employee, a graduate student in international affairs, and a permanent resident of the United States in the process of becoming a naturalized citizen. Like most Americans, I obsessively followed America's entry into wars in Afghanistan and Iraq. Of all the details of the time, what I remember most is how the more I watched and read about the wars, the more I worked myself into a soul-crushing depression. When I joined the Army, I met many others who shared that experience.

There are moments in life when the smart thing to do and the right thing to do don't necessarily align. By 2004, that defined my dilemma. The country was politically polarized, the wars were going badly, but none of that mattered to me. What mattered was my overwhelming conviction that if I did not do my small part in this broader fight, I would regret it for the rest of my days. Yet what if going to war cost me my life, leaving my daughter to grow up fatherless and my wife a single mother? There was no good answer.

There was, however, an imperative, felt by so many other Americans as well. Irrespective of their sentiments toward the wars, they were saying: here I am, send me. Why? Because they thought it was their duty as citizens. And so it was with me. On October 14, 2004, I became a naturalized US citizen. On October 15, I went to the Army recruiter's office and asked to enlist in the airborne infantry. I requested assignment to the 82nd Airborne Division, known by the nickname All American.

The Army has a way of bringing people together from all over America and giving them a home. The Army gave me a home too.

The 82nd Airborne lived up to its nickname. There were people of many different races, ethnicities, religions, and socioeconomic backgrounds—as well as, most surprising to me, immigrants from many different countries. The institution and its leaders created an environment where soldiers single-mindedly focused on the mission regardless of their differences, yet without compromising their individuality. Only two things mattered: whether you could perform and whether you gave your all. If you could and did, you were in. If you could not or did not, you were worthless, and there were plenty of superiors at hand to point it out.

Some of my experiences in training were memorable because they exceeded my expectations, and some were memorable for their endearing absurdities. At Fort Bragg, North Carolina, most of us were housed in dilapidated barracks built in the sixties, with ceilings falling apart and condemned rooms infested with mold. It was obvious, as our senior NCOs often pointed out, that the armed forces had been an afterthought in the minds of policymakers in the previous decade. And to say the IT system was antiquated would be an understatement. We joked that this was by design: no enemy can hack a system that does not work. Everyone turned their complaints into humor and had an attitude of "figure shit out and make it happen."

On the first day, another new guy and I walked into the dilapidated barracks bathroom. (At the time the unit was all male.) A senior noncommissioned officer with multiple combat deployments was sitting in a doorless stall with his pants around his ankles. One hand held a magazine on firearms, the other a spit-bottle for his mouthful of chewing tobacco. He casually looked up, spat into his spitter, and introduced himself as one of the NCOs who would be training the new guys to get them up to speed. "Let me pinch this turd off and link up with you boys in five mikes," he said. We had arrived.

An atmosphere of immediacy animated our unit. A sense of intensity and purpose made for a relentlessly unforgiving setting. We would deploy soon, and we had to be ready. The only way to be ready was to train. Train the way we fight and fight the way we train: that was the mantra.

All the senior NCOs and even most of the buck sergeants had combat experience, while most of the young officers and all the enlisted privates and specialists—the majority of the unit—had none. A long series of intensive training cycles and multiple organizational reforms eventually whittled our unit down to half its original size. This was by design. When our turn to deploy came, we were fewer in number, but we were ready.

When we arrived in Iraq, our job was to kill or capture high-value individuals. We had volunteered to be in the fight, had trained to kick down doors, and now were finally getting the opportunity to do the job. It was a dream come true. This was what we had signed up for.

Dreams in war have their costs. Our unit would go on to receive the Presidential Unit Citation, awarded for extraordinary heroism in action against an armed enemy. Along the way, we incurred a 21 percent casualty rate. That was considered high for this war—though as we kept reminding ourselves, it paled in comparison with earlier wars, where many dared far more and fared far worse. This kept us inspired. And while continuous combat was wearing us down, it was also making us better at our job. Experience sharpens intuition and increases one's confidence in making decisions of consequence.

Some members of the unit, after completing a six-month deployment, went home for less than two weeks and immediately returned as some of the first boots on the ground for the surge. By August 2007, some of us were approaching fourteen months of nearly uninterrupted combat. We had spent more time with one another in those months than with anyone else, and the shared experiences of combat create bonds that last a lifetime. We unequivocally trusted our leaders and one another.

* * *

SOLDIERS AND OFFICERS read, some more than others, and our unit was no different. We read about our trade, about tactics, and about politics at home. As the war polarized discussion back in America, we increasingly saw politicians and pundits trying to appropriate what was happening in Iraq in behalf of their own agendas. Iraq per se was irrelevant; how Iraq would affect domestic politics was all that mattered.

We took all this in with humor. In Iraq, we had become familiar with numerous insurgent groups, and many of these had what was referred to as a "spiritual leader," usually a high-ranking cleric. An Iraqi friend of ours explained the underlying dynamics. He saw these spiritual leaders as the worst of the bunch—peddlers of self-serving delusions in the guise of faith who gave real clerics a bad name. Fascinated by power, these leaders could never actually wield it directly. Instead, they used their spiritual authority to influence the action by leveraging their followers. And the best part of being a spiritual leader was that one was never held accountable for the consequences of one's thoughts and words. Ah, we thought: We know how this goes. We have the same thing in America, where commentators, columnists, and public intellectuals play out a profane version of spiritual leadership for their devoted following.

Soon, soldiers in my unit started speaking of the most prominent American public intellectuals and TV commentators as mirror images of Iraqi spiritual leaders. The TVs in our recreation tent were tuned to the Armed Forces Network, and the news broadcasts were mostly Fox News. But some genius or jokester at the network had decided to supplement these with the ribald commentary of Jon Stewart and *The Colbert Report*. The parodies, we thought, captured the reality of our experience much more accurately than the straight news programs.

Many of us felt that the extreme hubris of American politicians and the commentariat was responsible for the mess in Iraq. Our military leaders in Iraq were fighting tooth and nail to craft a winning strategy to salvage what was turning out to be an ignominious military and political failure. We found it enraging that the same folks who had breathlessly cheered the nation into war were now imparting half-baked wisdom from their safe confines about what our military leaders were getting wrong. The tragedy is that when American opinion makers mislead the public and misinform them about the realities of warfighting, it has a direct impact on how the war is waged. That's because the legitimacy of our combat power ultimately comes from the people in whose name we fight. As soldiers of an all-volunteer force in a democracy, we know our personal predilections regarding the mission we've been asked to execute are irrelevant. As long as it is legal and ethical, we've always believed that it is our duty to carry it out.

What was really going on in Iraq, meanwhile, had little to do with American military superiority. Our combat primacy was never in doubt. But we doubted the willingness of people back home to commit to what the realities on the ground required: the widespread use of lethal force. And we also recognized the struggles of our Iraqi counterparts. This was not because of any personal failings: committed Iraqi soldiers were as good as any of us. But they could not be the best versions of themselves, because the institutional structure was not there. The contrast in this respect between us and them was striking and disheartening. As American soldiers, we were kept immune from the political vicissitudes of the wider American society. Iraqi soldiers, on the other hand, had to worry about their ethnic, linguistic, sectarian, and political affiliations, because the Iraqi military was also a contested political space. That meant they always had to watch their backs, they could barely trust their comrades, and they could not trust their leaders.

American counterinsurgency strategy had two facets. One was the feel-good approach of winning hearts and minds. The other involved killing off the most extreme and getting the fence-sitters to choose: as we used to say, violence has a way of working on the heart by way of the mind. In this way, relying on our combat primacy, we had managed to create a tapestry of control in Iraq. But that tapestry held together only because myriad Iraqi groups recognized that we had a preponderance of resources and power. We may have set the stage, but the decisions of those Iraqi groups mattered as much as our own efforts. And what would come in our absence?

So at the tactical level—our particular interest, politics be damned—enabling our Iraqi colleagues to do their jobs meant that they had to take ownership of the war. They needed to claim a larger share of the killing, even if the outcome was going to be bloodier. Bloodier not because they sought gratuitous violence but because the Iraqi military hardly had the capacity to apply violence with a sense of surgical precision. They would have to overcome their shortcomings with a preponderance of indiscriminate violence. Though unpleasant, if applied with clear strategic goals in mind, it is a military tactic that goes a long way toward generating desired outcomes.

* * *

SOLDIERS IN WAR take their jobs seriously but rarely themselves. Maybe not taking themselves seriously is necessary for taking the job seriously. And it was no different with us. Between missions one day, we were once again kicking around those ideas about counterinsurgency tactics while making fun of the misguided pronouncements of some prominent American "spiritual leaders." Perhaps, we thought, "the troops" that the politicians and spiritual leaders kept reverently referring to should actually have a say, if only for a moment. "You knuckleheads should write something up," an NCO in the unit suggested. Sure, we said. We'll do it in the *New York Times*.

It was a joke, but also not. We knew Americans were not getting the straight scoop about why the Iraq War hadn't turned out as planned, and we wanted to provide a glimpse of the little corner of the war that we had become intimately familiar with. Now suddenly there was a dare and a wager. At stake were sublime libations—for soldiers are resourceful, and we knew where to find the right stuff. Nightcaps at dawn it was. Game on.

Irreverent as we were, we were responsible soldiers committed to the mission, and loyal to our leaders and the Army. We knew that we were operating around the limits of our freedom of expression, because when we'd raised that right hand, we chose to forgo some of our individual rights. We also knew that as enlisted soldiers and NCOs, we had a bit more maneuvering space in our ability to express ourselves than commissioned officers did.

That brought us to another dilemma. Should we ask our commissioned officers for permission? If we did, that would put them in a difficult position—and us, too, for if our leaders said no, we wouldn't disobey them. On the other hand, not telling them would inevitably put them in the hot seat when the piece came out. We decided to go with the latter alternative and just hope that the hot seat wouldn't be too hot. When all was said and done, the officers could comfort themselves by calling us the knuckleheads that we were.

And so it was that the *New York Times* wound up running "The War as We Saw It," coauthored by half a dozen NCOs from the 82nd Airborne and me. "We are skeptical of recent press coverage portraying the conflict as increasingly manageable and feel it has neglected the mounting civil, political and social unrest we see every day," we wrote. "The claim that we are increasingly in control of the battlefields in Iraq is an assessment arrived at through a flawed, American-centered framework. Yes, we are militarily superior, but our successes are offset by failures elsewhere. . . . A vast majority of Iraqis feel increasingly insecure and view us as an occupation force that has failed to produce normalcy after four years and is increasingly unlikely to do so as we continue to arm each warring side."

Part of the problem, we explained, lay in the bewildering tangle of the groups involved in the fighting: Sunni extremists, Shiite militiamen, al-Qaeda terrorists, armed tribes, unaffiliated criminals. The situation was made even more complex by the questionable loyalties of the Iraqi police and the Iraqi Army, which had been trained and armed at American expense. Even if their battalion commanders were well-meaning, they had little to no influence over the thousands of obstinate men loyal only to their militias.

After an armor-piercing explosive was detonated between two Iraqi-controlled checkpoints, for example, killing one American soldier and critically wounding two others, local Iraqis readily told us that that Iraqi police and Army officers had escorted the triggermen and helped plant the bomb. But these civilians couldn't alert us beforehand: the Iraqi Army, the police, or the local Shiite militia would have killed their families. And such incidents were virtually routine. Our enemies were determined; our allies, questionable at best.

Coupling our military strategy to an insistence that the Iraqis meet political benchmarks for reconciliation was also unhelpful. Political reconciliation couldn't happen at our command. It would occur only on Iraqi terms when the reality on the battlefield became congruent with that in the political sphere. There were no magnanimous solutions that would please every party. There would be winners and losers, and our only choice was to decide which side to take. Trying to please every party in the conflict, as we were doing, would only ensure hatred from all involved in the long run.

Meanwhile, we noted, "the most important front in the counterinsurgency, improving basic social and economic conditions, is the one on which we have failed most miserably." There were two million Iraqis in refugee camps in neighboring countries and almost two million more internally displaced, while cities lacked regular electricity, phone service, and sanitation. As for security, the fact that American observers could now safely walk down the streets of formerly violent towns was not the relevant measure. What the locals saw was a lawless environment where men with guns ruled the streets and simply engaging in the banalities of life was a death-defying act. When the primary preoccupation of average Iraqis was when and how they were likely to be killed, handing out care packages didn't do much good. It all added up to a situation where the best thing for American forces to do was to pull back to the margins and develop a nuanced strategy to assist Iraqis so they would take ownership of the fight. We simply pointed out "the war as we saw it," so that others could think of the broader implications.

* * *

Not by coincidence, our essay appeared just as our commanding general was attending highly publicized hearings on Capitol Hill. Having published the piece and won the in-house wager, we deliberately chose not to follow how it was received at home, though, for entertainment value, some of our colleagues would bring up from time to time bits of the more egregious commentary we provoked. Nor did we engage in any follow-up discussions on the topic. We had said all there was to say. Now it was back to continuing the mission.

Given the loud political cacophony at home, it was inevitable that the officers in our unit would have to address the piece. When one of them received complaints from prominent folks back in America about his soldiers talking to the press, his response to them was: "What appears to be the problem? I see no problem."

As for our senior commanding officers, when questioned about our essay, they first mentioned that almost all their staff agreed with our depiction of the multifaceted challenges on the ground. They commended us on work nicely done. Then they told us: "Given the adversaries we are facing, outfighting them means outthinking them. You are fighting soldiers but also thinking soldiers. Keep fighting, keep thinking, and as for writing, that is a right that we fight to keep. Keep writing!"

It is perhaps no accident that our senior officers were the only ones to see what we wrote through an objective lens. They were dealing with the same realities we were and, like us, could see the issues close up. Therefore, they saw our essay for what it was and knew us to be committed soldiers. For our part, we had always trusted our leaders, but this experience distinctly deepened our loyalty to the Army as a whole. While various spiritual leaders back at home were ranting their heads off, our leaders could be magnanimous and give us top cover, precisely because the institution allowed for it. In this case, the smart thing to do and the right thing to do went together. One could not say the same of many other institutions.

That was our experience with military dissent. The time, the place, the nature of the unit, and the leadership all play a role in how such events transpire. Perhaps we were naïve, but in truth we never really expected to get in trouble for our piece. We did expect at least someone in the military hierarchy to lose their wits over it, which would give us fodder for more humor. But that barely happened, we suspect because more astute heads prevailed.

At the end of the day, we had the confidence to do what we did because we trusted our colleagues and hoped that our leaders would cut us some slack even though we'd put them on a hot seat. Our leaders did not disappoint. They proved to take the job seriously but not themselves.

In no time we forgot our moment of passing notoriety, for we still had to continue our mission. In the end, of the seven of us that penned the piece, one passed away in an accident, one was severely wounded but lived, and two were killed in action. One of those two was a permanent resident in the process of becoming a US citizen. From a legal standpoint, a petition to become a citizen usually dies with the person. But during times of war, the military is allowed an exception. And just as our colleague lived up to his enlistment oath by making the ultimate sacrifice, the institution lived up to its own promise. The Army flew in some of his immediate family from his country of origin to attend the funeral. And a federal clerk showed up to the ceremony to make him an American citizen before the burial.

* * *

The Army provided me with a home, a purpose, and a tribe. Whether armies and wars bring out the best or worst in people will forever be debated. But what I do know from my experience is that the armed forces attract a self-selected group with some consistent characteristics. It seems that for those of us who join, something distinctive resonates in the deep recesses of our hearts. For the call to service is ultimately an affair of the heart.

Most of those who volunteer find a sense of meaning and purpose in life by belonging to something larger than themselves. And from day one of training, it seems everything is designed to inculcate a sense of mission and service. As some career NCOs would tell us: "If you are in the Army because you took a wrong turn somewhere—and you are—then it is our job to make sure it was the last wrong turn. We will make sure you end up at the right place. And if you take one more wrong turn, we will skull-drag you down the street out of love."

Senior officers, with a better vocabulary and better training in the art of eloquence, would say much the same thing in different words. "By raising your right hand, you have proved that you are committed. Now we will make sure you turn into the leaders that your soldiers deserve. And along the way, we will make great citizens out of you."

That animating intensity of purpose is what most soldiers miss when they leave the armed forces. And for the enlisted, that void is coupled with the painful realization that the skill set they acquired has little applicability to civilian life, at least if they were at the sharp end of the spear kicking in doors.

So it was for me when I left the Army. I needed to retool and acquire a new skill set. In addition to making good soldiers and great citizens, the military also teaches recruits about themselves. The Army taught me that I am innately goal-oriented, that I need to have clear objectives to live and not self-destruct. Warfighting taught me that I can think critically. And working with my commanders taught me that I can write and that I want to speak my mind. So, armed with multiple recommendation letters written in my behalf by the very officers whom we put on a hot seat, I walked into a fully funded PhD program in political science at a top university.

Academia showed me what true privilege looks like, and how absurd it is when people unaware of their privilege sustain a narrative of victimhood by indulging in a contrived siege mentality. Having been trained in the Army to speak my mind, I also realized that, contrary to all the highbrow claims, not all corners of academia allow a person to do that. In fact, outspokenness could be quite detrimental. I realized that academia would not be my natural home. I completed my PhD, but in my moment of success I once again felt a deep depression.

I had too many choices, and every choice seemed hollow. I had survived the war relatively unscathed, thankful to my colleagues, leaders, and God for saving my dumb ass. I carried in my heart the memories of all my comrades I'd carried to the medevac birds, injured or dead. The best way to honor those who made the ultimate sacrifice, I knew, was not to quit when things got tough, to keep going, to try to do better with every step. But what would be the most meaningful way to spend the rest of my life? How could I be of service again?

Once more, my colleagues and some mentors we'd put on a hot seat came through for me. They eloquently pointed out, as only dear friends can, that I am dumb as a box of rocks, that I have a bad attitude, that I run my mouth and I speak my mind. In other words, I am fundamentally unemployable—except in the military! Once again armed with their recommendations, cheerleading, and inspiration, I set out to get a job but ended up finding my calling. Now I teach at the US Air Force Academy, where I get to dissent to my heart's content while playing my part in improving our armed forces as we prepare for the next fight. And the true privilege is that I also get to play a role in the personal, intellectual, and professional growth of the next generation of our military leaders. Leaders with critical minds; leaders who, when necessary, will speak truth to power by providing constructive criticism while remaining unwaveringly committed to the mission, the armed forces, and the nation.

THE ACCOUNTABILITY-AVOIDANCE TWO-STEP

Jason Dempsey

As a young infantry officer in the United States Army, I spent a lot of time trudging through the woods. It was rarely the graceful, stealthy experience depicted in recruiting commercials, but rather the resigned shuffling of heavily burdened men walking with all the grace of turtles. Soldiers inevitably tripped and fell, and over time I noticed a recurring pattern. With a crash and quiet cursing, the turtle in front of me would fall on his back, having failed to negotiate a fallen log across our path. And then, while I was silently mocking my comrade for his inability to navigate an obvious obstacle, my own foot would catch the hole hidden on the back side of the log, and I would join him in a tangle of weapons and gear.

That experience, clumsy as it was both in reality and as metaphor, increasingly comes to mind when I consider the legacy of our post-9/11 wars. Having grown up in the aftermath of Vietnam, my father's war, I started my Army career with a firm belief that our military could learn from experience and adapt over time. Our conduct in Iraq and Afghanistan revealed that faith to be wildly naïve. World War II veteran Paul Fussell once said, "To become disillusioned you must earlier have been illusioned." For my part, I don't think I had many illusions about military service at the outset. But my military education inculcated them in me over time, and it took years for me to fully comprehend the plodding bureaucratic reality behind the failure of those campaigns.

My high school coming-of-age was marked by indecisiveness and indifference. Moving around the world in an Army family, I experienced the whiplash of beginning high school among military brats on a base in South Korea before ultimately graduating from a school in the middle of Missouri where anyone not clearly identified as Black or white might be casually referred to as a "half-breed." Although I'd grown up listening to soldiers gripe about the inefficiencies of the system, the Army didn't seem like such a bad way to get out of that place. That I was considering it at all, in a society increasingly divorced from the military, placed me in that small caste of Americans for whom military service is a family business.

Being one of the very few military kids in my high school, I also saw the visit of a West Point recruiter as a plausible excuse for skipping out of English class. My idea of military schools had come largely from the 1981 movie *Taps*, and I had no desire to plunge into the *Toy Story* meets *Lord of the Flies* atmosphere depicted there. But the recruiter's description of the actual United States Military Academy caught my attention. I decided that if I didn't know what I wanted to be when I grew up, there were worse places to figure that out than one that offered physical challenges and a free education. So began my illusionment.

For decades, Robert Heinlein's novel *Starship Troopers* has been taught in elective classes at West Point, and I first picked up a copy as a cadet. I found it fascinating: the certainty and righteousness of military service; the elevation of the military to the preeminent position in political life; the clarity and lack of equivocation about the utility of force. *Starship Troopers* told me everything I wanted to hear as a young infantryman-to-be, and I studiously highlighted and underlined the great quotes and insights into military life. After finishing it, I eagerly lent it to a civilian friend from high school. He returned it a few months later and thanked me for going out of my way to highlight the "especially fascist bits."

Written in 1959 by a young Navy veteran horrified by the advance of Communism, the book still appealed to a young soldier in the 1990s looking for validation of his career choice. Unfortunately, the political universe that Heinlein created could exist only in the context of a subhuman enemy—in this case, actual "bugs." Heinlein conjured up a world where the brave, facing hordes of arachnoid aliens, answered the call of duty while the selfish and cowardly offered excuses for not joining the fight. It made no sense to try to understand the aliens' point of view: they weren't human, after all. As for history, in humanity's hour of maximum danger, it was irrelevant. I liked to think of myself as having a slightly more refined view, but I could certainly appreciate a role in society where you could be both celebrated and paid handsomely for your work but still get to call yourself a servant.

I spent my first years in the military on the periphery of minor conflicts around the world. A U-turn at the southern tip of Florida during a planned invasion of Haiti—Raoul Cédras, the country's dictator, capitulated while we were in midair—was as close as I got to combat. Instead, I got to do a lot of training jumps out of airplanes, a lot of stumbling around in the woods, and generally lived what we called the Peter Pan lifestyle: playing soldier without having to grow up. That period of my life culminated with command of a company of tanks and infantry fighting vehicles cavorting across the deserts of Kuwait along the Iraqi border after Desert Storm, back when the United States still believed in deterrence. And then, as the saying goes, everything changed.

The morning of 9/11 found me in New York City. I had just started classes at Columbia University in preparation for a teaching assignment at West Point. In the chaos of the city that morning, I found my way to a fire station, explaining that I was an Army captain and ready to assist. The policeman taping off the area said I should get ready to deploy. But to my frustration, I was relegated to observing the unfolding conflict from afar.

Stuck in New York, far from the fight, I became acutely aware of America's relationship with its military. The American flags in every store made the city feel more welcoming to soldiers than normal. But as the months passed and the flags faded, I had a growing sense that this was a hastily arranged marriage, doomed to end in disappointment. The images of the technological dominance of the first Gulf War, followed by the daring, lightning victory over the Taliban in the first year of the War in Afghanistan, made the American public expect triumphant success from the military—and made members of the military expect unquestioning adoration from the public. But as the Iraq War contentiously began and then foundered, the American romance with "the troops" wore thin. Replacing it was a respectful indifference that would largely define the relationship for the remainder of the wars.

As for me, in 2005 I finally made it to Iraq. Having volunteered to deploy from West Point, I was assigned to a military cell in the Republican Palace in Baghdad, tasked with helping to coordinate military and diplomatic efforts. It was a great place to be for someone interested in political science, but not at all a place for bolstering one's confidence in the American war machine. Not only were our diplomatic and military initiatives completely separated—literally so by secure doors between State Department and military personnel—but we didn't even have a clue about what kind of war we were in. Were we withdrawing soon or settling into a long occupation? No one knew.

The rediscovery of a doctrine known as counterinsurgency offered glimmers of hope. After I redeployed home, Iraq's growing civil war and a political drubbing in America's 2006 midterm elections finally forced a hesitating commander in chief to try a different approach to the war, providing an opening for this rediscovered doctrine. Counterinsurgency calls for a merging of political and military considerations, focusing on winning the "hearts and minds" of the local population rather than just combat operations against insurgent forces. Back at West Point, I was a distant and, as it turned out, gullible consumer of encouraging news about the military's embrace of this concept.

The reality of units on the ground was much different. After returning to a conventional unit in 2007, I realized that there was actually little interest in employing counterinsurgency doctrine, nor any real capacity for it. With two wars in full swing, the period between deployments was a mad dash to change out chains of command, onboard new soldiers, and train as best one could while often unsure even which country one might be deployed to. Matters of culture and language understandably took a back seat to ensuring that units could meet the basic standards of tactical proficiency.

Even once uncertainty of our destination was resolved—we were going to Afghanistan—there was little chance of gaining an understanding of local politics. In the soup of reported terrorist and insurgent organizations, we could barely figure out whom we would even be fighting. In retrospect it didn't matter. The fact is, we were going to lump all our enemies together and ignore the politics anyway.

Shortly after my unit's arrival in Afghanistan in 2009, we were beset by an eager counterintelligence team from higher headquarters. They needed us to arrest a man by the name of Haji Jan Daad, identified as having connections with some unsavory characters. After some absurdist comedy involving confusion over which Haji Jan Daad we were supposed to roll up (there were two, it turned out, and they were enemies), we determined that the man in question was a contractor and power broker whom we met with regularly. Americans had worked more closely with him during the first years of our presence in Kunar Province, until they learned more about his violent past and stopped contracting with him directly. But he still controlled various construction companies that had a part in most anything being built in Kunar. As a consequence, the atrocities he was reported to have committed in the 1990s were largely overlooked.

My unit knew little about Haji Jan Daad's background and less about the intelligence connecting him to our enemies, so we had some doubts about detaining him. Still, we cuffed him and put him on a helicopter to the detention facility in Bagram. He never arrived.

We hadn't hidden his detention but arrested him publicly, and the word went out quickly. So quickly, in fact, that before the helicopter made it to Bagram, President Karzai's office called the senior coalition commander, demanding his release. Haji Jan Daad got a free ride to the presidential palace. And if that didn't make our error sufficiently clear, about a week after we arrested him, his son was appointed as deputy director of the National Directorate of Security (the Afghan equivalent of the FBI) for Kunar. Later that summer, Haji Jan Daad was one of two local elders appointed to head up Karzai's reelection effort in the province.

This should have been a dramatic wake-up call that we needed to better understand the relationships and motivations of our Afghan partners. But with summer approaching and the fighting season ramping up, we focused instead on taking the fight to the enemy. Someone else would have to untangle the complicated loyalties of local political leaders. And as my 2009 deployment wound down, it appeared that this "someone else" would soon appear: the State Department announced it would be flooding the country with advisors down to the district level. I also saw promise in our plans to assist the Afghans in building their own army, instead of doing all the fighting ourselves. Still naïvely optimistic, I lined up an assignment that would get me back to Afghanistan a few years later.

My optimism proved short-lived. By the time I returned in 2012, "green on blue" attacks—members of the Afghan military shooting Americans—had become increasingly common, and one of my first tasks was to investigate a point-blank shoot-out that had erupted when an American unit dropped in unannounced on an Afghan checkpoint. Figuring out what had happened was like untangling *Rashomon*. It was made even more difficult by the language barrier and the deaths of those most directly involved.

We interrogated the surviving Afghans at a detention facility where the officer in charge took special pride in highlighting how they had some of the best interpreters in the country. Attempting to find out what had transpired at the Afghan platoon headquarters prior to the attack, we asked a young soldier if he had interacted with the main shooting suspect. He replied that he had been at the *company* headquarters and had not seen the suspect. But the interpreter, not familiar with military terminology—a regular platoon has about forty soldiers; a company, composed of several platoons, might have well over a hundred—left out the word for "company." The interrogator could not believe the Afghan could have been at the small platoon headquarters and not seen the suspect in question. The conversation grew increasingly heated, to the point where I had to intervene. But when I explained to the interrogator that she and the Afghan had been talking past each other, she dismissed it in fury: "I just know he's been lying to me." And that was pretty much the state of our efforts in Afghanistan in 2012.

Meanwhile, the plans of a grand surge of civilian political advisors had never come to fruition, leaving the US military in charge and adrift. We continued to go through the motions of building a national army for a nation that did not exist, becoming increasingly frustrated with the Afghans for not having a country better suited to our plans.

Much of this work involved pouring billions of dollars into constructing military bases. Touring nearly fifty outposts and bases with my Afghan counterpart in the provinces of eastern Afghanistan, I saw remarkable uniformity, along with uniformly shoddy construction. Contracting for this construction was never done via Afghan military leadership; the responsibility was parceled out between American military engineers and contracting officers, who took their cues from the US commanders responsible for security in a given province. The occupants of these positions all reported to different chains of command and saw regular turnover, meaning there was little coordination. The cohort overseeing the construction could be several generations removed from those who had conceived of the project in the first place, ultimately leaving no one responsible for ill-conceived or poorly executed projects.

It was an insane way to run a massive construction effort, but a great way to avoid accountability for what we built. We could look at multimillion-dollar runways and military compounds sitting unused and unoccupied, and just shrug it off as a cost of war. The whole thing was on credit with the American taxpayer anyway. With that unique mix of blind ambition, profligacy, and indifference to results, it took us only a few short years to build an abandoned, colossal wreck that made the works of Ozymandias seem truly eternal by comparison.

Leaving Afghanistan in 2013, I returned a year later for a brief final visit to assess the advisory effort. The trip coincided with the Afghan presidential election, hailed as Afghanistan's first-ever democratic transfer of power. From a security perspective, it appeared to be a resounding success. There were few significant attacks, and I observed election day from an Afghan corps headquarters that was replete with tracking maps, quick reaction plans, and fire coordination cells. But it was all theater. The idea that the Afghans were securing their own election was a charade. Hidden behind the curtain was the US military, which was maintaining an air superiority blanket over the country day and night and frenetically using its intelligence assets to intercept car bombs coming in from Pakistan.

This effort, paired with the actual election outcome—a fractured government and accusations of widespread fraud—made clear that our final strategy was to prop up the Afghan forces until a government magically arose that could maintain security and be seen as legitimate by the people. It was disheartening but not unexpected. American military leaders kept rotating through, each rating his own individual effort as a resounding success. In the meantime, nobody at home seemed interested enough in the war to demand that someone take ownership of the overall failure.

* * *

On reflection, I've come to recognize three factors that turned our military's plan for the war into a shambles. The first is the perennial optimism unique to the military, which is a helpful mindset when asking soldiers to take on personal risk but not especially useful for taking on tasks one is not trained for. A common opinion among senior military leaders in the 1990s was that a unit that could handle high-intensity combat operations could easily handle any other type of conflict. This may have been true for pre-9/11 peacekeeping deployments and the like, but after 9/11 this attitude ballooned into a conviction that members of the military had skills well beyond those specifically related to warfighting.

The self-assurance reached the apex of delusion when military leaders bragged about young officers serving as de facto mayors for villages in Afghanistan and Iraq. It was true that by virtue of the war, these officers had the authority that came with weapons and a direct line to reconstruction funds, but their competence in handling a decidedly unconventional battlefield was another question. More important, no one ever thought about what the situation must have felt like to the locals. No one considered how an American town might react to a twenty-six-year-old from the federal government taking control of the local police force and major contracting decisions—let alone how we might respond if, say, Chinese military officers tried to run an American city.

In the early phases of the war in Iraq, I encountered several young officers embittered that their efforts to build schools and support orphans did not somehow settle long-standing religious and ethnic hatreds and local blood feuds. But then again, we never required officers to stick around long enough to force them beyond a superficial understanding of local politics. It was easier to blame our failures on local cultures than on our lack of interest in actually understanding those cultures.

Beyond the dysfunction that uncritical optimism can

produce, the second factor in our failures was the unstoppable momentum of military bureaucracy. Even when we realized, at least in theory, that it would be good to work "by, with, and through" our foreign counterparts as our doctrine espoused, it was not clear that we could adapt the military to that task.

As we grappled with the chaos of Iraq in 2005–6, many military leaders understood, and increasingly stated publicly, that the way out of Iraq was via building a new Iraqi army that could secure the nascent government. It therefore followed that training this army was the US military's most important mission. Except it never was. At the Army's Command and General Staff College, officers have some say in where they want to be assigned next, and in the mid-2000s taking an assignment to train the Iraqi army was decidedly the last-place option. It simply did not fit within established career timelines and paths to further promotion. The military's incentive structures were closely tied to conventional warfare, not counterinsurgency, and there was no intention of changing that.

The same dynamic manifested itself in Afghanistan as well. Stanley McChrystal, who took command of American forces in Afghanistan in 2009, was one of the military's smartest and most reflective leaders. When he visited our unit that year, he asked each of us: "What would you do differently if you had to stay until we won?" It was absolutely the right question. But in retrospect it was also a useless question. The answer was to get the right people into the fight, keep them there long enough to develop an understanding of the environment, and hold them accountable for progress. But that was not something the military was interested in doing. Instead, McChrystal and other commanders were tasked with winning the war without disrupting the established military personnel system, and they would stay in their lane even if it meant the effort was doomed to come up short.

To keep the existing career management and promotion systems intact, the military rotated personnel through Afghanistan like tourists. An entire unit would come into the country, stay for seven to twelve months, and then get swapped out again. We stayed just long enough to become exasperated with the locals for not meeting our expectations and to fulfill preconceived notions of what we should do while there. More often than not, this meant we pursued tactical measures of success with only superficial nods to training Afghan forces.

Faced with the complexity of Afghan politics, it was always easier, and institutionally more rewarded, to focus on metrics we knew. We executed ever-larger air assaults because it was the kind of thing we could compare to the battles and leaders we idolized from Vietnam. We even adopted the maligned Vietnam-era emphasis on body counts, just dressed up with new technology and called *targeting*. The illusion that we knew exactly whom we were killing prevented us from ever asking how many times we could possibly kill the "second-in-command" of a specific insurgent cell. It took a long time for many of us to realize that the ever-larger piles of dead enemies might not be a sign of success but an indicator of a fundamentally failed strategy that was pushing ordinary Afghans to side with our opponents. Then again, the emphasis on metrics of violence meant that the creation of a perpetual violence machine was a bonus for our individual careers, even if the whole endeavor was destined to fail.

We were allowed to drift nearly indefinitely in this fantasy of progress because of the third key factor: no one at home felt they could or should question those in the fight. With the advent of the all-volunteer force in the early 1970s, Americans no longer felt tied to the military unless they wanted to be. And with a force built around high-tech weapons systems, the military never needed more than a fraction of a percent of Americans in uniform.

This gap between the military and American society resulted in a significant shift in American discussions about war. No longer could there be said to be active antiwar and pro-war camps. Instead, the range of acceptable discourse about the military now stretched from respectful indifference to unquestioning fandom. Neither of these promoted criticism or even adequate oversight of the military effort. Without a war tax or a draft, those who did not approve of the way the conflict was being handled could look at it as just a remote, academic question that never required their sustained attention.

As it turns out, public indifference was harmful to the effort, particularly when combined with the norm of uniformed service members not criticizing or publicly questioning their orders or American foreign policy. The perennial optimism and mission focus of the military meant that the public only heard a steady stream of cheery can-do pronouncements from military leaders and silence from the junior service members who may not have shared that optimism but did not feel free to speak publicly. In that climate, political and military leaders could count on the public to tolerate the War in Afghanistan almost indefinitely, as long as the costs stayed relatively low—which after our drawdown in 2014 meant about $20 billion to $40 billion and a dozen American lives per year.

Yet while such indifference from large swaths of the public allowed our military efforts to drift for years without effective oversight, it is the unquestioning adoration of the military by much of America that continues to do the most damage. Amid a collapse in confidence in American institutions like Congress, the courts, the presidency, big business, and even churches, the American military is the last institution left standing. This should not be interpreted to mean that the public approves of what the military does, but rather that it remains enamored with the vision of what it believes the military to be.

Steeped in decades of action hero movies and industrial-scale propaganda about the military, it is no wonder that many Americans view military force as the easy-button solution to complex challenges. In the view of too many, American armed forces can not only defeat all enemies but also solve even nonmilitary problems. This gives the military a status and degree of autonomy unique among public bureaucracies.

Such absolute faith in the military has enabled a peculiar accountability-avoidance two-step that both generals and politicians find advantageous. Political leaders can appear strong by putting the military in charge of even the most inappropriate missions, like nation-building, without worrying that the public might ask hard questions about the mission's feasibility or the military's suitability for that mission. And ambitious military leaders can then play the role of soldier-statesmen, basking in public adoration, but with no responsibility for the outcome of their efforts. After all, if a plan does not work out, they were "just following orders," and the ultimate fault must lie with elected politicians. Ultimately, no one ends up being held accountable.

In the fallout over our fiasco in Afghanistan, politicians who largely ignored the conflict for twenty years dug into problems with our withdrawal with just enough fervor to score partisan points. Meanwhile, the military leaders of that war effort stepped up to cast blame on the politicians while ignoring their own crucial role in shaping policy.

Much of this was individual reputation management from those who became the public faces of the war. For members of the military in less high-ranking or high-profile positions, blaming someone outside the military was also a logical step. After all, as we rotated through Afghanistan, everyone's individual efforts were graded as an A, and every participant got a trophy at the end: end-of-tour awards doled out on the basis of rank and position, with performance being at most a tangential factor. So if the overall effort ended up as a failure, surely someone else besides the military was to blame.

To prevent another cycle of military debacles, veterans must take the lead in voicing criticism. Those who bore the brunt of the costs of this war are most familiar with its inefficiencies and shortcomings. They understand the vast chasm between the public pronouncements of our leadership and the reality on the ground. They are also the only ones with the standing to challenge an institution that has become the new third rail of American politics—an institution applauded at sporting events but never questioned about what it does overseas.

Unfortunately, challenging the public's veneration for the military is difficult, both for veterans and those still serving, who are increasingly likely to view themselves as part of a foreign, misunderstood tribe. In the cacophony of public debates, it is easiest to keep one's head down and let the politicians take the fall for post-9/11 military disappointments, in effect resurrecting the "stab in the back" narrative from Vietnam.

In the 1990s and 2000s, we told ourselves repeatedly that we had exorcised the ghosts of our fathers' war. The conflicts in Iraq and Afghanistan exposed this as delusion. Understanding how we replicated that failure therefore starts with recognizing that we are recycling the same excuses they made—excuses that gave them a reason not to learn from their own mistakes. Allowing those narratives to take hold increases the likelihood of stepping confidently into the next war, with no idea of why we tripped and fell in the last one.

FROM THE RUST BELT TO MESOPOTAMIA

Vincent Emanuele

Like most American boys who grew up in the 1980s and '90s, I was fully immersed in militarism. My older brother and I played with plastic toy guns. He was the cop. I was the robber. He was the cowboy. I was an Indian. He was the good guy. I was the bad guy. Or something like that. We dressed in camo, owned real guns by the time we were teenagers, and fantasized about parachuting into foreign lands and killing enemy combatants.

We watched and rewatched *Rambo*, *Commando*, *Navy Seals*, *Missing in Action*, and every other violent and patriotic movie featuring Chuck Norris, Steven Seagal, Jean-Claude Van Damme, Sylvester Stallone, Bruce Willis, or Arnold Schwarzenegger. The post-Vietnam era showcased a hypermilitarized culture, and my brother and I loved every minute of it.

My father had served in the military during the Vietnam War, but he didn't go to the war zone. While his friends died for a bullshit war in Southeast Asia, Pops was skiing in West Germany, keeping those Germans safe from their "commie" cousins on the other side of the Berlin Wall. He enjoyed his time in the Army but returned home to find his friends who'd served in combat dead, depressed, or addicted to drugs. He knew the US war in Vietnam was illegitimate but also appreciated his experiences in the military.

My grandfather had served as a basic infantryman during World War II. He'd fought Italian Fascists in the infamous Battle of Anzio, receiving two Purple Hearts for his troubles and a lifetime of nightmares and embedded shrapnel. He never encouraged my brother or me to join the military and never mentioned a word about his experiences fighting "the good war." He spent his later years mainly sitting silently on his reclining chair, smoking pipes, watching golf, and reading the daily paper.

By the time I was thirteen years old, I knew that school wasn't for me. I wasn't meant to go to university, at least not yet. I loathed sitting in classrooms and couldn't see the connection between whatever my teachers talked about and my life outside of school. The only classes I enjoyed were homeroom and physical education—bodybuilding and strength and conditioning. I was an active kid. I'm still active. I don't like to sit still, never did. And I enjoy the pain and suffering of intense workouts. They push me to the brink of exhaustion, and that's always made me feel more human, more alive.

Plus, I grew up in a dying Rust Belt region dotted with deindustrialized ghettos, suburban hellscapes, and rural poverty. Most teenagers in my neck of the woods leave at the first opportunity. Why wouldn't they? There's nothing for young people in Northwest Indiana. It's a hellhole of alienation and social conservatism. I wanted out. And with a 1.9 GPA, my only options were the Marine Corps or the steel mills. Looking back, as contradictory as it may sound coming from someone who's now a "war resister," I'm glad I chose the former instead of the latter.

In short, I joined for excitement and a change of scenery. I also wanted to test myself and see if I could make it through Marine Corps boot camp. My classmates were going to college to guzzle booze and sleep with as many strangers as possible, but I'd experienced enough of that in middle and high school. More important, I didn't want to end up doing what everyone else was doing. I hoped to chart my own path, and that's precisely what I did.

The events of 9/11 played absolutely no role in my joining the Marine Corps. I saw the planes hit the Twin Towers while doing dumbbell bench presses in my senior year of high school. At first we thought it was a movie. Then everyone gathered around the television hanging in the corner of the gym, watching with some combination of horror and indifference. To be honest, my only concern on 9/11 was whether or not we were getting the day off school. After all, it was early September, and the beaches were still open—a perfect day to smoke some joints down by the lake.

The Marines didn't have much trouble finding me. I walked straight into the local USMC recruiter office and told the two NCOs on duty that I wanted to be in the infantry. They were ecstatic. Later, when I got to boot camp at the Marine Corps Recruit Depot in San Diego, I was shocked by the number of doughy, scrawny, and exceptionally stubby people all around me. Weren't marines supposed to be the ultimate badasses? Muscular, ripped, chiseled jaws, and all the rest? I guess the propaganda had colored my expectations. That's why they call it propaganda.

For me, boot camp was a breeze. I quickly became a squad leader, then a platoon guide. The physical challenges were a piece of cake. Funny enough, I was in better shape when I entered boot camp than when I graduated! Lots of running in the Marine Corps and not much weight training. Guys who came in looking like marines from Hollywood movies left boot camp looking more like Lance Armstrong. I'd expected much more rigorous workouts. Psychologically, it was difficult being away from friends and family. There's no doubt about that. But overall, boot camp wasn't as hard as people make it out to be.

After boot camp, I entered School of Infantry (SOI) training at Camp Pendleton in Southern California. Much like basic training, SOI consisted of a lot of running, hazing, and hiking. We learned the basics of various weapons systems but mastered none. The NCOs in charge of our platoon were drunks. Their lives were in shambles: divorce after divorce, DUI after DUI, drunken brawl after drunken brawl. Once again I left training disappointed, and increasingly skeptical that I had made the right choice in joining the USMC.

By March 2003, I had graduated SOI and was sent off to Kuwait to prepare for the initial invasion of Iraq. It's hard to overstate just how little any of us understood about the war we found ourselves fighting, thousands of miles from the small towns most of us came from. Some of the guys I was serving with were looking to kill "sand niggers" and "towelheads"; others had joined to "defend the Constitution." Others had enlisted for college money and health care.

According to President George W. Bush and company, Saddam Hussein was buddies with Osama bin Laden, Iraq had supported 9/11, and it possessed chemical weapons or worse. We followed orders, as good soldiers and marines do. Information was scarce, especially for privates and lance corporals. All ties to the outside world were cut. We spent our time in fighting holes and barracks huts. We waited for the chemical attacks and rigorously tested our outdated gas masks and deteriorating protective gear. I went on a few patrols, some in brand-new Toyota SUVs. Thinking back, there was so much weird shit going on. Just the amount of money and equipment sloshing around was enough to blow your mind.

A few months into the deployment, one of our staff sergeants came into the hut with a piece of paper in his hand and said, "Emanuele, why don't you grab your smokes and come outside." As a young PFC, I was scared shitless. Any good grunt knows that it's best to stay off everyone's radar. "What did I do?" I sat down, lit my cigarette, and the sergeant told me, "Your mother has had a brain aneurysm. She's not dead, but she could go at any moment. She's undergoing emergency surgery as we speak. So your deployment is over, marine. Get your shit together because you're flying out of Kuwait City first thing tomorrow afternoon. You'll land in Ireland, then to Chicago. I'm sorry this happened. Take care of yourself. *Semper Fi!*"

The next thing you know, I'm sitting in the waiting room at Northwestern University, awaiting news from the surgeons and doctors. Fortunately, my mother made it out of that episode alive and, for the most part, well. But that summer taught me a lot. While I had been learning about discipline, life, death, and violence, my friends in college were learning about politics, culture, philosophy, sociology, anthropology, and so much more.

I started reading up about the countercultural movements of the 1960s and '70s. It turned me on to all sorts of writers and thinkers—people like Hunter S. Thompson, Jack Kerouac, and so many more. I liked the idea of sexual freedom. (I grew up Catholic, but that didn't stop me from experimenting at a very young age—in fact, it probably encouraged it.) I appreciated the absurdist and creative Merry Pranksters, the stories about protests and fighting the man. All of that sounded interesting to me.

Then I started to experiment with mind-altering substances, mostly psychedelics but also copious amounts of marijuana. Psychedelics opened up entirely new worlds of thought and consciousness. As a result, I started to ask more profound questions. What's life all about? Why are we here? Am I ready to die? Am I a good son, brother, partner, friend? Do I love myself? What is love? What is reality? Who am I? What's my purpose in this life? Why is it so hard to be vulnerable? What am I hiding?

All those experiences, reading, conversing, and experimenting, forced me to question why I was in the Marine Corps and whether I genuinely wanted to die for the cause. Turns out, I didn't. I had no idea why we were fighting a war in Iraq. And I couldn't understand my place within this entire mess. None of it made sense, but I knew I didn't want to be a part of it anymore.

Nevertheless, I went back to Twentynine Palms, California, where my unit was stationed. They were happy to be back from the deployment. Enlisted personnel and officers celebrated our victory over the Iraqi Army and the taking of Baghdad, and Bush gave his "Mission Accomplished" speech on the aircraft carrier. The boys were ready to hit the Pacific for the regularly scheduled tour of various Asian countries and Australia. Older marines who had yearned for an opportunity to showcase their fighting skills were happy to come home with war stories. After all, that's what it's all about, right? The stories we tell, most notably the ones we tell ourselves.

By the end of 2003, though, it became clear that the war wasn't going to be quick and easy like Donald Rumsfeld, Dick Cheney, Condoleezza Rice, President Bush, and others had predicted. In early 2004, we got word from command that our unit would instead redeploy to Iraq in August. That gave us eight months to get ready. Morale dropped. Marines started drinking heavily. Pills hit the scene, mainly acquired from the medics. Some guys, including myself, were smoking pot in the barracks daily. Others smoked meth, blew coke, and freebased crack in decrepit military base housing or in hotel rooms and back alleys of Tijuana, Las Vegas, Los Angeles, and San Diego.

This was by far the darkest period of my time in the Marine Corps. All around me, drinking, DUIs, assaults, overdoses, and suicides increased. The self-loathing, confusion, and anger were too much to bear. Alcohol eased the pain, and stress evaporated in bottles of Jack Daniel's or Joshua Tree whiskey—what we bought when we didn't have enough dough to get the good shit.

In July 2004, less than a month before we deployed a second time, a friend took me to a movie theater in San Diego to watch Michael Moore's documentary *Fahrenheit 9/11*. I laughed and cried during the screening. Moore nailed the absurdity, brutality, and banality of the war, and blew apart Bush and company's justifications for the US-led occupation. He also made soldiers and marines look like a bunch of uneducated dummies, which jibed with my personal experiences.

After leaving the theater, I called my father and told him that I didn't want to go to Iraq for a second deployment. He understood my reservations and protests but didn't have any suggestions. I could have deserted, I guess, but we were told that doing so would ruin your life. If a potential employer saw that you were dishonorably discharged, they'd never hire you—that's what we had heard. Of course, all of that is bullshit, but I didn't know it at the time. I was afraid, far from home, and unsure how I would explain to my fellow marines that I was running away while they were reluctantly sprinting into the fire.

Soon enough, we were back on the birds and on our way to Kuwait. Our destination: Al-Qa'im, a small town in Anbar Province. Located on the border with Syria, hugging the Euphrates about 250 miles northwest of Baghdad, Al-Qa'im had been the central location of Iraq's refined uranium ore production from the mid-1980s through the early 1990s. Most of the town, including the production facilities, was bombed out and destroyed during the Gulf War in 1991.

By late summer 2004, Al-Qa'im was at the center of the Iraqi resistance. Local Sunnis battled with US forces, as did foreign fighters streaming across the Syrian border. One officer told us that we were simply bullet sponges for the boys downstream in Ramadi and Fallujah. Our job was to intercept as many fighters and weapons as possible before they made their way to the country's interior.

In reality, no one knew what the hell was going on. Many officers went on patrol when the missions were safe and stayed back at the huts when things got bad. Those who did patrol with us ended up getting people killed because of their ignorance or bravado. Some of these guys were fresh out of college—baby-faced wannabe warriors, most of them.

Morale continued to drop during that second deployment in western Iraq. We started smoking weed on patrol and doing coke while setting up observation posts. We'd brought most of the drugs with us when coming over. I remember emptying the first aid kit latched to my flak jacket and filling up the pouch with as much weed as I could. Most of those drugs lasted only the first few months of the deployment, though. We'd planned to stretch our supply to the end, but it didn't stay secret for very long that we had good shit with us. And how could we deny anyone the pleasure of getting stoned under the brilliant, unprecedented Mesopotamian sky?

The deployment turned sour quickly, with several marines, including some of our commanding officers, killed in the first seventy-two hours. After that, things went from bad to worse. We shot at noncombatants. We tortured prisoners. We blew up civilian structures. We ran over, mutilated, and took pictures of dead Iraqis. As one headline in *Maxim* magazine put it, Al-Qa'im was the "Wild West of Iraq." Frankly, we did whatever the fuck we wanted. Eighteen-year-olds with machine guns, rocket launchers, and a license to kill, or so we thought.

I'm happy to say that I didn't participate in many of those "extracurricular" activities. I raised my voice about them on several occasions but was basically told to shut up unless I wanted to meet the same fate as Pat Tillman—the NFL star who enlisted in the Army Rangers and was killed by friendly fire in Afghanistan in 2004. I didn't shut up, though. I kept talking, and reading, and writing letters to my friends and family back home. At that point, I was regularly reading the *New York Times*, *Newsweek*, *Mother Jones*, and the *Nation*. I was a good liberal. I voted for John Kerry via absentee ballot and hung up antiwar stickers and postcards on the wall next to my bunk.

But I didn't know the first thing about resistance. I was reading about the countercultural and antiwar movements of the 1960s, but I didn't know anything about the modern antiwar movement. Even if I did, I wouldn't have known what to do as a marine deployed in the combat zone. Thank God for my friend and bunkmate Nick Epstein. He was one of the only marines in our platoon besides myself who was willing to speak up about the unjust and insane nature of the war. We both paid a heavy social price for our outspokenness. We were put on shit missions, in shit positions, usually the most dangerous or tedious ones. They did their best to break our rebellious spirits, but they lost. We were some hardheaded bastards. Still are.

By the end of my deployment, local Iraqis and foreign insurgents controlled the town of Al-Qa'im. Much as during the Vietnam War, local towns were destroyed, then captured by US forces, only to be retaken by the other side. With some of them it happened over and over again. Marines reportedly regained control of Al-Qa'im in May 2005, a few weeks after my unit left the country. In 2006 the insurgents took back the city and surrounding areas, and would maintain their dominance for years to come. In August 2014, even more extreme Islamic State forces took over the train station where our base had been located. Low-level fighting, drone strikes, and bombings have occurred in the area ever since.

I remember sitting in front of my computer screen back in 2014, watching as ISIS took over Mosul and Al-Qa'im. I couldn't help but laugh. The Iraqi resistance fighters were always going to control their country—no matter how long US forces stayed, no matter how brutal our attacks became. The Iraqis were fighting for their families, their land, their pride, their dignity. American troops were only in it for health care, college money, steady housing, or ideological nonsense. Almost none of us actually believed the people we encountered posed a threat to our homeland. And those who did believe that were absolutely out of their minds, as history has shown.

When I finally returned from that second deployment, I was shattered. I was drinking heavily and smoking so much weed that my eyes looked permanently glazed over. Eventually, I went home on leave. After long talks with friends and family, after many nights of solemn reflection, I decided that I could no longer kill people for the US military. I checked myself into a Veterans Affairs (VA) facility and entered a two-month inpatient drug and alcohol rehabilitation program. The doctors tried their best to convince the command that I should stay home, but my commanding officers disagreed and forced me to return to Twentynine Palms.

When I got to base, my fellow marines were excited to see me. Everyone else had returned from leave two months earlier and already received word about a third deployment. Back home, my father and uncle started writing letters to every

Senate and House Armed Services Committee member. Soon after, letters, phone calls, and inquiries poured into our unit's command offices. I was called in to speak with high-ranking officers and enlisted personnel—marines way above my pay grade. They talked to me about "the mission" and "American freedom" and all the rest. At that point, I not only knew they were full of shit but could also outtalk and outthink most of them. Nevertheless, I kept my mouth shut and kept repeating, "I will not go to the armory, and I will not board an airplane." They were gonna have to drag my unconscious body to Iraq if they wanted me to deploy a third time.

Eventually, the command acquiesced and offered me a "general discharge under honorable conditions." The bureaucratic pretext was my failure to complete the drug and alcohol rehabilitation process. Once a marine finishes the two-month inpatient program, they must also complete two months of outpatient treatment. Since my command never offered me that treatment, and since I never sought it out, they figured this was the easiest excuse to get rid of a troublesome and vocal antiwar resister. They would rather lose a seasoned gunner than allow me the opportunity to bring down unit morale.

They made the right choice. I'd promised myself that if I were forced to deploy for the third time, I would kill as many of my commanding officers as humanly possible. Anger and resentment flowed through my body, pumping faster than my blood after a long run. I was ready to kill, only this time for the right reasons. In hindsight, the Marine Corps avoided a disaster, and I avoided the death penalty or a lifetime behind bars. I was lucky, and so was Uncle Sam.

The day I left Twentynine Palms remains the happiest day of my life—even better than returning from the war. I was finally free. I remember lighting up a cigarette on California State Route 62 and sticking my head out the window like a dog. Smiling from ear to ear, I didn't have a care in the world.

Once I got back to Northwest Indiana, I ended up living with my parents for several months. I got a job as a rodbuster with Ironworkers Local #1 in Chicago. It was a good gig: I made great money even as a first-year apprentice, twenty-five dollars an hour in 2006. But I knew I didn't want to be an ironworker for the rest of my life. My father had been one for years until he fell off a scaffolding that collapsed, breaking his neck, back, shoulder, hip, and arm and blowing out both eardrums from his head smacking against steel beams before hitting the deck. That wasn't for me. The money wasn't worth it.

One day, my dad told me about an event at a local university that featured a debate about the war in Iraq, for and against. After the discussion, they asked for comments from the audience. I raised my hand and said that I was a former marine and combat veteran with two tours of duty and fully supported the antiwar position. Stunned, the audience whipped their heads around to see who the hell I was. After the event, a Vietnam-era veteran ran up to me and asked if I had ever heard of Iraq Veterans Against the War (IVAW). I had not, but took his advice and attended an IVAW event in Chicago the following week.

From 2006 to 2008, I traveled most of the country with IVAW. I gave antiwar speeches at union halls, religious services, universities, community centers, town halls, libraries, street corners, parks, and protests. I was interviewed by every media outlet under the sun—cable news shows, radio programs, magazines, newspapers, and all the rest. It was a whirlwind experience, culminating in the 2008 Winter Soldier hearings, when hundreds of veterans converged on Silver Springs, Maryland, for several days of testimony about US war crimes, sexual assaults in the military, drug abuse, and much more. Later that year, about a dozen of us officially testified before the United States Congress.

At the time, no one could tell us whether or not we would face legal repercussions from doing so. And even though IVAW had thousands of members, only a dozen or so were willing to testify, which really bothered me at the time. I should've paid attention to my instincts, because such cowardice was par for the course within the modern antiwar movement and broader left-wing political movements in general. People were afraid of the consequences of speaking on the record. I understand their position better today, but I still don't respect it. If you want to remain silent, that's fine. Go about your civilian life in peace. But if you're supposedly trying to stop a war, then you should be willing to sacrifice as much as those who are fighting it. If not, why bother?

Since then, I've gotten involved with every political movement under the sun: environmental efforts, Black Lives Matter, Occupy Wall Street, labor protests, union efforts, Fight for $15 campaigns, community organizing, and cultural projects. Each step of the way, I've learned a lot about myself and society, and I've grown because of it.

In the end, I can't say whether my particular form of dissent meant anything in the grand scheme of things. The antiwar movement never had the infrastructure, vision, discipline, or capacity to sustain resistance to the US war machine. Symbolic protests and street theater won't stop the Joint Chiefs of Staff in the Pentagon or mammoth defense contractors like Lockheed Martin. And pink-haired college kids and old Quaker grannies aren't the sorts of people I would choose to lead any serious political movement. In many ways, the antiwar movement was a joke. There were good people involved in the movement, but they were few and far between. Too much over-moralizing and not enough strategy.

Am I glad I resisted? Absolutely. Would I recommend others do it? Perhaps. I was fortunate in my circumstances: I'm close with my immediate family, who supported my decision to refuse orders for a third deployment. I had childhood friends in my corner. I had, and maintain, an excellent social network. And because of those connections, I never had a problem getting a job. Many veterans cannot say the same, and they shouldn't be shamed for not speaking out. That's an individual choice, not a collective choice, unless the collective is willing to take care of the individual dissenter and their family if and when they face repercussions.

These days, I've taken a step back from political organizing. In 2017, my best friend, Sergio Kochergin—a former scout sniper and briefly a platoon mate—and I cofounded a community cultural center called PARC (Politics Art Roots Culture) in Michigan City, Indiana. For several years, we offered a space for local progressive organizations and hosted open mic poetry slams, live music events, hip-hop shows, comedy showcases, art installations, documentary film screenings, soup kitchens, and an endless array of casual social events.

It was fun, but then the pandemic hit. We were able to hang on for fifteen months, only to have our landlord turn around and sell the building. Ain't capitalism grand?

Yet no bitterness on my part. My time in the Rust Belt has come to an end. As I write this, I'm actively making plans to live in New York City, close to my brother and fully immersed in the most diverse and culturally vibrant city in North America. I will carry forth the idea of PARC and hopefully reopen the space someday in an environment more conducive to cultural and political experimentation. In our "age of isolation," community and social bonds are that much more critical. They are the source of our collective strength. And I believe the more time we spend together, in person rather than mediated by screens, discussing and debating the major issues of our time—climate change, war, capitalism, race—the more likely we are to successfully address them.

If Americans were collectively organized, if working-class people had a voice, if unions were strong, if democracy truly flourished, perhaps we wouldn't ever have gone to Iraq in the first place. Maybe the US empire would be a thing of the past. Who knows. It may sound simplistic, but all we can do is try. In the meantime, I'm going to have as much fun and create as much as I can. Life is too short, and there's no time to waste. The war taught me that much. If you're not busy living, you're busy dying. I'm interested in living and embracing the infinite contradictions that color and shape our lives.

If you're reading this and you're a veteran, welcome home. Join a mixed martial arts gym. Stay active. Lift weights. Run. Get involved in sports and community efforts. Have lots of sex. Learn to play an instrument. Paint, draw, and sculpt.

Stay away from booze, TV, and social media. Listen to your family and friends. They've noticed changes you'll never recognize. And while you may not be the man or woman you once were, that, too, is okay. You're here now, and your mission is to stay alive, contribute what you can, and live the rest of your life with as much happiness, purpose, and dignity as humanly possible.

CANDOR AND INTOLERANCE

Paul Yingling

In 2007, I was moved to write an article in the *Armed Forces Journal* titled "A Failure in Generalship." Detailing the grave and deteriorating situation in Iraq, I argued that the debacle was attributable not to individual failures but to a crisis in the entire institution of America's general officer corps. The piece sparked a fierce debate within the armed forces, catapulted me from obscurity into the national media spotlight, and ultimately ended my military career. I became a dissenter, having declared war on an institution that I'd loved and loyally served for more than twenty years. It was not a role I had imagined for myself.

I joined the Army at the age of seventeen because I had few other options: I was a bad kid in a bad place. I wasted my adolescence drinking, smoking pot, and fighting. Growing up in Pittsburgh as the steel industry was dying, I needed a way out. In 1984, Pittsburgh put more recruits in boots than any other comparably sized city in the country, and I was one of them. I enlisted to straighten myself out, and it worked.

Being a soldier taught me self-discipline and self-respect, which was just what I needed. I enrolled in Duquesne University and graduated at the top of my academic class. I won an ROTC scholarship and was commissioned at the top of my ROTC class. I married my high school sweetheart, convincing her that I was not the aimless thug I had once been. I was a college graduate, an Army officer, and a married man, well on my way to a middle-class living and middle-class respectability. I could not imagine wanting anything more for myself.

I trained as a field artillery officer, and in early 1990 reported to the 1st Infantry Division at Fort Riley, Kansas. In one of my first field exercises, I was assigned as an evaluator for a fire support team as part of a large exercise involving infantry, tanks, artillery, engineers, and other supporting forces. Greg Fontenot, then lieutenant colonel and senior evaluator for the exercise, would gather the other evaluators together each night and lay out what would happen in the next day's battle: the plans of enemy and friendly forces, the decisions the commanders would make, the terrain and weather considerations that would influence those decisions, and the possible outcomes of the battle. He told all of us where to be and what to look for. At first, I was skeptical: How could he possibly know what would happen the next day at such a level of detail? After the first battle, though, I became a true believer. Fontenot was a master of battle command; he saw the battle unfold in his mind before it was fought.

Less than a year later, we were in an assault position in northern Saudi Arabia, preparing to attack Iraqi forces occupying Kuwait. My job was to give fire commands to eight cannon that supported the attack of the 1st Brigade, 1st

Infantry Division. The brigade's mission was to breach the frontline Iraqi defenses; we were expected to take so many casualties that follow-on forces would then have to take over the attack on the Republican Guard. Instead, we breached the Iraqi defenses with minimal casualties, conducted a hundred-mile maneuver, pulverized the Republican Guard, and ended the war in one hundred hours. I was as mesmerized by my senior commander, Lieutenant Colonel Harry Emerson, as I had been by Fontenot; he, too, had seen the battle unfold in his mind, prepared for every possibility, and brought the conflict to a swift and decisive conclusion. I looked up to my bosses and vowed to learn what they knew. I loved being a soldier: it was not merely a living but a good life's work.

Five years later, I was conducting peacekeeping operations in the former Yugoslavia. I had attended the field artillery's training course for newly promoted captains, where I had read about "operations other than war" in the "post–Cold War era." The Army used these clumsy terms to describe peacekeeping, humanitarian aid distribution, and just about any mission that didn't involve fighting the Soviets in Europe. I thought it odd that we would define operations and eras by what they were not. However, I was too pressed by more immediate concerns to give the matter much thought. My unit's mission was relatively straightforward: to monitor our assigned area for violations of the Dayton Peace Accords, which separated the Bosnian, Serb, and Croat factions in that country's bloody civil war. However, beyond that narrow task, everything seemed incoherent. I did not know how my small unit's task fit into a larger plan or what the end state of our operations was to be. Some of the same commanders whom

I had so admired in the Gulf War were unable to explain what we were doing or why we were doing it.

The Army selected me to attend graduate school at the University of Chicago and then teach international relations in West Point's prestigious social sciences department. Entering grad school, I was a capable tactician but no more. Chicago opened my mind to the political aspects of war and the use of military force as an instrument of policy. I read Livy's account of the campaign waged by Scipio the Younger in Spain during Rome's Second Punic War and Thucydides's record of operations carried out by Brasidas in Thrace during the Peloponnesian War of ancient Greece. These generals were not mere tacticians; they wielded military force and diplomacy with equal alacrity toward a clear political goal. I wrote my master's thesis on third-party military intervention in civil wars, finding a nearly uninterrupted record of failure. I studied extensively with John Mearsheimer, whose classic work *Conventional Deterrence* melds strategic and operational calculations into a rigorous and seamless whole. Just before graduation, I met Mearsheimer for drinks. He told me, "Paul, you're smart, and the Army likes officers who are smart. But not too smart. Be careful." I had no idea what he meant.

While at West Point, I met John Nagl, who over the next twenty years would become my best friend, intellectual sparring partner, and frequent coauthor. John had just finished his doctorate on irregular warfare, which would soon be published as the counterinsurgency classic *Learning to Eat Soup with a Knife*. John's thinking on military adaptation helped me make sense of my experience in the former Yugoslavia: the same officers who were so skilled in conventional warfare, I realized, had failed to adapt to the irregular conflicts of the Balkans. As Gulf War veterans, John and I were both proud of the Army's performance in 1991. But he was focused on the future. He asked: "After seeing what we did to Iraq, why would anybody fight us like that again?" That question should have shaped a generation of military thinking. Alas, it did not.

Meanwhile, my career continued to flourish. As a newly promoted and well-regarded major, I was chosen to attend the School of Advanced Military Studies (SAMS). The Army referred to SAMS graduates as Jedi Knights for their skill in war planning. This reputation was well earned: SAMS graduates had been among the principal planners of the Gulf War. The program combined graduate education—I read classical military theorists such as Clausewitz, Mao, and Galula—with military planning exercises. During the course's sophisticated war games, I served as Napoleon's chief of staff at the Battle of Leipzig and commanded a German corps in the World War I Battle of the Masurian Lakes. SAMS was the missing piece in my professional education. I had learned tactics on the battlefields of the Middle East and the Balkans, and had studied strategy and politics at Chicago; SAMS taught me how to connect the two. The 9/11 attacks occurred while I was at SAMS, and I was convinced those skills would soon be in high demand.

Upon graduating from SAMS in 2002, I was assigned as the chief of plans for the 2nd Infantry Division in Korea. In both geographic and intellectual terms, the assignment could not have been further from the irregular conflicts that would dominate the decades to come. My task was to develop, maintain, and exercise the division war plans intended to deter conflict, and to defeat a North Korean invasion of South Korea should deterrence fail. Korea was considered a "hardship tour"; my family remained in the United States while I worked eighteen-hour days in an underground bunker. I performed my work with due diligence, all the while recognizing its absurdity. I had analyzed the Korea scenario with Mearsheimer as a graduate student, coming to the conclusion that South Korean forces were more than sufficient to defeat any aggression from the North. Every exercise and every piece of intelligence that I would see during my time in Korea confirmed this judgment. I concluded that the Army's fixation on Korea had less to do with intelligence than with the Army's organizational and cultural preference for conventional conflict. Meanwhile, outside of the Korea bubble, the Bush administration was manufacturing a pretext for war in the Middle East.

John Nagl and I frequently discussed the prospects for war in Iraq. By the fall of 2002, it was clear to us that the Bush administration was determined to invade the country. Given the US military's conventional dominance, we were confident that it could topple Saddam. However, we saw that as the beginning rather than the end of the conflict. The precursors for a long and bloody insurgency were all present in Iraq: conflicting ethnic and religious identities, skillful and ruthless demagogues, ample supplies of money and arms, and a large pool of angry, ignorant, and disaffected young men. We feared that a US invasion would be the match setting this combustible mixture ablaze. While we were worried about challenging the Army too directly, we felt duty bound to raise these concerns. Citing just war theory, we argued that "an officer who wins the war and loses the peace is no more professional than a doctor who saves the patient's leg at the expense of his spinal cord."

My education and experience notwithstanding, I never in my life up to this point imagined that I had any role in shaping policy or strategy. I saw myself as a fighter and nothing more; the only thing that had changed was the character of the fighting. I could not picture a world in which important people would care what I had to say. But for John's friendship, I would never have written or spoken a word in public. John, though, insisted that we had an obligation to think and write about the challenges the Army would soon face in Iraq. This period began a nearly decade-long cycle of "writing and fighting," where we became increasingly outspoken about our concerns. We would alternately spend our time fighting in combat tours in Iraq and writing about the lessons we'd learned upon our return.

My first tour in Iraq began in August 2003, as second-in-command of an artillery battalion. Returning from my hardship tour in Korea, I had the option of declining to deploy but could not imagine doing so. My unit had been part of the initial invasion force, and I joined midway through its deployment. I went to the operations center and asked the battle captain to brief me on the current situation. Looking at the operations map, I saw an icon representing the 3rd Armored Cavalry Regiment (3rd ACR) on the Iraq–Syria border. I felt some glimmer of reassurance, as border security seemed a sound use of cavalry forces, which are designed for the reconnaissance and security of important terrain. However, I saw no other unit icon in the entirety of Anbar Province—Iraq's largest, with a population of 1.5 million and an area larger than the state of New York. I assumed this to be an error, but the battle captain assured me that the five thousand troopers of the 3rd ACR were the only forces securing this area. Next, I asked to see the campaign plan. The battle captain handed me a book of brief orders covering routine security and logistics matters. Ever the SAMS graduate, I explained that I needed to see the overall plan describing the desired end state in Iraq and the operations to achieve that end state. The young officer replied that he knew of no such document.

I returned from Iraq deeply concerned about the growing insurgency and the Army's failure to adapt to this challenge. In my tour, my unit had been assigned the task of training Iraqi Army and police forces. We did our best, but our efforts were entirely improvisational. In 2004, I began advocating that field artillery forces start planning and preparing for the task of developing Iraqi soldiers and police officers in support of counterinsurgency operations. At the time, I was second-in-command of a field artillery brigade in Fort Sill, Oklahoma. My boss, then-colonel K. D. Dahl, was supportive, but his boss—the commanding general of all the artillery brigades in the corps—dismissed the idea out of hand. He told us instead to "focus on Korea."

This guidance was utterly perplexing, especially since I had briefed that same general on Korea two years earlier during my time as chief of plans for the 2nd Infantry Division. I had told him back then that in a war between North and South Korea, a "counterfire fight"—an artillery duel—would break out immediately, and artillery forces from the continental United States wouldn't be able to deploy in time to affect the battle. In 2004, for our artillery brigade in Fort Sill to "focus on Korea" meant training thousands of soldiers for a hypothetical scenario where they couldn't possibly be relevant, instead of making adjustments we needed for the ongoing fight in Iraq.

Later that year, the same commanding general declined to complete an optional officer evaluation report on my performance, a move that derailed my promotion prospects. The overall selection rate for my peers was 90 percent, and the news that I was in the bottom 10 percent of my peer group came as a shock. I had previously been selected for every "top 5 percent" cut in my career—graduate school, instructor duty at West Point, early promotion to major, attendance at SAMS. Every evaluation report in my personnel file was "top block"—the strongest possible recommendation for promotion. Yet none of that counted now. This episode highlights the precarious tightrope that mid-level and senior officers must walk in the military's "up or out" personnel system. The general could derail my career simply by doing nothing. In such a system, officers can scarcely afford a disagreement with a vindictive boss; a single personality conflict can be a career-ending event.

Difficult as it may have been, my non-selection for promotion to lieutenant colonel was both a test and a gift. Like many successful officers, I had espoused the virtues of selfless service while my own service was constantly recognized and rewarded. Now, although I had done nothing wrong, my career nevertheless appeared to be over. I am ashamed to say that my initial response was self-centered: I prepared to chart a path for life outside the military, even as the wars in Iraq and Afghanistan spiraled further out of control.

But in late 2004, Colonel Dahl called me into his office. The 3rd ACR needed someone to lead a nonlethal effects team in their upcoming deployment to Iraq, he told me.

"Every lieutenant colonel in the brigade has said no. I'd like you to lead this team."

I was stunned. "Sir, why in the hell would I volunteer for another tour in Iraq after the Army passed me over for lieutenant colonel?"

Dahl replied, "We're going to send a team of soldiers to war, and you're the best officer to lead them. If you say no, you won't be able to live with yourself." He was right. The next day I volunteered for my second tour in Iraq.

The 3rd ACR was like every other heavy brigade combat team in the Army, only heavier. Every heavy brigade combat team had plenty of mobility and firepower—tanks, Bradley Fighting Vehicles, cannon, and the like. The 3rd ACR had all of that in greater numbers, and its own aircraft to boot. At the time, all the heavy brigade teams were struggling mightily to develop counterinsurgency tactics in the absence of a coherent Army doctrine for irregular warfare. The 3rd ACR took its commitment to this task to a whole new level. The regiment's junior leaders were as skilled at negotiation as they were at tank gunnery. The regimental staff had plenty of trigger pullers but also PhDs in history and native Arabic speakers. Most important of all, the regimental commander, then-colonel H. R. McMaster, was both soldier and scholar. A history PhD who earned a Silver Star in the 1991 Gulf War, McMaster had authored *Dereliction of Duty: Johnson, McNamara, the Joint Chiefs of Staff, and the Lies That Led to Vietnam*. The book was required reading for every Army officer.

My job was to coordinate the regiment's nonlethal operations, such as civil affairs, psychological operations, and reconstruction. In practice, that role required me to assist McMaster in dealing with Iraqi sheikhs, politicians, and occasionally leaders of the insurgency. More than once, I heard McMaster tell tribal elders, "I understand your grievances, and the proper place to resolve those grievances is politics. The time for honorable resistance is over. Don't make me kill your young men to convince you that I'm serious." I was reminded of Scipio the Younger in Spain maneuvering legions through the countryside, cutting Hannibal's lines of communication, and welcoming the tribes back to their loyal allegiance to Rome. The message in both cases was clear: politics or death.

The 3rd ACR's "clear-hold-build" method of counterinsurgency operations is the stuff of legend, and this space cannot properly do it justice. In short, the regiment was assigned responsibility for an insurgent-infested area in northwest Iraq, centering on the city of Tal Afar. The city of 250,000 people was entirely under insurgent control and served as a way station for fighters and supplies heading from Syria to the city of Mosul. The regiment, in combination with Iraqi Army forces, conducted a massive assault to clear Tal Afar of insurgents. Once cleared, these areas were held with Iraqi Army and police forces, supported as necessary by US resources and assistance. Having secured the population from insurgent violence, the regiment then assisted the Iraqi government in rebuilding essential services: health, education, transportation, and local government. McMaster pursued this operation with single-minded tenacity, while working to empower the Iraqi political and military leaders who would have long-term responsibility for the security of Tal Afar.

McMaster's success was in no small part due simply to his willingness to tell the truth. Most commanders in Iraq, whether because of self-delusion or willful deception, played a game with their reporting on security conditions. They would take over an area of operations at the beginning of a twelve-month tour and declare it a debacle. They'd report that it would take at least fifteen months to create the conditions that would permit handover to Iraqi Army and police forces. Every month of their twelve-month tour, they'd report incremental progress, and declare by the end of their tour that success was just ninety days away. Then a new commander would come in and repeat the same process. McMaster did not play this game. Instead, he cited the specific obstacles to progress, such as lack of Iraqi government ministerial support to forces in the field, corrupt and complicit officials, and inadequate logistics systems. If these conditions did not change, neither did McMaster's assessment. These blunt assessments infuriated McMaster's bosses but also garnered the regiment resources unheard of for other brigade combat teams, including national intelligence assets, de facto control of US Special Forces, and a massive infusion of reconstruction funds.

I returned from Iraq in early 2006 both hopeful and furious. The 3rd ACR's success had demonstrated the effectiveness of clear-hold-build. Nonetheless, Iraq was plunging into civil war. The February 2006 bombing of the Al-Askari Mosque set off a new wave of sectarian violence, even as senior US political and military officials lied about the actual security conditions in Iraq. With both of us back in the United States, John Nagl and I continued our collaboration. While I had been in Tal Afar, working without a coherent counterinsurgency doctrine, John had been working on that very doctrine. He was part of the writing team that put together General David Petraeus's celebrated FM 3–24: *Counter-*

insurgency. John and I wrote a piece for the *Field Artillery Journal*, arguing that artillery formations had little relevance in counterinsurgency but that artillerymen could remain relevant by training local army and police forces. In the *Armed Forces Journal*, we took on the Army's sclerotic personnel system, which had such a deleterious effect on risk-taking and adaptation. That piece included a passage that would later be quoted by Secretary of Defense Robert Gates: "The Army will become more adaptive only when being adaptive offers the surest path to promotion."

These works, along with our broader efforts in advocating for the counterinsurgency approach, generated some minor buzz but had little institutional impact. Civil war raged in Iraq, US casualties mounted, and US political and military leaders doubled down on their Pollyannaish "turning the corner" statements. John and I reached a crossroads: the US government was lying about Iraq, and the only way to stop those lies was to get the public's attention. However, the only way to get the public's attention was to state the case in terms so explicit that our careers would be over. Much to my surprise, during my second tour in Iraq I had been promoted to lieutenant colonel after all. I looked forward to battalion command but viewed the system that selected me for this honor with utter contempt. John, too, had been selected for battalion command; this position is the gateway to general's stars. We both had distinguished combat records, and our writing up to that point had made us prominent and controversial but hardly toxic. If we would shut up and play ball, our career prospects looked bright.

By late 2006, I was the deputy commander of the 3rd

ACR in Fort Hood, Texas; I would assume command of a field artillery battalion the following spring. One of my responsibilities as deputy commander was to represent the regiment at public events, including the monthly Purple Heart ceremony. At any given time, Fort Hood had nearly twenty thousand soldiers deployed to Iraq, and hundreds came back severely wounded every year. The ceremony to honor these soldiers was a somber one. An adjutant would read the names of the wounded, and the soldiers would come forward, visibly scarred, sometimes in wheelchairs, other times with the assistance of a buddy, parent, or spouse. The senior officer representing the unit would then shake hands with the wounded soldiers, thanking them for their service.

I extended my hand, but for the first time in my life I could not look a soldier in the eye. The soldiers had done their duty: they had faced the enemy in battle and shed their blood in the service of our country. We senior officers had not done our duty: we had not adequately visualized the conditions of combat and prepared our soldiers to face those conditions. We were failing to connect—or adapt—the tactics we preferred to the strategic outcomes we claimed to want. I knew the solutions to these problems but lacked the courage to speak that truth. I was valuing my recently revived career prospects over the lives of the soldiers standing in front of me. Bile rose in my throat; my eyes burned with shame at the realization of my complicity and my cowardice.

I began writing "A Failure in Generalship" that night. My focus was not on one officer or group of officers but on the entire system that the US military uses to select its senior leaders. I accused America's generals of wasting decades preparing to fight the wrong war. I found them guilty of misleading Congress and the public about the intensity of the insurgency. I excoriated the services for their refusal to hold commanders accountable for battlefield failures, noting that "a private who loses a rifle suffers far greater consequences than a general who loses a war." I sent a draft to John, whose keen analytical mind and judgment I found invaluable. He added a section calling on Congress to be involved in the solutions, as congressional interventions are more enduring than any internal service reforms. We circulated drafts to a wider audience of respected soldiers and scholars. Around thirty of our peers made helpful and occasionally contradictory suggestions. On two points they were unanimous: we were right, and publishing this article would end our careers.

After months of revisions, we were ready to publish, with only one point of disagreement: authorship. Whose name would go on the byline? John suggested anonymous authorship; I found an anonymous call for moral courage impossibly self-contradictory. We finally agreed that I would publish the piece in my name alone. John was making incremental progress in the "inside game" of defense reform. We saw little point in setting two careers on fire when one would do.

"A Failure in Generalship," as we predicted, created a firestorm. The *Washington Post* ran a front-page story titled "Army Officer Accuses Generals of 'Intellectual and Moral Failures.'" The *New York Times*, *Wall Street Journal*, CNN, Fox, NPR, and other national media outlets followed suit. Junior military members began openly questioning senior military leaders about our allegations of failure in Iraq. Members of Congress weighed in, publicly praising the candor of the piece and privately warning the Army against retaliation. The great paradox is that so many people were shocked by the argument, yet it contained little original thought. Sergeants had known for years about the shoddy counterinsurgency training and equipment, as well as the lack of accountability among senior officers. Captains had long decried the lack of effective irregular warfare doctrine in private conversations. However, the article gave both permission and a pathway to make these concerns public.

As expected, the article ended my career. America's soldiers have suffered far worse fates than mine, and I see no value in going into the particulars. Instead, I'll merely point out that the last five years of my military service were a cacophony of absurdities. I took command of my battalion, but the Army reassigned all my soldiers to perform counterinsurgency missions under other commanders. My work was taught at the Army War College—a program for senior officers considered to have significant potential for promotion—but the Army did not select me to attend the program myself. I was promoted to colonel after all but was passed over for command at that rank. The chairman of the Joint Chiefs of Staff summoned me for a private audience to express concern about my career prospects but declined to intervene to alter those prospects. In private emails and whispered conversations, politicians and generals confided that they agreed with me, but none of them spoke out publicly. In 2012, I retired from the Army to take a job teaching high school history. I refused to have a public retirement ceremony, as such an event would necessarily involve a boilerplate statement about how much the Army valued my service. I knew this statement to be a lie, and I could not tolerate any more lies.

Reflecting on a tumultuous decade as a military dissenter, I know both contentment and regret. Where much is given, much is expected, and my countrymen had every right to expect much of me. By the grace of God, I was blessed with a capacity to make powerful arguments. By the generosity of the American people, I was able to use that gift in the country's service. I published tens of thousands of words on leadership and adaptation, and I will not recant a single one. My arguments were not mere scholarly abstractions; I put those words into action during my service in Iraq. For a time, the Army seemed to take those arguments seriously, undertaking reforms in personnel policy and irregular warfare doctrine. However, as the pressures of the battlefields of the Middle East recede, the Army seems to be reverting to form. Still, though, the play goes on; I am content to have contributed a verse.

Even so, I regret how I treated people along the way. For ten years, I burned with a white-hot rage that frequently boiled over into self-righteousness. I used my gifts to not only advance my ideas but also humiliate those who disagreed with me. When the longtime editor of *Field Artillery Journal* balked at publishing the article that John and I wrote about field artillery's growing irrelevance, for example, I went over her head to force the issue. Attacking her life's work with the same ruthlessness I had applied to America's enemies on the battlefield, I got a two-star general to overrule her objections. No matter whom I clashed with, the only options I could imagine were cooperation or elimination.

I did not seek out the perspective of those who disagreed with me. In fact, I scarcely recognized their humanity. I was in a hurry, and they were in the way. Being able to make others look foolish is a dangerous talent, and I went at it with abandon. Only in hindsight do I see the irony in a purported counterinsurgency expert who used power so indiscriminately and made enemies so profligately.

I regret not having been kinder.

A SAILOR'S STORY

Jonathan W. Hutto Sr.

October 2003 outside a Wendy's in Prince George's County, Maryland: I am sitting in my decade-old Volkswagen Jetta, sobbing. I've just left a fifth-grade classroom with no intention of going back. I've failed miserably at becoming a teacher, my attempt at a new career after several years in the nonprofit world. A three-week "transition to teaching" crash course, it turns out, isn't nearly enough to take on the immense challenge of teaching middle schoolers in an underserved community. My life is unraveling, and I have nowhere to turn.

Although born into Atlanta's Black middle class, I had experienced difficulties growing up, especially as a teenager. My parents divorced, and my mother married a financially unstable Vietnam War veteran. Living in reduced circumstances, we became transient, moving on average once a year. By age sixteen, I was convinced that the way to improve my life was through education. I set my sights on attending Howard University.

With an up-by-the-bootstraps spirit, I worked very hard during my final two years of high school. The effort paid off as various philanthropic organizations—including the Vietnam Veterans of America—awarded me scholarships that would enable me to make ends meet as a student. When Howard University offered me admission, it seemed my dream had come true.

I arrived at Howard intent on making a difference and quickly committed myself to student activism. By the fall of my sophomore year, I was coordinating a campus-wide voter registration project. This catapulted me into leadership positions, first as an elected advisory neighborhood commissioner in the District of Columbia, then as president of the Howard University Student Association and undergraduate representative to the university's board of trustees. But by 2003, those days of collegiate enthusiasm and success seemed oh so distant.

Now things were about to change again. When I left my Jetta to buy a cup of coffee, a US Navy recruiter spotted me. A young, sharp-looking Black man with spit-shined shoes, he walked right up to me and launched into his pitch, promising me "a new lease on life." When he got to the part about the Navy repaying student loans, I began to listen and to ask a few questions of my own.

It was October 2003, half a year after the George W. Bush administration had launched the US invasion of Iraq. I had no desire to kill anyone or to risk my life fighting on foreign soil, especially on behalf of what I viewed as US imperialism. So I never even considered enlisting in the Army or the Marine Corps. But like Randle McMurphy from *One Flew over the Cuckoo's Nest*, I thought I could leverage the system to my personal advantage. The Navy could provide me with a steady paycheck for a while, I figured, and then I could proceed to the next stage of my life.

Indeed, my eagerness to begin collecting a paycheck almost cost my recruiter his catch. Training in most of the then-available Navy specialties, known as "rates," wasn't starting for another six months, and I did not want to wait that long. He was undeterred, however, and called me a few days later with news of a rate available sooner: photographer's mate. I knew little about photography, but was willing to learn. I took the plunge and enlisted.

My unwillingness to serve as cannon fodder connected directly to the tradition of Black resistance to the Vietnam War. Embodying this dissent was Stokely Carmichael, later known as Kwame Ture, who had chaired the Student Non-violent Coordinating Committee in the 1960s. Ture visited Howard University, his alma mater, during my time there, and compared himself with General Colin Powell, a university trustee. "We both faced the draft for Vietnam," he said. "Powell told them 'Yes,' and I told them 'Hell, no, I ain't going.'"

By the time I joined the US Navy, I occupied a middle ground between Powell and Ture. In no way did I intend to make the military a career and become a tool of America's ruling class. At the same time, I was hardly an ideological purist. I genuinely believed that a term of military service would benefit me. On this point, I was in for a rude awakening.

The human rights champion Paul Robeson once stated, "The battlefield is everywhere." I found that despite the military's supposed inclusivity today, it offers no escape from racism and white nationalism. And this racism is directly connected to the acts of aggression and even war crimes committed by the US military overseas.

* * *

The nine-week Navy basic training was tough, mostly from a physical perspective, but I hung in there and graduated. Next came an assignment to the Defense Information School at Fort Meade, Maryland, to learn the basics of still photography. Here things began to go south. On the first day of class, students were asked to state their reasons for enlisting. I responded by saying that the military was the best affirmative action employer in the country. My use of the phrase *affirmative action* provoked the military instructors, and from then on, they were intent on getting me. If I was even one second late for class, or if they could find any minor infraction, I'd be written up. Still, I managed to graduate, in no small part thanks to the support of other Black recruits.

In July 2004, my training complete, I reported for duty aboard the aircraft carrier USS *Theodore Roosevelt*. At the time, the carrier was undergoing shipyard repairs in Portsmouth, Virginia, in preparation for a six-month deployment the following year. Given my experience at Fort Meade, I joined the ship with limited trust in the chain of command and the Navy in general. My first day at the ship's photo lab foreshadowed the struggles that lay ahead.

The problem began with a white sailor from upstate New York. After observing me for roughly ten minutes without my having said a word, he bluntly stated, "You're one of those Real Black People, huh." Though initially shocked, I eventually came to understand what he meant. He was an overt racist who praised Adolf Hitler, performed Nazi salutes, and openly referred to Dr. Martin Luther King as "a coon." What was most disheartening to me wasn't his attitude but the internalized oppression displayed by Black sailors around us, who would either ignore him or uncomfortably laugh.

The situation was made worse by the tyrannical petty officer who ran the ship's media division. He talked down to everyone, barked and shouted orders, mistreated workers, and ran the shop with an iron fist. On only my third day in the photo lab, he remarked that my photography was the worst he had ever seen in his life. By December it became clear that he was intent on driving me out of the Navy.

The following month, I traveled to Washington, DC, to attend my son's birthday party. While I was there, a snowstorm hit, preventing me from returning to the ship as required by seven o'clock Monday morning. Such minor offenses are usually overlooked as long as the sailor involved alerts the chain of command and describes the mitigating circumstances. This courtesy was not extended to me, however. I was written up and brought before the draconian disciplinary review board, composed of high-ranking chief petty officers. The master chief presiding over the board was the senior enlisted sailor on the ship, outranking all but the carrier's executive officer (XO) and its commanding officer.

It was here I came face-to-face with the real Navy, live and uncensored. The board was diverse in terms of race and gender, but that made little difference in the way I was treated. I was forced to do multiple parade-ground-style "facing movements" while being screamed at repeatedly. One grisly-looking master chief, a white man, banged on the table and threatened to "kick my ass." Another chief, a Black woman, mockingly asked me if I'd ever heard of Hallmark: next time, she said, I had better send a card and forget about my son's party. Ultimately, the presiding master chief decided that I had not demonstrated sufficient contrition, and therefore should submit to an executive officer inquiry—the final step before a "captain's mast," a disciplinary hearing convened by the ship's commander.

At this point, I'd had enough of the Navy. The bullying that followed solidified that decision. After the disciplinary review board's hearing, I was ordered to stand rigidly at attention in the photo lab while awaiting a sea bag inspection—petty harassment disguised as a way of ensuring that I had all required uniforms and clothing. I had never been so humiliated in my life. After standing at attention for more than thirty minutes, I made a break for it. I grabbed a few personal articles, made my way to the quarterdeck, left the ship, and caught a cab to the nearest rental car facility. I didn't know exactly where I was going, but I knew I would not be returning to the United States Navy. I was going AWOL.

Of the several calls I made as I drove toward Washington, DC, one was to Rodney Green, an economics professor at Howard University. He'd been foundational to my development in college; as a student, I had participated in my first demonstration alongside Rod and the International Committee Against Racism. He also had personal experience with the military, having been drafted into the Army in 1969. Now Rod invited me to come over to his home the next morning for a chat and chew.

I was unprepared for the advice he gave me. Rod believed my going AWOL was both ill advised and harmful to my future. He spoke about his experience organizing against the

Vietnam War from inside the Army and said that my actions went against the principle of building working-class solidarity and cohesion among the enlisted "grunts." Rod's most striking assertion was that a number of my fellow sailors probably felt much as I did but expressed their unhappiness differently. He challenged me to report back aboard ship, accept whatever punishment I had coming, and then gradually work on building the deeper relationships and support needed to more effectively challenge the chain of command.

I returned to the ship after forty-two hours of unauthorized absence. Two weeks later, I stood at the executive officer's inquiry, inwardly fuming while the XO personally admonished me for behavior unbecoming a sailor. Believing I was "trainable," the executive officer decided against escalating my case to a captain's mast and instead assigned me extra military instruction, to be overseen by the despotic petty officer running the lab. *Extra military instruction* was a euphemism for dirty work. For the next month, I stayed after work for hours each evening—shining brass, stripping and waxing the photo lab deck, scrubbing ladder wells, cleaning deck drains, and so on. It was very humbling, yet the entire time I heeded Rod's advice and kept my eye on the ball.

Soon thereafter we were at sea, and I kept busy as a photojournalist in the ship's public affairs office. Then, on January 10, 2006, came the events that will always be burned into my memory. That night, I went to the photo lab to inquire about the military's joint photojournalism program with Syracuse University and saw three white petty officers in conversation there. Reaching into a vent duct, one of them pulled out a hangman's noose and grabbed his crotch. It was beyond shocking, as was the fact that the other two just stood there smirking. When I spoke up in protest, the man holding the noose replied that another Black sailor of our acquaintance could use a lynching as well.

I stormed out of the photo lab in utter disgust. Two hours later, I sent an email to the three petty officers demanding an apology and acknowledgment of their wrongdoing. I included some background on the legacy of lynching in America, explaining why their actions were the very opposite of funny. The next morning, when I went to the photo lab, the noose was still there, tied to the top of the vent duct. I wasn't prepared for the emotions I felt as I untied the noose. I wept uncontrollably as I recalled images of Black men tortured and killed, savage crimes for which there have been no real accounting and no reparations to this day.

It was evident the next day, upon seeing the smirk still on the face of the man who'd pulled out the noose, that no apology would be forthcoming. At this point, I decided enough was enough. Months earlier, I had already alerted my immediate chain of command to the oppressive culture within our workspace. I described an environment where racist remarks, including favorable references to the Ku Klux Klan, were constantly being made. But instead of investigating my complaints, the supervisors had accused *me* of being a racist.

With no hope of finding justice within my shop, I decided to send a letter of complaint to our ship's equal opportunity advisor. The Navy's ethos emphasizes handling situations at the lowest level, but I saw that as just sweeping problems under the rug. I was determined not to let that happen.

When asked to fill out paperwork, the target of my complaint designated a Black senior petty officer to serve as his advocate. A Black man serving as an advocate for an overt racist might seem absurd, but in reality it is far from surprising. Internalizing oppression is all but a requirement for African Americans who want to ascend the Navy's ranks.

To his credit, the officer conducting the investigation surveyed the sailors in my shop to assess my allegations. Remarkably, nearly a third of them affirmed that an oppressive culture existed there. Those who spoke up represented a cross section of the shop: three Black men, two white men, a Latino man, and a white woman. The lone woman had been victimized by having misogynistic pictures of her plastered on the wall of the photo lab, which the shop's chain of command clearly ignored.

The investigating officer ruled in my favor, charging the petty officer who'd brought out the noose with violating two articles of the Uniform Code of Military Justice. Eventually, he was restricted to the ship, reduced in rank, and fined. One of the other petty officers, the most senior sailor who'd witnessed the incident and done nothing about it, was reduced in rank and fined as well. Rod's advice to be patient, build collective solidarity, and "dig deeper" had paid off. This time my immediate superiors were the ones feeling the heat.

To my frustration, though, much of their punishment was suspended, to be wiped away if they committed no further misconduct in the next six months. Given the severity of the offense, it felt like they were getting away with just a slap on the wrist. I decided to appeal the outcome to higher authority. I felt strongly that the light punishments were inconsistent with the Navy's purported "zero tolerance" of racism and sexism. In my view, both of them should have been court-martialed, making them subject to much graver consequences.

* * *

WHILE DOING SOME research to strengthen my appeal, I came across the Center on Conscience and War. From them I learned that every member of the military is allowed to contact their member of Congress without going through the chain of command or getting prior command approval. In the spirit of causing some of the "good trouble" he famously urged, I contacted the office of civil rights icon John Lewis, who represented the Georgia congressional district where my parents resided.

Congressman Lewis subsequently wrote a letter to the Navy regarding my concerns. The Navy wrote back to him that it did not intend to take any further action. However, just by responding to Lewis about my concerns, the Navy made my case part of the public record, an example for present and future generations of enlisted personnel who encounter racism and sexism within the ranks and who may be looking for guidance on how to organize and resist.

While all this was going on, I had occasion to see the documentary *Sir! No Sir!*, which chronicles the history of dissent by active-duty troops who mobilized to end the Vietnam War. It added historical context to my own struggles. Here I encountered the testimony of Greg Payton, an Army veteran who took part in the 1968 uprising of Black soldiers being held at Long Binh stockade in Vietnam. I came to appreciate how the US military's domestic racism is part of a pattern of dehumanization that, at the extreme, leads to events like the

My Lai massacre in Vietnam and the killing of civilians in Fallujah during the Iraq War.

Payton compared being called *nigger* in the United States to GIs referring to the Vietnamese as *gooks*—later echoed by US troops disparaging Iraqis as *hajjis*. (Contrast this with the famous phrase often attributed to Muhammad Ali: "I ain't got no quarrel with them Vietcong. No Vietcong ever called me nigger.") Payton's story also helped me gain a deeper understanding of the noose incident. It was clear that as a Black sailor, I had been insufficiently submissive in the eyes of the white petty officers, so they felt a need to put me in my proper place.

Around the same time, Rod sent me a copy of *Soldiers in Revolt*, which also documents the Vietnam GI resistance movement. First published in 1975 by David Cortright, a veteran of the movement who later became a professor of peace studies at the University of Notre Dame, the book had just been reissued for its thirtieth anniversary. One chapter in particular captured my attention. Titled "Black on White," it describes the struggle against the racism afflicting the Navy during the early 1970s, culminating in the shipboard rebellion on the USS *Kitty Hawk* in October 1972.

Shortly before we returned from deployment, I emailed Cortright and invited him to give a talk in Norfolk, *Theodore Roosevelt*'s home port. To my delight, he enthusiastically accepted. The event drew about seventy-five attendees, including several active-duty sailors and a few marines who drove down from Quantico.

The highlight of the evening came afterward, when ten active-duty service members met with Cortright at the home of another local professor. There we engaged in a two-hour discussion centered on the question, "What could we do in this present moment?" All members of the group were united in their opposition to the ongoing post-9/11 wars and occupations. Cortright pledged his support, yet was cautious as he recalled his activist comrades from the prior generation being jailed and harassed for speaking out. We departed that night with a commitment to continue the fight.

Throughout that summer, Cortright and I had many conversations as we sought to envision a framework for active-duty opposition to war. The foundation of our vision was the Military Whistleblower Protection Act of 1988 coupled with Defense Department Regulation 1325.6, "Handling Dissident and Protest Activities Among Members of the Armed Forces." The Whistleblower Act gives an active-duty member the right of appeal to a member of Congress on any issue, without prior command approval. Regulation 1325.6, meanwhile, gives active-duty members the right to participate in political demonstrations while off base and out of uniform, so long as these occur within the United States and avoid slandering the president and other high officials.

I soon began to discuss this proposed framework with a handful of like-minded service members. Cortright began mobilizing the broader peace-and-justice community, including Veterans for Peace, Iraq Veterans Against the War, and the Center on Conscience and War. Our immediate aim was to mobilize GI opposition to the Iraq War. We drafted an Appeal for Redress from the War in Iraq, which we hoped other soldiers, sailors, airmen, and marines would sign. The text was respectful and to the point: "As a Patriotic American proud to serve the nation in uniform, I respectfully urge my political leaders in Congress to support the prompt withdrawal of all American military forces and bases from Iraq. Staying in Iraq will not work and is not worth the price. It is time for U.S. troops to come home."

We launched the appeal in October 2006. Tony Snow, President George W. Bush's White House press secretary at the time, stated during a press briefing that we had the right to appeal for redress but that our movement was not representative of the military as a whole. Within a few weeks, however, we had roughly six hundred signers from around the globe. CBS interviewed more than a dozen of them for the news show *60 Minutes*. The *Nation* magazine spoke to another twenty-four for a cover story called "About Face." On Martin Luther King Jr.'s birthday, we announced that the number of signers had surpassed a thousand. Immediately following the announcement, Representatives John Lewis and Dennis Kucinich became the first members of Congress to endorse the appeal. Clearly, we were onto something.

In October 2007, our burgeoning movement was both honored and humbled to receive the Letelier-Moffitt Human Rights Award from the Institute for Policy Studies (IPS). The award ceremony was attended by an intergenerational crowd of peace activists and organizers, including IPS cofounder Marc Raskin, who had been David Cortright's dissertation committee chair. By the end of the year, we had upward of two thousand signers serving in ten countries around the world, including Iraq and Afghanistan. Eighty-five percent of them came from the enlisted ranks, with 60 percent having served at least one tour of duty in the Iraq War.

The struggle against racism aboard *Theodore Roosevelt*, coupled with my work on the Appeal for Redress, left an indelible imprint on my activist soul. I saw that military dissent is of inestimable value as a resource to end America's ongoing imperial wars. The spark for the Appeal for Redress came directly from the Vietnam-era GI resistance movement, which demonstrated how members of the armed forces can fight for their interests even in the face of opposition from military and political leaders. In a myriad of ways, GIs had dissented, resisted, and, by the early 1970s, rendered the US armed forces virtually ungovernable and all but useless as a fighting force. In a different time and in different circumstances, our Appeal for Redress was building on their example.

My experiences within the US Navy taught me that enlisted personnel have an untapped power that, if organized, can potentially help change the course of history. By and large, enlisted members hail from the margins of American society, rural towns and blighted urban centers all but abandoned by the elites. Whether they come from Appalachia, West Virginia, or Washington, DC, young enlistees share a wide range of common interests. My fervent hope is that the Appeal for Redress can inspire a new generation of peacemakers within the ranks of the armed forces.

RECLAIMING MY MORALITY

Matthew P. Hoh

Dissent is a difficult topic for me to address. This is not because it brings up thoughts or emotions I find troubling or overwhelming. Nor is it because I don't want to revisit my past experiences and what led to them. Rather, the problem is that my journey of breaking from the military, the wars, and the US empire was not a simple one. It is not anything like a straight line.

In high school, I applied to West Point (the US Military Academy), to Annapolis (the Naval Academy), and for a Reserve Officers' Training Corps (ROTC) scholarship. The military academies require both a standard academic admissions process and also a nomination from one's member of Congress. I was academically accepted at West Point but only received a congressional nomination to Annapolis. I could have delayed college for a year and asked my member of Congress to nominate me for West Point instead, but I chose not to. And while I was offered an Army ROTC scholarship for college, I declined that as well.

This change came about because of the Gulf War. In 1990, a few weeks before my senior year of high school began, Iraq's dictator, Saddam Hussein, invaded Kuwait. Initially, I supported US intervention in the region. I believed the situation with Saddam and Kuwait was analogous to the oft-cited example of Hitler annexing Czechoslovakia. Even as I was filling out my applications to West Point, Annapolis, and ROTC, though, I started to recognize that the rationale for the war—let alone any moral foundation for it—was fluid and inconsistent. I realized that my intellectual critiques and moral principles did not square with what I was seeing happen in the Persian Gulf.

When the US invasion began, I was aghast at the slaughter. On both an intellectual and moral level I was angered by US hypocrisy, by our government's blatant manipulation and destruction of lives for purposes of US geopolitical and economic primacy. Even a high school senior could notice that the United States had only recently armed and supported Saddam Hussein, providing him with weaponry, equipment, money, and intelligence during the Iran–Iraq War of the 1980s. When Saddam had used chemical weapons, not just on Iranians but also on his own people—weapons that had been directly and indirectly supplied and approved of by America—the United States provided him with political cover at the United Nations. But now, in 1991, the same officials who had supported Iraq in the 1980s as members of the Reagan administration (including President George H. W. Bush himself, Reagan's vice president) were turning on Iraq and Saddam simply because it was politically convenient to do so.

The Gulf War was over before I graduated high school in

the spring, and I went to college that fall. I had applied to college wanting to study international relations. When one application essay asked me to imagine my future self delivering a commencement address, I chose to write it as if I had become secretary of state. But as a result of the Gulf War, I turned inward. Rather than studying foreign affairs, economics, and political science, as I had imagined only a year earlier, I studied religion, philosophy, literature, and classical mythology. I went from being a high school kid with a subscription to the *Economist* to a college kid with a passion for the poetry of John Milton.

Throughout my time in college, I gave little thought to the military, politics, and foreign affairs. After graduating, I worked in finance and operations for publishing companies. I did that for about two years before my boredom and restlessness became too much. Above all else, I was afraid that I would pass my time as a young man without ever having *done something*. Those years of inward focus in college had been enough. Now I was haunted by the idea of waking up one day at forty years old and realizing that I had never challenged myself, never served others, never exposed myself to danger, never participated in the world or the making of history.

I looked into becoming a firefighter, but the fire department where I lived wasn't hiring for another year or two, and I didn't have the patience for the residency requirements of fire departments in other cities. One day, frustrated, I saw an advertisement in the *New York Times* for becoming an officer in the Marine Corps. I called the telephone number and began the process. Nine months later I arrived at Quantico, Virginia, for Marine Officer Candidates School (OCS).

I needed to be of service, to be a hero and take part in something bigger than me. I thought I would find that in the Marine Corps.

At this point, my understanding of history, while pretty thorough for someone of my age, was disjointed. I recognized and understood the downfalls and the deceits of our society, but I didn't tie them together. I did not see history as a continuous line that runs through events; instead, I perceived historical events as separate episodes, with only loose associations of cause and effect. I was familiar with the genocide of the Native Americans and the conquest of the continent, the invasion of Canada in the War of 1812, the war against Mexico, American interventions in Asia (including the "opening" of Japan by Commodore Perry), the coup in Hawaii, the Spanish–American War, the centuries of American involvement in Central and South America, and assorted post–World War II coups, interventions, occupations, and proxy wars, up through and including the Vietnam War. All those incidents and wars I recognized, disliked, and denounced. Still, I didn't truly understand them as the coherent story of American empire that they were.

When I entered OCS, I could say that the Vietnam War was awful, what the United States had done in Central America in the 1980s was terrible, what we did to Iraq in 1991 was horrible. But I failed to see that the same forces, and often literally the same people in government, were driving events in the present.

I was initially stationed with the Marine Corps in Okinawa, Japan, then assigned as a staff officer to the Pentagon, working for the Office of the Secretary of the Navy. That's where I was when we invaded and occupied Iraq in 2003. As the realities of the Iraq War assaulted my moral and intellectual foundation, the initial excuses I'd made for being part of this enterprise fell away, but new ones arose. My disagreements with the American wars, and my internal justifications for continuing to be involved with them, were never static: they competed against each other, mutated and evolved, each rebutting the other in turn. That's why I left active duty in the spring of 2004 and went to Iraq as a government official on a State Department reconstruction and governance team. Even though I was convinced of the illegality of America's war there, its mendacity, and its counterproductive nature, I thought that as an individual, I could make a difference. If I went to Iraq, I told myself, I could do good there. Where others harmed, I would help. I believed I could be a moral actor in an immoral environment.

I spent a year in Iraq, handing out millions to local political leaders for reconstruction efforts. Two safes in my bedroom held as much as $24 million in cash at a time. I worked closely with Iraqis of all backgrounds, saw many of them suffer and die, and all of them, along with their families and neighbors, endure lives of hellish fear. I left Iraq with a clear sense of the folly of the war, the cruel damage being done to the people there, and the potent mixture of US ignorance and arrogance.

After coming back to the United States, I went to work as a consultant on the State Department's Iraq desk. Now my thinking wasn't so much that I could do good right away, but that if I stayed involved, I might be able do so in the future. I knew that as a junior or mid-level person in government, I couldn't change things. However, I thought, if I stuck around, maybe I could make a difference as a senior official in the years and decades to come. The work I did at the State Department belied this optimism, though. I had seen senior people at the Pentagon allow themselves to be misled, and now I saw the same at the State Department. Whether they embraced the war openly and eagerly, or were passive in their ignorance, the lies of the war were circulated and celebrated throughout Washington.

For a while at the State Department, I was responsible for writing the *Iraq Weekly Status Report*. This report, in classified and unclassified versions, went to many people in Washington: government officials, the media, members of Congress, admirals and generals. It was placed on the desks of the secretary of the state, the vice president, and even the president. So, among other tasks, I would spend my time each week trying to assemble "good news" about the Iraq War. Of course, there was none. The weekly status report was a complete work of fiction, as anyone with any degree of intellectual or moral honesty would recognize. However, it was promoted, disseminated, and cited, and I did my part.

How could a system that was so rotten and corrupt—and so incentivized for that rot and corruption to succeed—ever be changed? What could someone within it possibly do? Once again, my justifications for my involvement in the war began to change. While working at the State Department, I was also a reserve officer in the Marine Corps, and one day I received an email from the Marines looking for volunteers for Iraq. The first position in that email immediately appealed to me: they needed a captain to command a combat engineer company being deployed to Anbar Province in Iraq.

My argument for staying in the war now became that I was a good officer, better than most. This was a combat unit

I would be taking over, with some 150 sailors and marines, and I knew I could bring those young men home to their families. I would be protecting and taking care of others.

This is a common excuse seen throughout the military, held by many officers and senior enlisted personnel throughout their careers. But it involves shrugging off any responsibility for what you are taking part in, denying your duty to understand whether the orders you are following are legal or illegal. There may be some truth to your commitment to take care of others, but it means dismissing the overall reality of the war. And this excuse is used to such an extent by people in leadership positions in the military that it has become a washing of the hands, a self-absolution that ignores one's complicity.

It was a difficult and violent deployment. From late summer of 2006 through the early winter of 2007, in many parts of our area of operations attacks and combat happened almost daily. Our armored vehicles and body armor saved many lives and limbs; some of my marines had their vehicles hit by ten or more IEDs during our time there. (Whether they truly escaped unharmed is another question. These days the Department of Defense requires anyone within fifty yards of an explosive blast to be evaluated for traumatic brain injury, but that standard did not exist during our deployment.) Most of us had stories of roadside bombs, rocket and mortar attacks, rifle fire, grenades, and so forth that in previous wars—or even in the first year of the Iraq war—would have killed or maimed us. Now, thanks to our equipment, we just brushed ourselves off and continued with our patrols and operations. The Iraqis, of course, had no such protection.

Things started to change around the end of 2006, when

American officers began speaking directly with Sunni insurgents and trying to address their grievances. Those grievances amounted to no more than the well-understood consequences of having a people occupied and abused, by both foreigners and a sectarian conflict driven by America's divide-and-conquer strategy. Answering these grievances meant turning control of Sunni areas over to Sunni leaders. In return, those leaders abandoned al-Qaeda and other jihadist groups, and violence began to drop quickly. Such reactionary religious groups had never amounted to more than a few percent of the insurgency, which raises the question of what would have happened if we'd spoken to the Sunnis right from the beginning. Of course, never invading Iraq in the first place was always the correct answer, but just how wrongheaded and counterproductive a strategy the United States pursued afterward—never mind how massively immoral—was clear to anyone with the courage to see it.

So when I came back from that second Iraq deployment, I demobilized from active duty as soon as I could and resigned my Marine Corps commission. I wanted to step away from the war entirely. There was an enormous dissonance between what I had taken part in during my time in Iraq and who I thought I was as a person. The dissonance was causing chaos, dismay, and desolation within my mind and spirit. This was moral injury: the harrowing feeling of having transgressed—whether through thought or deed, action or inaction—against your moral code. It is a betrayal of who you thought you were.

Moral injury also occurs when a person is betrayed by organizations or other people whom that person had believed in, respected, and cherished. And in the case of the military, it's not only a matter of what groups and people one identifies with or wishes to emulate: these are institutions and leaders for whom a person is willing to make the most extreme physical sacrifices, to die and to commit violence against others. I had betrayed who I thought I was by being morally and intellectually dishonest, and I was betrayed by others who were conducting a war based on lies.

I was in a bad way. I cannot emphasize enough the destructive effects—mental, emotional, and spiritual—of moral injury. It is believed by many to be the primary driver of combat veteran suicides. It is much more than mere guilt, shame, and regret, which it incorporates but supersedes in its manifestation and symptoms. The deaths of both Iraqis and Americans, the ongoing suffering of the Iraqi people, the anguish of American families bereft of their hoped-for futures were a burden on my soul. And I had not only witnessed the slaughter but taken part in it too. My hands had been covered in blood and brains, fragments of ligament and bone. I was a perpetrator.

To deal with the moral injury and perpetration-induced traumatic stress (PITS), I self-medicated with alcohol. Daily I would numb myself to accept who I was. By keeping closed the doors of intellectual and moral honesty in my mind, by not allowing myself to recognize what the war truly was, and by consuming alcohol in massive quantities, I neutered myself into a piece of meat that was happy to have been a servant of the US empire.

* * *

After demobilizing in 2007, I expected to find my employment in the private sector. But just as I was about to accept a job offer with an HVAC and plumbing subcontractor in Baltimore, I was invited to work with a Pentagon unit that was building and acquiring technology to protect US troops from IEDs, suicide bombs, and the like. The recruiter told me: "Hey, I saw your résumé, and based on your skills and experience I think you can help save a lot of lives." The argument caught me just when I was most susceptible to it, and I went back into the wars once again. I thought I could help save others. I felt I owed it to them.

Not very long after I started working at the Pentagon, I had a chance to receive a direct appointment into the Foreign Service—something relatively rare—and go to Afghanistan. I was excited about the opportunity. I believed President Barack Obama's administration would be different from the Bush administration. I concurred with what General Petraeus said about needing to pursue a political solution to Afghanistan rather than a military one. I had been in the Sunni parts of Iraq during the Sunni Awakening that began in late 2006, and had seen how dialogue with the Sunnis brought about a temporary cease-fire and the near destruction of al-Qaeda in Iraq. (Optimistically, I thought the cease-fire would hold, once again ignoring the continuity of American history and warfare.) If the United States similarly met the grievances of the Afghan insurgency, I thought, the war there could be brought to an end.

I thought I could be of use in Afghanistan. I also felt that Afghanistan could be of service to me. My relentless consumption of alcohol was a slow and steady form of suicide. The idea of dying in Afghanistan was more attractive to me than dying in the United States: I could kill myself in America by drinking or with a gun, or die seemingly more honorably in service abroad. Being back in the war was what I needed and where I belonged. As soon as I landed in Afghanistan, in April 2009, my issues with PITS and PTSD quite nearly vanished. All felt right.

It didn't take long, though, for those feelings to dissipate. Perhaps it was the absence of drink: I could no longer water my brain with alcohol every day, as if it were a pesticide to keep back the weeds of intellectual and moral honesty. Perhaps those weeds were beginning to bloom again. Whatever the reason, I was confronted in Afghanistan with the same realities I'd experienced in Iraq.

It soon became apparent the only difference between the Iraq War and the Afghan War was that one had been run by a Republican and the other by a Democrat. As weeks and months went by, I was again sickened by what I was taking part in. As the late veteran-turned-antiwar-activist Jacob George put it, the United States was sending poor farmers overseas to fight poor farmers. Just as in Iraq, I saw local villagers get ripped apart, bodily and mentally, with no promise that their suffering would ever mean anything. I saw American men and women go home in coffins to families to whom I could not justify their sacrifice.

Event after event confirmed the agreement of the Afghan War with the Iraq War, as well as with the multitude of previous wars fought to establish and ensure American primacy, devastating all but the few who profited from them. Naturally, there were some things unique to Afghanistan, such as the drug trafficking (largely dominated by our allies in the Afghan government). But by and large, the Afghan War was the identical twin sibling to the Iraq War. Arguments I was making to myself foundered, and my reasons for being there quickly began to feel silly or selfish. The thought of a government career as a neocolonial officer of the American empire was nauseating.

The lack of alcohol was not the only reason why my intellectual and moral strength returned. There was a searing column written by Bob Herbert of the *New York Times* on the passing of Defense Secretary Robert McNamara, "Lyndon Johnson's icy-veined . . . intellectual point man for a war that sent thousands upon thousands of people to their utterly pointless deaths." And there was a letter I received from my father, which made me realize that I alone could decide what I did next. Only I could determine my morality and ascertain whether my life was an honest one. By my fifth month in Afghanistan, sleepless, sickened mentally and emotionally, I submitted my resignation from my post with the State Department.

My resignation occurred as Obama was preparing to send an additional thirty thousand soldiers into Afghanistan, to go along with forty thousand US troops he'd added to the war almost immediately upon entering office, plus tens of thousands more security contractors (that is, mercenaries) and NATO soldiers. The war was distinctly immoral, a pursuit of military victory solely for the sake of glory for the White House and the Pentagon—quite akin in that respect to George W. Bush's crusade in Iraq. It was also strategically unsound, counterproductive, and futile. The Taliban were fighting an extension of a civil war that went back to the 1970s, a war largely caused by American interference and manipulation meant to stymie the Soviet Union. The bulk of the Taliban's soldiers were in it not for some religious ideology but because they wanted to end foreign occupation. This was not my lone opinion, but the assessment of nearly all my diplomatic, military, and intelligence colleagues.

After I returned home, a chain of *Forrest Gump*–like events led to the *Washington Post* interviewing me about my resignation. They ran the piece as a front-page, above-the-fold three-thousand-word profile. The morning it was published, I woke up to three TV trucks outside my apartment; by the end of the day, I had received more than seventy-five interview requests. Within a few days, I had six book offers and was heading to New York City to be on the *Today* show. I asked the *Washington Post* reporter, Karen DeYoung, why she had given me such extensive coverage. Karen replied that it was because she had asked everyone she knew at the White House, the State Department, the CIA, and the Pentagon about what I had written in my resignation letter, and no one had disagreed with me. Not one person, though, went on the record to support me.

There was never any single moment when I decided I could not lie to myself any longer and keep participating in the wars. The sense of what is fair and honest just overtook me by degrees. Perhaps it's as simple as being an alcoholic without alcohol on hand to subdue his feelings. The entire US government, including our military, intelligence, and diplomatic corps, was—and is—full of people who don't believe in America's endless wars, don't believe in our supposed reasons for fighting them, and don't believe that the sacrifices and costs are worthwhile. The extent of their lying, to themselves and to the public, has been well documented, not only for Iraq and Afghanistan but for all American wars of this century, and most wars of previous centuries as well.

In 2019, the *Washington Post* reported on the Afghanistan Papers, a confidential trove of interviews conducted by the Office of the Special Inspector General for Afghanistan Reconstruction with more than six hundred US officials, both military and civilian. The report laid bare the systemic lying of the entire US government regarding the Afghan War, just as the *New York Times* unveiling the Pentagon Papers in 1971 revealed the systemic lying of the US government regarding the war in Vietnam. Yet our elected officials have made no attempts to address the unmitigated mendacity. Britain's Parliament, to its credit, has held formal inquires regarding the wars in Iraq and Libya, confirming that those wars were started and sustained upon lies. In the United States, we have not had justice or truth-telling from our leaders.

Chelsea Manning showed the world video of US helicopters massacring journalists and an ambulance crew; she was imprisoned, while lies disavowing such attacks (to say nothing of the attacks themselves) remain unpunished. CIA officer John Kiriakou spoke out about the agency's torture of prisoners; he, too, went to prison, while the torturers were untouched. Actual US assistance to al-Qaeda, the Islamic State, and other jihadist groups in Syria and Libya has now been so thoroughly documented—by journalists and whistleblowers, leaked documents and recovered weapons—as to be undeniable, yet there has been no investigation, no accountability, no justice. Instead, there has been a subordination of mind, soul, and spirit at all levels of the US government. I'm speaking of not simply generals and top political leaders but the men and women who fill out the ranks of the military, the intelligence community, and the diplomatic corps. And the same goes for Congress and the mainstream American media as well.

Since coming home in 2009, I have spoken out against the wars and worked with peace movements. I have tried to live a life that aligns with my principles and values. But I am still dealing with the effects of moral injury, still reckoning with what I did in the wars, whether in Afghanistan, Iraq, or Washington, DC. My suicidal tendencies grew even worse after I resigned my position, peaking years after I had done "the right thing." They are still something I grapple with daily.

The great cowardice that kept me participating in the wars, the willful ignorance of how history runs unbroken through the events of our lives, and the ravenous desire to be a part of something bigger than me even if it meant destroying myself and others—all these may be behind me now, but they are still things for which I must atone. I do not know when or how I will meet the dictates and requirements of atonement. When will my guilt, regret, and shame be satiated? Perhaps never, and that is fair, for I helped wreck lives not solely in the current generation but for generations to come. But I do not believe the answer is to punish myself, although I sometimes struggle with that instinct. Instead, I've come to believe that it is to live a life according to how my mind, soul, and spirit dictate—to be intellectually and morally honest for the remainder of my days.

TRUTH, LIES, AND PROPAGANDA

Kevin Tillman

It took me over a year after leaving the military to write my first public dissent against the Global War on Terror. It was late 2006, and the death toll was mounting in Iraq and Afghanistan. By that point, both countries were essentially failed states. Nearly all Iraqis wanted US forces to leave—after all, Washington's illegal and immoral 2003 invasion had turned their country and society upside down. The world was a far more dangerous and intolerant place than it had been when I enlisted in the US Army in July 2002. Hundreds of American soldiers were being killed and injured monthly, and the moral fabric of our country seemed to be unraveling. On a more personal note, in 2004 my older brother, Pat, had been killed in action while we were deployed together in Afghanistan. In short, I was hardly in the best headspace.

Transitioning out of the military and back into civilian life was a struggle. Fairly or unfairly, I had trouble relating to civilians, who seemed to be carrying on with their usual lives unconcerned by America's actions overseas. I generally kept to myself. Most of my time was spent watching C-SPAN and reading books on philosophy, science, and American imperialism. Life seemed directionless and without purpose. I wanted to have as few feelings as possible; remaining stoic and isolated seemed to serve me well. Thinking about the military and foreign policy, on the other hand, brought an upwelling of disbelief, disappointment, rage, and survivor's guilt. At times I would degenerate (speaking loosely and unclinically) into feeling suicidal, homicidal, or both.

Somehow, though, I managed to steer myself into something I felt was productive and cathartic: writing an article for Robert Scheer's progressive online journal *Truthdig*. The piece began by recalling a conversation I'd had with Pat before we joined the military: "He spoke about the risks with signing the papers. How once we committed, we were at the mercy of the American leadership and the American people. How we could be thrown in a direction not of our volition. How fighting as a soldier would leave us without a voice . . . until we got out."

There were a few nightmare scenarios we had discussed prior to enlisting. One of those was that our service might be used as a tool of profit and power, not to defend the country or for the good of humanity. But we hadn't imagined just how bad things would get. After Pat's death, a phrase kept running through my head: *how the fuck is it possible that . . .* followed by one disaster after another. The *Truthdig* article was the first time I wrote (or even spoke) publicly, so for the purposes of the piece I substituted "somehow":

> Somehow we were sent to invade a nation because it was a direct threat to the American people, or to the world, or

harbored terrorists, or was involved in the September 11 attacks, or received weapons-grade uranium from Niger, or had mobile weapons labs, or WMD, or had a need to be liberated, or we needed to establish a democracy, or stop an insurgency, or stop a civil war we created that can't be called a civil war even though it is. Something like that. . . .

Somehow profiting from tragedy and horror is tolerated.

Somehow the death of tens, if not hundreds, of thousands of people is tolerated.

Somehow subversion of the Bill of Rights and the Constitution is tolerated. . . .

Somehow torture is tolerated. . . .

Somehow reason is being discarded for faith, dogma, and nonsense. . . .

Somehow a narrative is more important than reality. . . .

Somehow being politically informed, diligent, and skeptical has been replaced by apathy through active ignorance. . . .

Somehow nobody is accountable for this.

I hoped my voice could in some small way affect the congressional elections that were taking place the following month. More important, though, I needed to release what was bottled up inside me, regardless of whether anyone cared or listened.

It has been fifteen years since I wrote that article. Frankly, I don't see myself as a true war dissenter in the traditional sense, although I am grateful and honored to be considered one. That designation, I believe, needs to be earned through persistent, relentless public advocacy against illegal wars and immoral military policy. I am also not an intellectual, journalist, or whistleblower immersed in foreign policy conversation. Nor am I a high-ranking military official critiquing national military strategy. I'm simply a veteran who enlisted in the Army to defend this country on the front lines after the 9/11 attacks.

The main impetus for my war dissent was a sense of moral obligation. There was a massive disconnect between the stated laws and ideals of my country, on one hand, and the stark realities that were unfolding in front of me.

* * *

I GREW UP in San Jose, California, in a small historic mining town called New Almaden. Our house was tucked against the mountains of Almaden Quicksilver County Park. It was an ideal environment for me, my two brothers, and our parents to thrive—safe, quiet, and with lots to do outside. Not particularly gifted in the classroom, I gravitated toward athletics. Competitive sports offered a controlled physical environment where I could display skill, courage, and discipline, as well as a chance to regularly fail or succeed.

Everyone in my family really enjoyed history, not from a particularly academic, PhD-level perspective but in the broader sense of regularly reading about and discussing it. There were always books around the house about the Civil War, both world wars, the Korean War, and Vietnam. We did talk mostly about military history, rather than economic, scientific, religious, artistic, or other varieties—presumably because, like most kids our age, we had grandparents and other family members with significant military backgrounds.

Naturally, the war that came up most often was World War II. Our grandfather had been stationed at Pearl Harbor during the attack, which filled us with pride and curiosity. We saw the soldiers defending the world from fascism as the gold standard of what it means to serve both one's country and the global community. That "greatest generation" had fought for the good of all humanity, and made a positive difference in the world, something I think every kid and adult wants to do.

As a teenager I found myself gravitating toward the military more and more. I viewed being a soldier as the only real way of displaying the ultimate courage and virtue. (Of course it is not true, but my experience and perception were limited at the time.) Since I played a lot of sports, I was involved in a lot of events that began with ceremonial renditions of "The Star-Spangled Banner" and it always gave me goose bumps. It was striking how everyone came together to celebrate our history and offer appreciation for those who had sacrificed so much—often everything—so that I could swing a bat for fun. I felt a real sense of gratitude for what past generations of veterans had endured and accomplished.

I also felt a sense of inadequacy. I gravitated toward books about the Green Berets, Army Rangers, Delta Force, Marine Recon, Navy SEALs, and other specialized elite units. These soldiers possessed a level of skill, bravery, and discipline linked to something bigger than a sport. What they were doing was not a game; it was real.

Both my parents grew up Catholic but stopped attending church well before they had kids, so I never had any kind of religious upbringing. Religious concepts like heaven and hell, sin and salvation, gods and scriptures, faith and prophets, and the like played no role in my life. Theism just wasn't a thing in my family or circle of friends growing up, nor was it a major focus or issue in my community. My worldview is science-based, what might be termed naturalistic or, more aggressively, atheistic. Books like *On the Origin of Species* or physicist Sean Carroll's *The Big Picture* have always been more palatable to me than the Bible or other religious texts. (I do, though, appreciate liberation theology used as a moral framework to fight oppression, as well as individuals such as Martin Luther King Jr., who used religious teachings to promote equality, freedom, empathy, peace, kindness, and self-determination.)

My interest in history and life's big questions is why I chose to be a philosophy major in college, at California Polytechnic State University in San Luis Obispo. My upbringing and my background may also explain both my loyalty to the United States and my sometimes skeptical attitude toward it. I've always loved the nation I was born into—its beauty, freedoms, opportunities, high standard of living, college football, and all the rest. But I had no illusions that it was divinely created, or that our leaders were infallible. I saw no individual, no institution, no nation, no book as being above reproach. Nor did I think that any people had been "chosen" from above through divine Providence, or possess more worth than any other people on earth. All aspects of life are fair game for scrutiny.

I knew American history was both wonderful and troubling. But I had a natural bias toward America: it was my country, and I wanted the best for it. So even when I would read about our belligerent foreign policy, it didn't seem to represent the overall character and ethos of the nation or where we were headed. It was only on September 11, 2001, that I truly felt my own life starting to connect with America's history and its actions overseas.

* * *

When the World Trade Center and the Pentagon were attacked, I was twenty-three years old. I was an infielder with a minor league affiliate of the Cleveland Indians, getting paid (although not very much) to play a game. I had recently undergone shoulder surgery and was doing physical rehabilitation back home in California. That morning, I watched in horror as the planes smashed into the Twin Towers. My brain had trouble believing what I was seeing. The crystal clear blue sky in the background added to the devastation, as people burned alive and some jumped out of the buildings to their deaths. It was gut-wrenching. Firefighters and other first responders were risking their lives to save people in that cloud of destruction. I was three thousand miles away from it all, haunted by a feeling of powerlessness and inadequacy. I wanted to help but I couldn't.

Up until then, I'd spent the greater part of my life trying to make it onto the forty-man roster of a major league baseball team. But I felt uneasy about those dreams in the wake of that horrible September day. As much as I loved baseball, the idea of continuing to play a game no longer seemed an acceptable path.

Thankfully, any decision I made would go relatively unnoticed outside the immediate circle of my friends and family. That was not quite the case for Pat. When the attacks occurred, he was in his fourth year of playing for the Arizona Cardinals in the NFL. There were quite a few football fans who watched him play and appreciated him as a person, both on and off the field So there ended up being a lot more attention for him to manage.

Ultimately, each person makes their own decision about whether to join the military; after all, the country ditched the draft at the tail end of the Vietnam War. Joining is certainly not for everyone. And while people who sign up for military service tend to be driven by similar motivations, the exact reasons are always personal, nuanced, and unique. In my own case, it was September 11 that caused me to enlist. The place where I was then in life, my age, my physical capability, my ethical framework, and my worldview made that decision seem obvious and morally obligatory for me.

As for Pat, he never publicly commented in detail on the reasons why he enlisted, and it's not my place to speak for him. In my opinion, his actions speak for themselves. However, for context, in an interview with NBC News the day after the attacks, he commented: "My great-grandfather was at Pearl Harbor, and a lot of my family has gone and fought in wars. And I really haven't done a damn thing as far as laying myself on the line like that. So I have a great deal of respect for those who have." A few months later, in a diary entry that has since become public, he wrote: "After recent events, I've come to appreciate just how shallow and insignificant my role is. I'm no longer satisfied with the path I've been following. . . . My voice is calling me in a different direction. It is up to me whether or not to listen."

So it was that in July 2002, Pat and I enlisted in the Army as infantrymen on a "buddy contract." This enabled us to go through training together, with follow-on orders for the two of us to join the Army Rangers—part of the US special operations community—if we passed the requisite courses. Our goal was simply to do our part and serve our country honorably, nothing more and nothing less.

* * *

Ever since I was a kid, there always seemed to be a lot of noise about Iraq's leader, Saddam Hussein. During the first Gulf War, in 1990–91, I was in middle school and didn't have a clue about what was going on. After the 9/11 attacks, I noticed an uptick in aggressive rhetoric directed Saddam's way. In January 2002, President George W. Bush called out Iraq in his infamous "axis of evil" quip during the State of the Union, lumping the country together with Iran and North Korea. Still, it wasn't until I was in basic training in late 2002 that the possibility of invading Iraq became real to me.

During basic training, we heard some comments about what was brewing in Iraq and how we should start mentally preparing for a new war. We had little to no access to the outside world at the time, so the information felt vague, indeed disturbingly so. However, at the time my focus was simply on getting through basic training, advanced infantry training, Airborne School, and the Ranger Indoctrination Program—the last of these, the final prerequisite before joining the 75th Ranger Regiment. As long as we passed all of them, Pat and I would end up where we wanted to be in order to serve our country on the front lines. After months of long and grueling training, we finally made it, joining the 2nd Battalion of the 75th Ranger Regiment in Fort Lewis, Washington.

It was only when we got to our unit that the talk of going to war with Iraq really sank in. We were not getting ready for

Afghanistan; the focus was 100 percent Iraq. And now that we had regular access to the same information as the rest of the American people, we also realized that this war was seemingly preordained, a fait accompli. Stories of weapons of mass destruction, mobile weapons labs, links to al-Qaeda, impending mushroom clouds over New York City, and all kinds of such fanciful shit were being served up by the Bush administration as justifications ostensibly requiring the United States to invade Iraq and remove Saddam Hussein. None of it seemed tethered to reality. It felt like such nonsense should have been dismissed out of hand by everyone, but it wasn't.

It was at this time that I started to notice war-dissenting voices more clearly—and recognize that they had a direct connection to my situation. The propaganda shoveled to the public was being fact-checked and scrutinized in real time. I was grateful for the insightful and skeptical voices in the conversation. But even after the United States and the United Kingdom failed to secure an authorization at the United Nations to use force against Iraq, the powers that be in Washington simply didn't care. Days before the invasion, an article in the *Washington Post* pointed out that the Bush administration was preparing to attack Iraq "on the basis of a number of allegations against Iraqi President Saddam Hussein that have been challenged—and in some cases disproved—by the United Nations, European governments and even US intelligence reports." Sadly, if international governing bodies and the US government's own intelligence reports were being disregarded, war dissenters hardly stood a chance of stopping the invasion. So invade Iraq we did—with Pat and me part of the invading force.

Being certain that we were participants in a war of

aggression—what the Nuremberg Tribunal called "the supreme international crime"—was disheartening, to say the least. My childhood delusions of saving the galaxy like Han Solo, Luke Skywalker, or Lando Calrissian were met with the stark reality of being a mere storm trooper for the US empire. Pat never spoke to the press during his enlistment, but a fellow Ranger, Russell Baer, later told a reporter about a scene that took place during the invasion. "I can see it like a movie screen," he said. "We were at an old air base, me, Kevin and Pat; we weren't in the fight right then. We were talking. And Pat said, 'You know, this war is so fucking illegal.'"

United Nations secretary-general Kofi Annan has said the same thing in no uncertain terms. Asked in an interview about the invasion of Iraq, he declared: "I have indicated it was not in conformity with the UN charter. From our point of view and from the charter point of view it was illegal." The United States is a signatory of the charter. But the sad reality is that the United States has veto power as one of the five permanent members of the UN Security Council, so the council will never formally address the illegality of the war. The Bush administration will never be convicted or even censured for its profound crime. Instead of being locked up, the architects of the aggression against Iraq walk the streets as if nothing happened and are even glorified.

As a soldier, I was prepared to serve wherever our elected officials and the American people sent me. I willingly relinquished that aspect of my volition when I enlisted in the US Army, and I was not going to renege on my commitment. However, I didn't volunteer to risk my life for America only to have officials motivated by profit and power use me as a glorified state-sponsored terrorist. Nor had I wanted to be cheered on by a manipulated, apathetic, and largely deluded citizenry. I felt, then and now, that Americans who voluntarily don the uniform should know for certain that their service is being used to *defend* this country and further the good of humanity. Anything less is a betrayal of the service member.

* * *

THE BETRAYAL BECAME more personal after we redeployed to Afghanistan, where Pat was killed on April 22, 2004, in a friendly fire incident. The Bush administration didn't like the optics of a high-profile soldier like Pat, in a Ranger battalion no less, being killed by friendly fire. In addition, the Abu Ghraib prison scandal had just hit the headlines. So the government lied to us—his family—and to the American public with a manufactured story about him dying by enemy fire, then used him to promote more war. For maximum effect, they awarded him a Silver Star, one of the highest military honors. It was all based on fabricated witness statements and a false narrative; they didn't even bother to find out what courageous actions he actually took on the battlefield. Our family did not start getting even fragmentary versions of the truth until about a month later and then in large part only because the coroner refused to sign the fabricated autopsy report.

Our family labored through multiple investigations, first within the US Army, then with the Department of Defense, and eventually the US Congress. Our mother, Mary, was without a doubt the driver of this effort, relentless in the fight for truth. The rest of the family, lots of friends, journalists, soldiers, veterans, and eventually elected officials contributed to it as well. However, none of it was initially motivated by a desire to dissent against the war. Rather, we simply wanted to uncover facts and get justice and accountability for Pat.

As the investigations mounted, it became clear that Pat was not the only service member who'd been used for political purposes during this time. Three years after his death, my mom and I testified before the House Committee on Oversight and Reform alongside Jessica Lynch. Lynch had been taken prisoner at the onset of the Iraq War when her supply convoy got ambushed in Al Nasiriyah. Several soldiers died in the attack, and she was badly injured. A rescue mission took place at the Iraqi hospital where Lynch was being held, and our forces were able to free her. Although she had been knocked unconscious at the very beginning of the attack, after her rescue there was a false narrative created for public consumption about, as she put it, "the little girl Rambo from the hills of West Virginia who went down fighting." These were stories she didn't create, didn't ask for, and couldn't get to stop.

What I learned from the experience is that this wasn't personal: for certain elements inside the power structure of the US government, this was purely business. The Bush administration and the US military were not trying to harm Pat or Jessica or any particular family with their lies, omissions, and deception. It could have been anyone. They were simply doing what they reflexively do when presented with global and domestic situations, good or bad: manage, control, and manipulate the optics to be favorable to them, and if possible use the situation as an opportunity to promote their agenda. The experience also helped me understand just how the US power structure functioned. It didn't matter who called the shots inside our unaccountable empire: the result would generally be the same.

This lesson was reinforced for me when President Barack Obama replaced Bush in January 2009. Like many others, I hoped—or, rather, felt certain—that the country's first Black president would promptly rein in America's belligerent foreign policy. By most accounts, Obama is a kind, smart, reasonable, hardworking, and thoughtful person. Even so, it wasn't long before he escalated the war in Afghanistan, expanded our global drone campaign, recolonized Africa with US troops, not-so-secretly helped turn Syria into an apocalyptic wasteland, and extended America's economic warfare against countries like Venezuela. This, from a Nobel Peace Prize laureate! My disappointment with Obama's foreign policy proved yet another reminder that the problems we face are structural and systemic—wired into the national DNA. I had counted on Obama's election engendering a paradigm shift. Instead, he continued nearly all the Bush administration's policies, only with far more sophistication. For both presidents, the main concern was expanding the American empire, or what US officials term "advancing American interests."

History now began to take on a whole different dimension for me. Beyond Afghanistan and Iraq, I started noticing how the various other American acts of international aggression—all those "police actions," coups, illegal sanctions, meddled elections, and smaller-scale military interventions—seemed to show up everywhere. I'd been reading anti-imperialist authors like Greg Grandin, Eduardo Galeano, and Noam Chomsky for years, but now I could actually recognize the little games Washington was playing overseas nearly in real time. It was all so offensively transparent.

* * *

IN FEBRUARY 2019, I published another article on *Truthdig*, this one headlined "A Call to Halt an Illegal Invasion of Venezuela." The US government was in the middle of staging yet another obvious coup in that country. President Donald Trump and the covert apparatus of the United States were colluding with an unpopular, unqualified Venezuelan impostor named Juan Guaidó, who'd declared himself president of Venezuela when he didn't like the results of his country's free and fair presidential election. It was all conducted so ham-handedly and unprofessionally that it seemed clear Washington's power players weren't even trying to hide it, which made it all the more offensive.

At the same time as our country was making the Venezuelan economy scream through unlawful sanctions, the Trump administration simultaneously communicated its intent to smuggle humanitarian aid into the country. The goal was to bait the Venezuelan military into violently engaging the convoy, which would presumably create enough chaos for the United States to intervene with an old-fashioned—though apparently still very much in vogue—Uncle Sam–driven regime change. Since Venezuela is not the banana republic it's made out to be, and actually has a legitimate army that refuses to be bought off by American dollars or fold under American bullying, the whole scheme was stillborn. However, the event itself felt somehow prophetic.

Two years later, the January 6 insurrection at the US Capitol was, for me, the decisive moment when the moral rot of decades (if not centuries) of America's overseas belligerence finally came crashing home. The failed coup was the inevitable result of an empire whose leaders had mired the citizenry in a constant state of war and endlessly lied about it all.

As I put it in a piece I wrote shortly thereafter for the indispensable *TomDispatch*: "On January 6, the US became a foreign country." The United States removing democratically elected leaders of other countries is a commonplace of our modern history, I pointed out. We replaced Iranian prime minister Mohammad Mosaddegh with the Shah of Iran in 1953; overthrew Guatemalan president Jacobo Árbenz in favor of the military dictatorship of Carlos Castillo Armas in 1954; supplanted Chilean president Salvador Allende with General Augusto Pinochet in 1973; supported the coup against Honduran president Manuel Zelaya in 2009. In other words, this isn't a matter of a few one-off mistakes or a couple of "dumb wars." Invasions, military coups, soft coups, economic sanctions, fueling of existing conflicts, secret funding of candidates of Washington's choice—all these are known and accepted US foreign policy strategies and behavior.

Such behavior inevitably leads to blowback, which in this case was a homegrown coup attempt on January 6, 2021. Trump, his countless enablers in Congress, his appointees, and his loyal followers did not like the outcome of the 2020 election. Their faith and fealty to the creed of "Make America Great Again" simply would not be stopped by political process, democracy, the Constitution, or other laws of the land. For these folks, the end would justify any means. So the president did what US leaders so often do when they don't like outcomes in nations around the globe: he tried to steal the election by force and through illegal political manipulation. January 6 was not a riot or a protest. It was the culmination of a coup attempt orchestrated in plain sight over multiple weeks by Trump and his followers, with the express purpose of staying in power by stopping the certification of President-elect Joe Biden.

It didn't matter that Trump's Big Lie about the election was transparent, verifiable nonsense. Nor did it matter that the actions of the insurrectionists at the Capitol were tantamount to sedition and treason. After all, when it comes to America's invasions around the globe, our leaders rarely care about illegality, because they are never held accountable. When they want something they just take it. Trump and his followers were simply imitating our foreign policy behavior in a domestic setting. And true to form, there has once again been a disgraceful lack of accountability. As of this writing, the January 6 select committee is still filling in the details of the coup as it continues its investigation, but the essence of it should have been obvious to anyone paying attention at the time.

My *TomDispatch* article ended with a plea for our leadership to change course. "There is truth and there are lies," Biden said in his inaugural address. "Lies told for power and for profit. And each of us has a duty and responsibility, as citizens, as Americans, and especially as leaders . . . to defend the truth and to defeat the lies." I called on him to live up to this rhetoric not only domestically but also internationally. To stop destroying vulnerable nations. To stop displacing families and starving foreign populations through economic sanctions. To stop sending American troops to die for "lies told for power and for profit."

Belligerent US foreign policy not only creates victims in other countries while getting our soldiers killed and injured but inevitably reverberates at home—with violence and corruption replacing political process and the rule of law; with reality subverted by false narratives; with a flourishing of fear, ignorance, and hate. War dissenters understand this, historically and conceptually. That's why war dissent is reasonable, necessary, and morally sound. In some cases, depending on your ethical framework, it is even obligatory.

* * *

THROUGHOUT AMERICAN HISTORY, there have always been citizens calling out the country's war crimes and illegal interventions—journalists, authors, political analysts, academics, activists, whistleblowers, and sometimes even combat veterans themselves. Across history, the list includes such famous figures as Mark Twain, Martin Luther King Jr., Malcolm X, James Baldwin, Muhammad Ali, Marvin Gaye, and Howard Zinn. There are also many crucial voices speaking out in our own day, including Angela Davis, Chris Hedges, Michelle Alexander, Juan Cole, Tom Engelhardt, James Carroll, and John Pilger. Arguably the most prolific antiwar activist and writer of the last century has been Noam Chomsky. There are also war resisters, like Rory Fanning, who served with Pat and me in the same Ranger battalion—a courageous man, who, after his deployment to Afghanistan, put down his weapon when ordered to go to Iraq.

War dissent comes at a price, however. Conscience has a cost. In many cases, dissenters get labeled by some members of the media and the general public as traitors, cowards, and distinctly unpatriotic. They are subjected to childish insults—that to be antiwar is to be anti-America, to be "in bed with the enemy," to be unsupportive of our troops, and similar nonsense. Meanwhile, our political leaders—the ones who so often lie to the American people, commit war crimes, and send American soldiers off to needless deaths—are somehow hailed as true patriots. The rank absurdity of it all makes it difficult to take such discourse seriously.

However, if the dissenter has the power to sway public opinion, or provides damning evidence against the US administration, then the price to be paid can be very real. Such people can find themselves classified as "enemies of the state." This can mean government-backed discrediting campaigns, harassment, and imprisonment. Most of these more extreme cases involve whistleblowers like Daniel Ellsberg, Chelsea Manning, and Daniel Hale, who see crimes and wrongdoing from inside the US power structure and believe the American people need to know.

One very well-known dissenter exposing American wrongdoing is not even a US citizen: Julian Assange of WikiLeaks. His platform is a treasure trove of information that puts powerful institutions in a state of panic. Their reaction is itself instructive. It is well documented how much the governments of the United States and allied nations want Assange silenced. At the time of this writing, he has been held in a maximum-security prison in London for nearly three years and faces charges in the United States that could see him imprisoned for life. After examining him, a UN expert reported that "Assange showed all symptoms typical for prolonged exposure to psychological torture."

President Obama insightfully asked in a 2015 speech:

"What greater form of patriotism is there than the belief that America is not yet finished, that we are strong enough to be self-critical?" Those who choose to speak up and be self-critical about American wrongdoing are in many ways the moral conscience of the nation, the counterpoint to unchecked, unchallenged power. War dissent is committed by those with a deep love for the country and its soldiers, for honesty, justice, humanity, and the rule of law. They bring light to situations clouded by secrecy, lies, and propaganda. The cost can be high, no doubt—for some even more than others—but the collective reward of providing transparency to the American people and global citizenry is priceless.

It is reasonable to think that war dissenters have had at least some impact throughout US history in helping to limit abuse of American power. But in truth, the effect seems minimal, given the sheer amount of destruction America has repeatedly caused around the globe. At every turn, in every generation, our government has managed to invent a new enemy that urgently needs to be destroyed or helpless victims who must be liberated. Seeing the same playbook used against our own democracy on January 6 was beyond discouraging.

The hard and discomfiting truth is that today's wars cannot be stopped by just a small number of war dissenters. We live in an ostensible democracy, so the onus ought to fall directly on the American public—preferably *all* of We the People. America's leaders perform their indecent acts in all our names, under our common banner. Thus, it is up to every one of us to cry foul immediately when they make such illegal and immoral policy decisions.

This, of course, is made more complicated by what has been called America's "civic religion of patriotism." The relentless worshipping of our flag and other national symbols goes hand in hand with the overt omission of our barbaric foreign policy from the national conscience. As I mentioned earlier, I grew up with the narrative of America and its allies destroying the evil Nazi empire, which is perfectly true. However, to this day, that one war manages to drown out almost everything else we have inflicted on the world since. Paying no attention to the evil we are doing right now because we destroyed a different form of evil seventy-five years ago is not tenable. This nation has been living off the virtue of the greatest generation for most of a century in order to systematically pillage the planet. It's an insult to everything that generation fought for in the first place.

All evidence suggests that we as a nation remain a long way off from fixing our foreign policy. We are likely to keep reading courageous, clarifying, and insightful pieces of war dissent while American soldiers die, vulnerable nations get destroyed, and the moral rot spreads at home. However, in the long term, I think real sustained progress can and will be made, and war dissent will reach critical mass both in America and around the globe—tipping the scales in favor of peace, diplomacy, and accountability. This assumes comparable progress in other areas, such as racial justice, economic equity, and environmental preservation. In the end, these issues are all interconnected. Until then, let us hope war dissenters continue their courageous work of providing transparency, honesty, and optimism to us all.

WHAT I LEARNED IN BAGHDAD

Gian Gentile

My father served in World War II and my older brother served during the Vietnam War, so I always felt that joining the armed forces at some point in my life was a natural and reasonable thing to do. My father had not been in a direct combat role—he was a supply specialist with the US Army Air Forces, helping fly supplies "over the hump" from northern India to the AAF's forward bases in China. Still, I grew up with stories my parents told about his deployment to India and my mother's wait for his return. These stories did not glorify war or whitewash the moral ambiguities of the American war effort. Even so, they instilled in me the conviction that wars could be fought and won for righteous causes.

My parents were politically toward the left and very critical of the US war effort in Vietnam. Their opposition was not to war per se, though, but rather to Washington's rationale for entering that particular war in the first place. They drew a distinction between wars and those sent to fight them. A war could be fought for the wrong reasons, but that didn't make the soldiers fighting it equally wrong. Not everyone would make that distinction, especially not the strident critics of US involvement in Vietnam. But my parents did see a difference there, and their thinking stuck with me.

Drawn to the idea of military service, I signed a contract with Army ROTC at UC Berkeley. In 1986, I graduated with a bachelor's degree in history and a commission as an armor officer.

Two decades later, I found myself and the armored reconnaissance squadron that I commanded caught in a vicious, deadly, and complex civil war in Iraq. By the time I returned to the United States with my squadron at the end of 2006, the Army was beginning to embrace counterinsurgency doctrine as a formula for victory in the country. The subsequent propagation of overly simplistic solutions to lowering violence in Iraq, along with the hagiographical celebration of certain Army generals, is what set me on the path to military dissent.

* * *

I DON'T BELIEVE I ever had a firm expectation of what war would be like. In the months leading up to our invasion of Iraq in 2003, I was so busy and so worried about doing my job correctly that I had little time to think about the character of the war in which I was about to participate. As the executive officer of a brigade combat team, I had the primary responsibility for moving a very large unit—four thousand soldiers and fifteen hundred vehicles—from Fort Hood, Texas, to Tikrit, Iraq. The complexity of that operation, at a time when the Army had few recent experiences moving those kinds of forces halfway around the world, practically consumed me.

Only during my second deployment, in 2006—this time as a squadron commander—did I find time to reflect on what I expected the war I was in to be. Early on in that deployment, I remember feeling frustrated that I had not experienced direct fire combat. By the time my cavalry squadron began operations in west Baghdad the level of attacks against US forces had dropped precipitously. I remember being bothered by the notion that I might go through an entire year and not take part in actions against the enemy. Looking back, I am embarrassed to say that I wished I would get hit by a deep-buried IED or something similar so I could earn the Army's Combat Action Badge.

My cavalry squadron was part of the 4th Brigade Combat Team, 4th Infantry Division. We were initially assigned a very large area in southwest Baghdad called West Rasheed. In late December 2005, we spent about ten days doing "relief in place" of an infantry battalion that had been responsible for that area for most of the year—having them introduce us to the territory, places of importance, key individuals, and troublesome areas that still contained a modicum of enemy activity. In January, we took over responsibility for the area and began operations.

The mission of the 4th Infantry Division at the start of 2006 was to finish up the training of Iraqi police forces, which at that point were dominated by Iraqi Shiite militias aided by Iran. I remember how a few months before we deployed, our division commander at the time, Major General J. D. Thurman, said that 2006 was going to be "the year of the Iraqi police." He meant that in a positive way: like the rest of us, he believed that by the start of 2006 Iraq was well on its way toward democracy. The Iraqis had already held some of their first democratic elections, and it seemed that creating a competent police force would essentially complete the US mission dating from the 2003 invasion.

Indeed, from my narrower tactical perspective, the first two months of 2006 appeared to confirm that Iraq was well on its way toward stability. My cavalry squadron, which at that point consisted of around a thousand soldiers, experienced no kinetic strikes, whether by IEDs or small arms. In fact, the overall coalition commander in Iraq at the time, General George Casey, had developed what was called an "off-ramp plan." That meant that since levels of violence were so low, and the basic institutions of democracy were apparently taking root, the United States could start reducing its overall level of commitment. As part of this plan, the 4th Infantry Division was scheduled to redeploy back to the United States nearly three months early. Such was the rosy, hyper-optimistic view of things that the US military and political leaders held in early 2006.

Then, on February 22, 2006, al-Qaeda militants—Sunni Islamist extremists—struck the Al-Askari Mosque in Samarra, Iraq, a highly revered Shiite holy site. A huge explosive device detonated inside the mosque, toppling its beautiful golden dome into an ugly mess of rubble.

That single spectacular act of destruction by al-Qaeda plunged my squadron into the middle of a civil war between Shiites and Sunnis. Yet that civil war did not suddenly begin on February 22. What I later realized was that it was really driven by America's decision, after our removal of the Saddam

Hussein regime, to rebuild Iraqi institutions and society along the lines of American representative democracy.

Under Saddam, Sunnis had enjoyed a privileged place in Iraqi society and politics. Instating representative democracy in a country where Shiite Iraqis accounted for about 70 percent of the overall population and Sunnis only 20 percent meant that Sunnis would inevitably lose that privileged status. It was this prospect that put Iraq on the path to civil war. The Askari bombing only brought things out into the open.

I remember in the first couple of weeks after the Askari bombing getting numerous calls on my cell phone from sheikhs at Sunni mosques, begging me to send forces to defend them from reprisal attacks by the Iraqi police and Shiite militias. At first these calls puzzled me. I remember thinking there was some mistake. How could it be that Iraqi police were attacking mosques in Baghdad? This was "the year of the police"; with our help, they were supposed to be developing into an institutional pillar of Iraqi democracy. But witnessing the attacks firsthand, and through the lenses of drones flying high above, made it evident to me very quickly that the real situation was quite different.

A clear indicator of what the civil war entailed was the growing number of dead bodies we would find each day strewn along the streets of west Baghdad. It was hard to discern the specific motives behind individual deaths, as Iraqi civilians were usually unwilling to talk to us. But we got enough to understand that the killings were part of a process of sectarian cleansing. Dead bodies in a largely Shiite district, for example, meant the purging of the few remaining Sunnis who, for whatever reasons, had refused to leave the vicinity.

Iraqi government institutions such as the Shiite-dominated Ministry of the Interior were themselves complicit in the civil war. In the second half of 2006, my squadron was shifted to northwest Baghdad, where we concentrated most of our effort on the restive, al-Qaeda-dominated district of Amiriyah. We quickly learned from residents of their frustration that the local bank branch in Amiriyah had been closed by the Ministry of the Interior and the similarly Shiite-dominated Ministry of the Treasury. The motive was clear: force Sunnis who needed to draw cash from the bank to leave the safety of their predominantly Sunni district and go to bank branches in Shiite districts instead. Doing this would force them to cross Iraqi police checkpoints, where they could be captured for ransom or killed on the spot.

In the middle of this civil war, attacks against the soldiers in my squadron grew steadily. We suffered more than 350 IED strikes, along with car bombs, suicide bombers, small arms attacks, and occasional snipers. The worst IEDs were the Shiite-made explosively formed projectiles, which were lethal even against our armored vehicles. Over the course of 2006, the squadron lost five soldiers killed in action, while another fifteen suffered life-changing injuries.

Some of the scenes that I came across during that year have stuck with me, and even now I see them like they only happened yesterday. Scenes like the woman weeping in the Amiriyah district that October, holding her dead baby in her arms while her husband lay dead on the street nearby. Her baby had been shot in the head by the same Sunni fighters who killed her husband—all because he, who was Sunni, had returned to Amiriyah with a Shiite wife.

But beyond the images of death and destruction, what

most sticks with me from that year is the complexity of the problem my squadron faced: how to stop the warring factions in a civil war from killing each other, while staying alive when those same warring factions were trying to kill us too. It was a difficult situation that could not be resolved by simplistic solutions. In fact, the application of US military forces offered little by way of help, given that those very forces had played a considerable role in creating the problem in the first place.

What my year in west Baghdad showed me, combined with my previous tour in Iraq during the invasion in 2003, is that it is much easier to break a country and its institutions than it is to put everything back together. Rebuilding a country after it has been broken by military force requires a massive amount of resources, time, energy, and commitment. Replacing what you've broken takes more than some fancy new doctrinal approaches credited to savior generals.

Two factors put Iraq on the path to civil war. The first was the decision by US policymakers to invade Iraq and remove the Saddam Hussein regime. The second, equally significant, was the decision to rebuild Iraq political institutions by installing a representative democracy in Iraq, regardless of demographic, ethnic, and sectarian realities. Those two critical choices are what created the conditions that erupted in the violent civil war in Baghdad in 2006.

* * *

THE LESSONS THAT the US Army took from events in Iraq differed from my own. And in my view, its conclusions were wrong.

In the fall of 2006, after much debate on the home front

about what to do with the apparently failing military effort in Iraq, President George W. Bush decided to commit an additional twenty thousand troops in hopes of reducing the high levels of violence stemming from the civil war. Bush's new senior commander in Iraq, General David Petraeus, arrived in Baghdad along with these reinforcements in early 2007. Petraeus also brought with him, as news reports put it, an "enlightened" new approach to counterinsurgency, centered on protecting Iraqi civilians and winning hearts and minds. This kinder and gentler way of warfighting was described in the Army's new counterinsurgency field manual, FM 3–24, which Petraeus himself had helped to write. Published some months before, it now received glowing attention and acclaim.

Very quickly the American press, along with many military pundits and a few retired US Army four-star generals, began trumpeting Petraeus's success in turning the war around. By the end of 2007, journalists and policymakers alike settled on a narrative that went like this: The reason the US Army had been failing in Iraq in 2006 was because it didn't understand and apply proper counterinsurgency doctrine. But then a savior general, armed with FM 3–24, arrived on the scene and immediately began doing counterinsurgency correctly. He instilled innovative tactical and operational methods in his forces, and the result was a precipitous decrease in internecine violence. The forward-thinking generalship of David Petraeus—a warrior-scholar, his followers often noted, with a PhD in political science from Princeton University—had made all the difference.

Based on my own experience in Baghdad in 2006, before Petraeus arrived on the scene, all of this struck me as seriously mistaken and dangerously misguided. Exposing the error became for me a mission of sorts. I attacked the false narrative of the savior-general in two ways. First, I published scores and scores of articles in local and national newspapers and numerous professional journals. Second, I undertook a sustained public-speaking effort, making my case to various civilian, academic, and military audiences.

In the summer of 2007, I arrived at West Point to take up an assignment teaching history. Shortly thereafter, I wrote one of my first published pieces on the topic, offering a critical view of the celebrated FM 3–24 counterinsurgency manual. At its core, I argued, the manual was based on an overly simplistic and generalized view of populations caught up in an insurgency.

A figure in the manual's opening chapter depicts "support for an insurgency" in the form of a rectangle. A line near the top of the rectangle shows about 10 percent of the population consisting of hard-core insurgents, who can't be flipped and will have to be either killed or captured. At the bottom of the rectangle is a similar line showing another 10 percent of the population as people who support the counterinsurgent's cause. The remaining 80 percent represents the rest of the population, the fence-sitters. The authors of FM 3–24 insist that this tripartite 10–80–10 division would always apply: "In any situation, whatever the cause, there will be an active minority for the cause, a neutral or passive majority, [and] an active minority against the cause."

The problem I had was that this depiction did not reflect in any way whatsoever the population that I had encountered in west Baghdad in 2006. That population wasn't made up of about 80 percent fence-sitters who were waiting to be won over to either the insurgent or counterinsurgent side. Instead, the population in Baghdad was divided smack-dab down the middle, with one side being Shiite and the other side being Sunni. As an approved Army doctrine, FM 3–24 was supposed to be authoritative. Yet its description of a population's support for insurgency, and the assertion that all populations will look like the one described, suggested to me that the new doctrine was based on false assumptions.

The manual also contained a deeply flawed cause-and-effect schema. It posited that if a counterinsurgent force provides the local population with benefits such as security, work, access to medical care, schools for the children, and so on, then the population will side with the counterinsurgents and turn against the insurgent fighters. But as I argued in an essay that appeared in *Armed Forces Journal*, my own unit had pretty much done those things in west Baghdad in 2006 without notable success. So why, I asked, had they not worked?

The answer from Petraeus's advocates, of course, was that prior to the surge in 2007, few in the US Army actually understood how to do counterinsurgency correctly. It wasn't until the surge and the arrival of Petraeus that the Army finally started to "get it" and thus turned things around.

Such dismissive responses to my critique of FM 3–24 prompted me to undertake further research and analysis. I wanted to compare the fundamental tactical and operational approaches used during the surge with what had come before. I wanted to assess the continuities and discontinuities between the generalship of Petraeus and his predecessor, General George Casey. What my research showed was that there was no fundamental shift in how units on the ground had operated. True, during the surge there were a few more "combat outposts" manned by US Army soldiers sprinkled in a few Baghdad districts. But they were too few in number to make the kind of difference that the surge narrative was postulating. And even though Petraeus was a more charismatic, press-savvy general, Casey's and Petraeus's overall approaches to command in Iraq were more similar than not.

At the same time that I was publishing numerous articles critical of FM 3–24, I was also calling into question the "surge triumph" narrative that had so firmly taken hold as an explanation for why violence in Iraq declined during 2007. That narrative attributed the lowered levels of violence to additional troops applying FM 3–24 under the stellar generalship of David Petraeus. The assertion seemed highly problematic to me.

The counterargument I made was that the reduction in violence had less to do with the surge and more to do with the Sunni Awakening that spread from Iraq's western provinces in 2006 and into Baghdad in 2007. Fed up with al-Qaeda's strict moral codes and violent actions against Sunni civilians who didn't conform to their ways, many Sunni insurgents professed a willingness to make common cause with the American military in fighting al-Qaeda. This Sunni Awakening happened at the same time that a large number of Shiite militias in Iraq decided to stand down their attacks against Sunni civilians. These two factors, not the surge of US troops practicing enlightened counterinsurgency doctrine, were the primary reason for the decline of violence in Iraq.

By 2010, I had been at West Point teaching history for nearly four years since my return from Baghdad. During those four years, in addition to taking on FM 3–24 and the surge triumph narrative, I also evolved a sustained critique of the US approach to Iraq and Afghanistan in general. FM 3–24, I pointed out, was not just a doctrinal manual on how to fight an insurgency, but essentially a prescription for armed nation-building. That was exactly what the United States had been doing in Afghanistan and Iraq for many years. I argued that armed nation-building made no sense unless undertaken in concert with a workable overarching strategy. Any such strategy would have to acknowledge that using foreign military forces to rebuild (or build from scratch) the major institutions of a country would entail a generational effort consuming huge amounts of American blood and treasure. To consider that prospect was to confront a fundamental question: Why undertake such an effort in the first place except in situations where genuinely vital interests were at stake? On that score, neither Iraq nor Afghanistan justified any kind of maximalist effort.

This is where the defects of FM 3–24 and the fallacies of the surge triumph narrative combined: together they suggested that nation-building at the barrel of a gun was a reasonable task to undertake. Indeed, John Nagl, one of the original prophets of US counterinsurgency and one of the authors of FM 3–24 itself, wrote in 2008 that "winning the Global War on Terror [will] require an ability not just to dominate land operations, but to change entire societies."

"Change entire societies"—there it was, encapsulated in a few words by one of the leading proponents of American counterinsurgency. The Army's ostensible success in Iraq provided a template for what future savior-generals would do again and again in other countries. In essence, it was this fundamentally wrongheaded and deeply flawed belief in the unlimited capacity of US military power that pushed me toward full-out military dissent. I felt compelled to challenge the notion that a US Army that had made everything work out in Iraq could go on to do the same in other troubled spots around the world.

What I did in my seven years of professional military dissent from 2007 to 2013 was argue the opposite. I believed, and still believe, that there are huge limits to what military power can accomplish. I believe further that war must be seen not as the best option for fixing the world's problems but as the last resort.

My dissent, therefore, was not antiwar or anti-Army. I am not a pacifist. Nor am I an isolationist, as many critics have accused me of being. I do believe that the United States needs a strong military to protect the nation and, when needed, to secure its important interests abroad. My dissent, therefore, was aimed specifically at fixing a delusion that I believe my Army had fallen into as a consequence of Iraq and Afghanistan. It was never a dissent directed at the Army writ large or its role in the national defense.

From what I can tell, those seven years of professional military dissent had no impact on the actual US strategy and the conduct of operations in Iraq and Afghanistan. Nor did my critique end the Army's infatuation with counterinsurgency. Still, I think my efforts mattered. I believe I educated leaders within the Army and the Department of Defense. If nothing else, by pushing back against the Army's embrace of counterinsurgency and challenging the triumphal surge narrative, I provided the Army with a much-needed alternative in thinking about our recent wars.

I like to imagine that the generation of US Army officers

who as young lieutenants read and absorbed my arguments came to appreciate that sometimes it's necessary to confront conventional wisdom. If my efforts helped convey the importance of thinking critically, whatever the current institutional version of truth, then all the work that I put into my dissent was worth it.

One thing I know for sure: given a chance to do it all over again, I would.

MY GOOD WAR

Gil Barndollar

Guy Crouchback had a good war. Though an English Catholic aristocrat and nearly forty years old, Guy finagled a commission with an infantry regiment and then the commandos. He endured challenging training, served in half a dozen countries, and saw a few skirmishes, but emerged none the worse for wear. Guy came out of World War II healthy in body and mind, despite his disgust with his country's compromises and betrayals. A young bride and a tidy inheritance waiting back home were ample salves for that.

Guy Crouchback's battles were confined to the page; his service was as the protagonist of Evelyn Waugh's Sword of Honour trilogy. Nonetheless, Crouchback embodies something real: the very British idea that one can have "a good war." This is largely absent from American war literature, but it is an entirely possible outcome of wartime service. I know because I had a good war in Afghanistan.

In late May of 2009, I found myself standing erect in

a squad bay straight out of Stanley Kubrick's *Full Metal Jacket*, staring across at another fellow attempting to take his leave of civilian life. Both of us were trying not to show our amusement with the theater of "pickup," as screaming drill instructors tore through our belongings in the opening hours of Marine Officer Candidates School.

Like that other candidate across from me, a lacrosse coach with a law degree who was well north of thirty, I'd taken an odd route to this odd summer camp. A drink-derived broken ankle and a scholarship for graduate school in England had eaten up four years of my life; by the time I put on the uniform that summer, I was just a few months shy of needing an age waiver myself. Thankfully, surgery to saw off bone spurs on my foot—Donald Trump's road not taken—had been a success and I was in decent shape for the rigors ahead.

What was I doing in Quantico, Virginia, running and rucking and yelling in a ten-week job tryout?

I didn't come from a military family. Soldiers and sailors were the heroes in 90 percent of the books I'd ever read, but I didn't actually know any. My dad, like most of his cohort, had managed to avoid Vietnam, while diabetes had kept his father out of World War II. One of our earliest ancestors had been briefly jailed for opposing Hamiltonian tyranny during the Whiskey Rebellion, but we weren't a family with much military heritage to speak of.

What there was came on the losing side of both world wars. My maternal great-grandfather Otto, sent to the Western Front in World War I, had been a lucky *Landser* (German foot soldier)—lucky enough to survive the trenches, anyway. His son, my grandfather, was drafted in 1944 at age eighteen, as the Wehrmacht marched relentlessly in the wrong direction. He, too, was extremely lucky: one of just eight survivors in his company after a battle near Smolensk, he was captured and shipped to Siberia. He didn't return home until four years after the war ended.

The brother of his future bride was not so fortunate. My great-uncle, a smiling, boyish medic, disappeared on the Eastern Front as the Red Army neared its final victory.

Such service under the swastika was not spoken of with shame in my grandparents' quiet brookside home, but it was certainly not celebrated. My Pomeranian grandmother, her village now a part of Poland, would still cry in her seventies when speaking of her lost brother. She would always end with a simple conclusion: "*Krieg ist blod.*" War is stupid. I heard her, but I didn't listen.

I came to military service without any external pressure or expectations. What I did have was an ideological attraction to the military.

I had spent college as a callow campus conservative, throwing darts from school newspapers at liberal professors, *The Vagina Monologues*, and other easy targets. Defending the Iraq War, launched during my junior year, was on brand. A 2004 summer internship at the American Enterprise Institute, then the beating heart of neoconservatism, didn't dull my chairborne ardor for a crusading post-9/11 American foreign policy.

Graduate school, luckily, did. Ensconced in England for four years, I got to watch Iraq fall apart from a remove—far from both the battlefield and America's domestic Sturm und Drang. Thank God for that. I'd like to think if I'd been back home I would still have resisted the temptation to cheerlead for the team and become a dead-ender for America's worst blunder in generations. But who knows. As we've learned in spades over the past two decades, political tribalism is a hell of a drug.

I spent those four years in the UK studying imperialism and insurgencies, albeit wars that had ended on the edge of living memory. Looking at Britain's decades of "small wars" helped reinforce the utter folly of America's campaign to remake the Middle East. By the time I returned to the United States in September 2008, I didn't believe Iraq was anything other than an unmitigated disaster, regardless of the newest self-aggrandizing narrative about a surge of troops having turned the tide.

But while home in New Hampshire the previous summer, I had walked into a US Marines recruiter's office—because I did and do believe in citizen-soldiers, republicanism, and an apparently archaic ethos that says a healthy young man probably ought to spend a few years wearing his country's cloth. America's vaunted "all-volunteer force" is in many ways a delusion, a way to pass the buck on the heaviest burden of citizenship, our collective guilt assuaged with lip service and idolatry, unearned pride and undeserved pity. But I was a volunteer.

Some blend of genuine patriotism, desire for adventure, lifelong fascination with war, and the benchwarmer's need to prove he could play drove me to seek a Marine commission and combat service. And though by then I had accepted the reality of the Iraq fiasco, I still basically bought the idea that Afghanistan was "the good war": morally justifiable, necessary, and salvageable. I chose the Marines because a friend was headed that way and told me that the Marine Corps had higher standards and would always be the "first to fight."

Officer Candidates School was both a blur and a slog. One slept little, ran much, marched everywhere, and learned the basics of the Marine Corps in sterile classrooms and barracks discussions. Leadership was evaluated in field problems, all of which seemed to conclude with the frenzied firing of blank rounds and a charge into the Quantico tree line. Our platoon had a score of prior enlisted marines, who were generally ready and willing to help us civilians. Most of the platoon graduated.

TBS (the Basic School) and IOC (the Infantry Officer Course) followed. Despite a penchant for blisters and being a pull-up or two shy of the max score, I put infantry at the top of my wish list at TBS. I was a garrison slacker but did fine in the field and the classroom. I also got lucky. The selection process for most Marine Corps officer jobs is done in order of TBS class rank—but broken into thirds, to ensure a "quality spread" across the most coveted positions. When selection time came, I sat at 99 in a class of about 285 and had my pick of jobs. A better day on the rifle range or at land navigation, and I would have been at the very bottom of the first third, bound for an adjutant's office or a supply warehouse.

IOC, shrouded in mystique and a code of omertà, was mostly TBS on steroids. For the less athletic or masochistic among us, it was "the best time you never want to have again." One lieutenant, more of a gym stud than most, went down on a run with a core temperature of 107 degrees and never stood in front of a platoon. The rest of us benefited from nearly three months of incessant field training, numerous live-fire ranges, and instruction from handpicked captains. All were Iraq or Afghanistan veterans, many both.

I and a dozen other newly minted infantry officers volunteered for light armored reconnaissance, the Marine Corps' Stetson-less cavalry, and we were soon living on the beach in lieutenant-filled McMansions in Southern California, awaiting the return of our battalion from its latest Afghanistan deployment. Unlike previous generations of new Marine officers, we didn't join units already in combat. The battalion came home, took post-deployment leave, and then we butter bars—new second lieutenants—were each handed responsibility for about two dozen marines and four eight-wheeled armored cars.

We had nearly a year before the battalion returned to Afghanistan, but the training flew by. I stubbed my toe more than most lieutenants, but forbearance from subordinates and seniors alike enabled me to begin to grasp what leadership looked like. The marines, I slowly realized, were incredible. Heavily tattooed, a cigarette or a dip never out of reach, but baby-faced as often as not, the lance corporals would run through a brick wall for you, the corps, or, most of all, their buddies.

Two things were hammered into us during that lengthy predeployment workup: counter-IED and counterinsurgency.

IEDs (improvised explosive devices) were homemade roadside bombs, responsible for the vast majority of casualties in Afghanistan by the time I got there. Our evil spirits, they were warded off with electronic jammers, metal detectors, bomb dogs, and plenty of dispersion—spreading out our vehicles and marines to minimize casualties. Some battalions were finding themselves in veritable minefields in southern Afghanistan's Helmand Province. The 3rd Battalion, 5th Marine Regiment had a horrific deployment there a year before us, with twenty-five marines killed in action and nearly three dozen amputees. The specter of their experience was always in the back of your mind.

Counterinsurgency was the doctrine, if not the dogma, of the day. Largely reliant on cherry-picked examples of decolonization campaigns from the past century, counterinsurgency preached "the people are the prize," "courageous restraint," and "money is a weapon." Like latter-day Episcopalians, few of us ardently believed, but we all mouthed the hymns when required.

The Marine Corps had decided its cavalry was best employed in the most open country available, so our battalion was sent to "the Fishhook," the southernmost area of operations in Helmand Province. Named for a pronounced curve in the Helmand River, the Fishhook was remote even by the standards of a remote, rural region. The outgoing commander in our new area, a short, lupine Southerner, pronounced it "the West Virginia of Helmand Province." A desert shelf descended to a small, flat, greenish cultivated zone named Wazirabad. Only a few kilometers wide, the strip of farmland hugged the river.

The adult male illiteracy rate in the Fishhook was over 80 percent. Most farmers wanted to be left alone by both the insurgents and the government. The Taliban, the outgoing marines told us, were nowhere to be seen.

It was something, but it wasn't war. One of the other

companies got in a few gunfights and hit the occasional IED, but for us in Alpha Company it was police work, only with an extra few dozen pounds of gear on your back. Miles of slow foot patrols every day, endless cups of tea with local elders and heads of households, the Helmandis invariably polite but indifferent. There would be new American faces soon.

I hadn't expected Fallujah or the Tet Offensive, but I also hadn't expected this.

On our very first patrol, I was introduced to counterinsurgency's fruits. A dozen marines eagerly set out from our dusty patrol base on the shelf down to the line of small villages and extended family compounds below. Bushels of dirty cotton were rotting in many of the fields we passed. Villagers told us that the Afghan government had pushed them to grow cotton as an alternative to opium poppies, then reneged on promises to purchase the crop. The farmers, fooled once, prepared for a poppy harvest the following spring.

Despite the lack of enemy activity, there was a steady drip of evidence indicating that the counterinsurgency campaign was going nowhere fast.

Knowing little of the area, we detained a young village mullah based largely on the fact that he looked too polished, too clean, too wealthy for Wazirabad. We narrowly avoided a riot as we hustled him out of the village. Back at the patrol base, one of our Afghan interpreters, the only real points of continuity in a campaign of seven-month rotations, quietly told me that the mullah had been there for quite a while. He was returned home with hollow apologies.

A squad from the elite Afghan National Interdiction Unit, their version of the Drug Enforcement Agency, was sent to assist us for a week. Their American advisor, a retired narcotics agent, admitted to me that he was nonplussed: Why were his trained plainclothes investigators now in uniform, tasked with searching random motorbikes in the back of beyond?

Our census operations, a counterinsurgency totem and thus a daily metric of progress, depended on biometric devices that the Afghan police would never use—if we would even hand them over when the pullout came.

And then there was the master sergeant who advised me that if you could manage to sleep twelve hours a day, the deployment was really only three and a half months long.

Risk aversion was the order of the day. We went "op minimize," hunkering down in place, for sandstorms (when medevac helicopters couldn't fly) and also for big American holidays—no one wanted to tell a mother she'd lost her son on Christmas Day. It was manifestly clear that, contra Vince Lombardi, winning wasn't everything; it wasn't even anything. We were, as that master sergeant fully grasped, just marking time.

Lacking either enemies to hound or friends to mentor, we did the American thing: we threw money around. After many rounds of tea with village elders and heads of households, we determined that the best thing we could do for the Wazirabad villagers was provide a basic primary school. A hospital and cell phone service were well beyond our powers and patience, but a one-room schoolhouse? That we could do.

A hatchback full of Afghan contractors drove down to us from the relative metropolis of Nawa, four hours north. Despite their evident fear and disdain for the backward Fishhook farmers, these men built a crude schoolhouse in a few days, while my bored marines stood guard, smoked, and cracked wise. It seemed to matter little that there was no schoolteacher nor any school supplies.

After the school was complete, I returned with a patrol to examine their handiwork. I'd never built anything more advanced than a machine gun trench, but this . . . didn't look good. There were already holes in the masonry, and the windows were held in place by slim red-painted bamboo poles. The Wazirabad school, the ostensible crown jewel of our efforts here, looked like an Afghan child mass casualty incident waiting to happen. My company commander, initially skeptical of my architectural assessment, came out to look and quickly agreed with me. Our new school could collapse on its future occupants at any time.

I duly trudged down to Wazirabad the next day and went door-to-door, shamefacedly telling elders that the school was unstable and their children must not even play in it. They immediately one-upped me: they'd never wanted a school, they told me with straight faces, and wondered why we'd built it. Whether this change of heart was the result of threatening Taliban night letters or some more mundane mercurial Afghan tilt, we never found out.

The Wazirabad school stood as an empty white elephant, a small monument to slapdash American counterinsurgency practice—and a danger to whoever might wander into it. Luckily, as they'd always preached to us student lieutenants in Quantico, "the enemy gets a vote." A couple of weeks later, just after dark, the patrol base was rocked by the sound of a blast close by. Racing to a guard tower, I grabbed a thermal binocular from the marine on post and saw the school's smoldering ruins and a car tearing off into the desert. A patrol the next day confirmed that the Taliban had saved

US taxpayers a couple thousand dollars and the battalion engineer officer a headache. I still haven't found a better metaphor for our war in Afghanistan than the Wazirabad school.

The morning after the school blew up, our towers came down. Our company had new duties a few dozen miles down the river: a new base to build, new villages to patrol, perhaps a little more excitement. Patrol Base Wazirabad, the supposed guarantor of security in the region, was just a scorch mark in the sand when we drove away.

At our new patrol base, created in a week by marine engineers, we had housemates: a company of the Afghanistan Border Police. The paramilitary ABP was near the bottom of the barrel among the alphabet soup of Afghan security forces. Our partnership was mediated by a border advisory team, a grab bag of marines from different specialties. Some were great fits for the challenging advising mission. Some weren't.

The border police had a distinctive gray chocolate chip camouflage pattern, ball caps, and cheap sliding-stock AK-47s. They occasionally accompanied us on patrol but mostly did their own thing, roaming about in green "Danger Ranger" pickup trucks, so named for being unarmored death traps. Marines, of course, patrolled exclusively in heavily armored vehicles.

A month or so after we built our shared outpost, a marine from the advisory team told us that the frequent ABP patrols into the nearby villages were foraging trips. The men hadn't been fed by their own supply system in months. Rumor was that their cancer-stricken colonel in the provincial capital was pocketing their ration money.

We turned the patrol base over to them that spring and

departed with little more than a halfhearted "good luck." The ABP abandoned the remote outpost and followed us back north two weeks later. No one could blame them.

One thing we weren't doing was killing insurgents. In seven months, my entire company of 150 marines killed exactly one Talib, a participant in a foolish motorcycle-borne attempted ambush of one of our foot patrols. This luckless machine gunner ended up having a 500-pound bomb dropped on his head, with no civilian casualties and relieved high fives around the combat operations center.

On the journey home, awaiting a flight while snacking on popcorn and beer at our way station in Kyrgyzstan, I did the math. It cost roughly $1 million to keep one American service member deployed overseas to a combat zone for one year. Add in daily air support, all those engineering assets, satellite communications, and broken gear . . . I figured the American taxpayer had spent about $100 million for us to kill one Talib. Just how little the Taliban had spent to keep us there was unknowable but even more depressing.

We could claim some other successes, to be sure. One of my sergeants collared an actual bomb maker, a scared kid who was then entrusted to the vagaries of the Afghan justice system. My talented group of NCOs, lacking visible enemies, became bloodhounds, reading the terrain and using handheld metal detectors to find scores of buried weapons caches. There was some satisfaction in that: taking machine guns, bombs, rocket-propelled grenades, radios, and a lot of ammunition off the battlefield. But we'd still spent $100 million to kill one Talib.

I left Afghanistan and quickly set to figuring out how to

get back. I hadn't scratched the itch. I knew I should have felt fortunate, but I didn't. I sought out the advice of our battalion gunner, a universally admired warrant officer who'd fought in three wars and was the best marine mentor I'd had. He gave it to me straight: "Don't go back to Afghanistan thinking you're going to fix anything over there. Go back if you want to test yourself and try to improve your skills as a marine and an infantryman."

It was justification enough for me. I was slated to sail the Pacific with a marine expeditionary unit when a friend and fellow lieutenant told me that he'd been picked for some oddball Afghanistan advisor deployment with a battalion from the Republic of Georgia. Surf and Singapore sounded like a better deal to him. We spoke to our executive officer and got approval to switch. I was off to the Caucasus a few months later.

Serving as a combat advisor with the Georgians only compounded the absurdity of Afghanistan. Georgia had signed on to both of America's major post-9/11 wars, though at one point they had to ferry their men home from Iraq to fight the Russians. Undeterred, the Georgians eventually committed a two-battalion force to Afghanistan, though they seemed barely able to manage it.

Georgia's outsized troop contribution was driven by the country's quixotic bid for NATO membership. But though they wanted to make the Americans happy, the Georgians were understandably less than eager to bleed for an alliance they didn't belong to. Our job as marine advisors was to ensure that they did the bare minimum, which in this case meant protecting a dirt track that was the main supply route for the dwindling coalition force in northern Helmand. Our request to get "Hessian" as our advisor team's radio call sign was swiftly denied.

The outgoing unit had had a rough deployment. They had lost ten soldiers to a pair of suicide bomb attacks on their bases. The Georgians had then gunned down an Afghan family on a motorbike, in what was officially described as a botched escalation-of-force incident. Preventing our battalion from killing any more Afghan civilians was nearly the top priority for us.

The idea of victory was even more absent than it had been two years prior. The word would have provoked laughter had it ever been uttered.

That winter, I was told point-blank by a superior officer: "Nothing here is worth the life of a marine." He probably meant it. But like the rote invocation before a live-fire exercise back home at Camp Pendleton—"Safety is paramount!"—the words were immediately invalidated by the circumstances that provoked them. However true, it was better left unsaid.

We got through the deployment without losing any of our marines or Georgians, but there were a few close calls. One marine was shot in the hamstring as we maneuvered to kill a rare Taliban sniper who actually could shoot. Another got shrapnel in the neck from a rocket-propelled grenade. Numerous vehicles struck IEDs. A Taliban recoilless rifle round shredded our base's outdoor latrine, but at a rare moment when no Georgian or marine was relieving himself into the PVC "piss tubes."

My team escaped fatalities, but a unit supporting us lost a marine in the final weeks of our deployment. A teenage lance corporal, he drove one of the hulking mine-resistant vehicles for a route clearance platoon, a combat engineer unit that periodically swept our dirt-track "road" at a glacial five miles per hour—about as unenviable a task as could be had by marines in Afghanistan. A massive bomb tore through his vehicle one December day, flipping it on its side. We watched, helpless, from a couple miles away, our surveillance blimp recording the explosion, the medevac, and finally the resumption of the engineers' slow progress down the route that had brought us all there.

We were united by country and corps, but none of us on the advisor team knew him. The route clearance marines were only occasional visitors to our patrol base. They slept in our dusty parking lot every few weeks, sharing quips and hot rations, then saddled up and were gone in the morning. The loss, and the letter home, weren't ours to bear.

At the end, we demilitarized (a euphemism for "demolished") some of our bases and turned the remainder over to tired paramilitaries from the Afghanistan National Civil Order Police (ANCOP). The ANCOP were in a battle for their lives as soon as we drove away.

Between and after my deployments, I talked to friends about the war and read as much as I could. I tried to force myself into open-mindedness and intellectual humility. Yes, Helmand was a mess, with the Taliban just waiting us out as we squandered blood and treasure in pointless exertions—but perhaps elsewhere in Afghanistan we were winning?

If we were, I could find scant evidence of it. Everywhere you looked, the Taliban were either enduring or ascendant. The Afghan security forces remained brittle and corrupt. Stories of them failing in combat were legion. Like our South

Vietnamese clients before them, they had been molded into an army that knew only the American way of war, which they would never be able to properly apply—or afford.

Friends who had served in other corners of Afghanistan had stories similar to mine. An enlisted Navy SEAL friend dismissed his work on the opposite side of the country. America's elite raiders, he told me, were spending most of their time killing "dirt farmers." When John Sopko, the US government's relentless and honest special inspector general overseeing Afghanistan reconstruction, came to Camp Pendleton to interview other combat advisors, a friend who was there was shocked by the candor with which these marines laid out story after story of waste, abuse, and failure. Sopko, he told me, "didn't bat a fucking eye." He'd heard it all before.

All wars, per one recently depedestaled American rebel, are terrible. But unlike Iraq, Afghanistan was not a war of American aggression. The attacks of September 11 demanded retribution for reasons both moral and practical. We had gone in legitimately, and we did try to fight a clean war among the people, however impossible that was.

Where we failed was in vastly misjudging our probability of success. Had American soldiers returned home after a short and sharp punitive expedition—however atavistic such a campaign might appear to modern eyes—the war would have achieved something. But we stayed for another two decades, attempting to accomplish what we couldn't even adequately explain.

At some point in their training, military officers usually learn about Napoleon's corporal. The story, probably apocryphal, is that Napoleon would bring a lowly corporal into the room when his marshals were drawing up their plan for a battle. If the plan didn't make sense to the corporal, Napoleon told them to toss it out.

Our battalion commander was a good man: cerebral, caring, extremely competent. He led by example, coached and mentored constantly, and was the last man to turn in his vulnerable light armored vehicle when it was belatedly accepted that these Cold War reconnaissance platforms weren't built to withstand IED strikes. Yet on the eve of the deployment, when a noncommissioned officer had the (laudable) temerity to publicly ask the colonel what our mission was in Afghanistan, he struggled to lay out something that would have satisfied Napoleon's corporal.

In choosing to waste both American and Afghan lives in pursuing unattainable and incoherent maximalist goals, our just war became immoral. My battalion lost two marines in that slow spring of 2012, both blown apart by Taliban bombs while fighting for gains we all knew were meaningless. They both died for their buddies: one walking point on patrol, the other taking the most dangerous place in a vehicle, the driver's seat, to give a promising young lance corporal some time in the turret. There is undeniable honor in that. But they shouldn't have been there.

I left the Marine Corps on New Year's Eve 2016. I made my way to Washington and sought to help reorient American foreign policy toward prudence, resilience, and realism. Absent a true catastrophe, this may be an even more Sisyphean task than transforming Afghanistan. But in our post-9/11 world of surrogate patriotism, American veterans have a uniquely powerful moral voice on matters of war and peace, unhealthy as that may be in a republic.

Since boxing up my cammies and dress blues, I have done

what I can to bear witness to the foolishness and hubris of our wars in the Greater Middle East. "Ending endless wars" is now conventional wisdom, earning lip service from even the most hawkish politicians and pundits. But I watched the announcement of bin Laden's death from my couch in California, six months before I deployed for the first time. It took America another full decade to withdraw from Afghanistan.

I came by my knowledge of America's wars honestly but easily. I returned home with stories, self-knowledge, a Combat Action Ribbon, all my limbs, and, most important, all my marines. The few Taliban we managed to kill were at far range, annihilated by rockets or air strikes. We avoided any Afghan civilian deaths. In time, my interpreters even made it to the United States. I sleep soundly at night. I had a good war.

Many of my friends who served have not been so lucky. One left a leg in Kandahar. Several will struggle with post-traumatic stress for the rest of their lives. Relaying the words of a Spetsnaz veteran of Russia's war in Afghanistan, one close friend told me: "It's like having the TV on in the background. You can turn it down but you can't turn it off." Most veterans I know have lost more friends and comrades to suicide than they did to the enemy.

What the Afghans call "the American War" ended suddenly in August 2021. As the final American forces withdrew, the Afghan government in Kabul collapsed with surprising speed. Everywhere I served in Helmand had fallen to the Taliban years earlier. Thanks to either Providence or dumb luck, I paid little price for my participation in America's longest foreign war. Our country can't say the same.

FROM SOLDIER TO WITNESS

Elliott Woods

My recruiter's name was Spicer. He was Army, but I don't recall his rank. He was average-looking in every way, and I remember little about him or his office in Richmond, Virginia. It was July 2001 and I was in a tough spot, having just failed out of college and gotten word from my father that there would be no help from him if I wanted to try again in the fall.

Working two minimum-wage jobs and feeling pretty down on myself, I was ripe for the picking. Spicer left a flyer on my windshield while I was at work one day, offering full tuition at any state university and a stipend for books and living expenses, all for the low price of one weekend a month and two weeks of annual summer training for six years. The Virginia Army National Guard was hard up for combat engineers that year, which meant Spicer was able to sweeten the deal with an $8,000 bonus. Truth is, the bonus wasn't really necessary. I would've paid to get out of Richmond right about then.

I was an easy recruit: I didn't need any medical or physical waivers, I had no criminal record, I passed the military aptitude tests with flying colors, and, best of all, I was desperate. Looking back, I can't remember asking any questions at all when I visited Spicer's office to go over the enlistment paperwork. I didn't even bother to tell my family until it was already a done deal.

My parents were supportive—thrilled, in fact—because they were worried about me. They hoped, as I did, that the military would straighten me out. It had worked for my dad when he was a wayward youth. He'd flunked out of college, too, then went to sea at nineteen as a deckhand on a merchant marine ship. This led to an appointment to the US Merchant Marine Academy in Kings Point, New York, and then a career as a naval aviator and eventually a Navy surgeon.

I didn't have a grand vision for a military career of the kind my dad had found at Kings Point. But I was in a hurry to redeem myself, and I remember thinking that what had worked for my dad just might work for me. What none of us knew that summer was that two wars were looming just out of view—wars that would require unprecedented deployments of reservists, including members of the National Guard. Those wars would consume my life for nearly two decades, first as a soldier and then as a civilian journalist. They would galvanize my opposition to existing US foreign policy and cause me to question the foundations of my identity as a citizen and as a veteran.

Hardly any aspect of my worldview has been left untouched by the wars. I've seen what relatively few Americans from my generation have seen—the fear, injustice, poverty, and violent death that accompany war. I've also seen the marks that grief leaves on the faces of parents who've lost their sons. Some of their sons were my friends.

My military service and my years as a journalist covering the Middle East, Afghanistan, and veterans back home have given me rare insight. Yet this insight has come at a heavy price. It's a price that wasn't worth paying—not for me, not for our country, and not for the countries that we left in ruins.

* * *

I WAS FOLDING clothes in the stockroom of the Banana Republic at Regency Square Mall in Richmond—one of my two jobs—on the morning of September 11, 2001. There was a little radio in the back and I was listening to some dumb morning drive-time comedy show. The hosts started talking about a plane crashing into one of the World Trade Center towers in New York City. At first it seemed like a simple accident. My shift ended at nine o'clock, and by the time I got home, the second plane had already hit the South Tower. My decision to enlist suddenly seemed a lot more serious. A month later, I was on a flight to Missouri to begin basic training.

The Soviet Union was a decade in the grave by the time I showed up at Fort Leonard Wood, where the Army trains combat engineers. But we were still training to fight the Soviets in the Fulda Gap, or at least that's what it seemed like to me. On the rifle range, we shot plastic silhouettes with red stars on their chests nicknamed Crazy Ivans. It was the twenty-first century, but barely. Some of my drill sergeants had been stationed in Germany or Korea, and most of them had deployed to the Balkans or to the Persian Gulf War of 1991. They taught us how to blow up an obstacle with Bangalore torpedoes, just like the engineers in the opening scene of *Saving Private Ryan*, which had come out only three years earlier.

It's weird thinking about it now, but even though the last big war had been Vietnam—a brutal counterinsurgency fight against an often invisible enemy—we mostly trained to fight conventional forces in set-piece battles. We learned how to build eleven-row concertina wire fences to stop speeding tanks, how to sweep for all different kinds of mines and probe for them on our bellies. We also learned about explosives, from shape charges to cratering charges and C-4. I loved all of it—especially the range days, like the time we set off so much demo that car-sized chunks of mud flew fifty feet in the air and clods came thumping down on the roof of our observation shack a couple hundred yards away.

If there was one throwback to Vietnam that particularly stood out, besides the instruction on claymore mines, it was the class on booby traps. The ones we were shown were usually small and attached to trip wires—the kinds of things you might run into if you were crawling through a Vietcong tunnel. Some of the mock-ups I remember were clever to the point of being ridiculous, such as a little bomb embedded in a book. However, I don't remember hearing the term *improvised explosive device* (IED) at any point during my engineer training. I wouldn't receive any formal counter-IED training until years later, on the eve of my deployment. The first generation of post-9/11 recruits, we would go on to witness the rapid evolution of a weapon that would kill thousands of

Americans and tens of thousands of Iraqis and Afghans, but all of that was unknown to me at the time.

Not that there weren't plenty of clues about what lay ahead: the 1983 embassy and marine barracks bombings in Beirut, the Khobar Towers bombing in Saudi Arabia in 1996, the East Africa embassy bombings in 1998, and the USS *Cole* bombing in 2000, to name just a few. All these attacks, along with horrific domestic terrorism incidents—the bombing of a federal building in Oklahoma City in 1995 and the Atlanta Olympics in 1996—offered ominous warnings about the emerging threat of homemade explosives in the hands of guerrillas and terrorists. But the future had not quite arrived at Fort Leonard Wood in the waning days of 2001 and the first months of 2002. Instead of learning counter-IED tactics and training on the anti-mine vehicles many of us would eventually drive, we shot at Crazy Ivans and blew tank ditches, training to fight the war that never was—the Cold War.

I don't blame my drill sergeants and classroom instructors for failing to school us on counter-IED techniques. They were simply teaching the doctrine they themselves had received. And besides, the most important thing I got out of basic training had nothing to do with tactics. For me, the payoff after fourteen weeks was that I would get my life back. I was fit and confident, ready to get back to college the next fall. More than anything, I was proud that I could go back to my family knowing that I had taken a big step in the right direction after disappointing them for so many years.

For a while after I first arrived at Fort Leonard Wood, the drill sergeants had me convinced that I would ship out to Afghanistan as soon as I graduated, and since I was cut off from the world, I had no reason to doubt them. I had a general idea of where Afghanistan was, and vague memories of watching footage of the mujahideen during the Soviet war in the 1980s, when I was a kid. But I had no idea what I would encounter if I were ever deployed to fight there. I knew nothing about the Taliban and almost nothing about al-Qaeda. At any rate, for me Afghanistan never happened. By the time I hit the halfway point of my basic training, in December 2001, al-Qaeda had been mostly chased out of Afghanistan, and the Taliban government had collapsed. My deployment would come two years later, to a new war in Iraq.

We received the alert order in late 2003 and spent January and February of 2004 in mobilization training at Fort Dix, New Jersey. It happened to be one of the coldest winters in memory, so it was almost a relief to touch down in the sweltering Kuwaiti heat en route to Mosul, Iraq. I would go on to spend a year in northern Iraq, my unit assigned to carry out a variety of odd jobs that rarely seemed to build toward any greater objective.

My platoon was ordered to an old Iraqi air base in Qayyarah, about seventy-five miles from Mosul. We ran convoy security missions, pulled gate guard, and built triple-strand concertina fences around the base perimeter. Sometimes I drove a Humvee for my squad leader; other times I manned the machine gun or grenade launcher mounted on top of the vehicle. At some point during our tour, we got a Husky—a South African–designed minesweeping vehicle engineered to absorb the blast of a land mine without injuring the driver. From that point forward, I was one of the platoon's Husky drivers, responsible for operating the machine on counter-

IED patrols up and down Highway 1, also known as Main Supply Route Tampa.

On days when I didn't drive the Husky, I manned the turret in the gun truck that followed behind. That's where I was when our convoy hit an IED on the way back to base one day in the summer of 2004. Fortunately for all of us, the brunt of the blast passed between the Husky and the vehicle in front of it. I remember seeing the fireball rise up from the road and passing through the smoke cloud seconds later. I scanned my sector from the turret, but there was no one and nothing to shoot at. The desert on either side of the highway was empty.

During my year in Iraq, the relative post-invasion calm would be shattered by the emergence of a ferocious insurgency. In April and November 2004, the First and Second Battles of Fallujah destroyed any hope of a simple exit from Iraq for the United States. But all of that seemed far from Qayyarah, where things stayed eerily quiet except for the occasional rocket or mortar attack. That one occasion when an invisible IED triggerman fired on my convoy and missed was the only time in Iraq when I felt as though my life was immediately threatened. Not everyone from my unit was so lucky.

On December 21, 2004, a suicide bomber sneaked into Forward Operating Base Marez in Mosul, where my battalion was headquartered, and detonated his vest in the chow hall. The blast killed twenty-two people, including two young soldiers from my company—Nicholas Mason and David Ruhren. They were both twenty years old. I wasn't there that day because I was in Qayyarah with my platoon. We learned what had happened later that evening when our company commander called us down to the command post to break the news. I remember the withering intensity of that moment. And all these years later, I still have no good answer for why it was them and not me. I have no good answer for why any of the deaths in Iraq or Afghanistan were necessary either. They didn't buy us more national security, they didn't avenge any of the 9/11 dead, and ultimately they didn't improve the lives of the people on the ground.

The soldier's old comfort is to think that death and sacrifice on the battlefield aren't really about the bigger picture—they're about love in the brotherhood of arms, about protecting the guys to your right and left. But that never got me very far. What is the meaning of personal sacrifice in foolish and wasteful wars with ill-defined objectives that hardly any of us understood even while we were serving in them? And if the big picture didn't matter—if we served just for the guys on the right and the left, or because it was our job—then how were we different from mercenaries?

I was most of the way toward recognizing myself as a dissenter by the time my unit returned from Iraq in early 2005. I had never really believed the case for war against Saddam Hussein, and I wasn't surprised when the canard about weapons of mass destruction fell apart. While I was in Iraq, I heard about how maybe what the war was *really* about was avenging the genocidal attacks Saddam launched against the Kurds in the 1980s and early 1990s. But that didn't make much sense to me, because the United States had done nothing to stop Saddam's massacres at the time—on the contrary, Saddam had been a US ally when he ordered chemical weapons attacks against Iraqi Kurdish towns in 1988, killing as many as ten thousand people. I read about all of this during my thirty-minute sessions on the base's computers, in the vast recreation center that had sprouted fully formed from the Iraqi dirt.

Somewhere along the way, I encountered the phrase *fraud, waste, and abuse*, and that seemed to fit the grotesque outlay of resources on the large bases where I spent time. As much as I appreciated our air-conditioned chow hall, and the steak and the crab legs and the Mongolian stir-fry, I couldn't help thinking that it was all a bit much. Sometimes it felt less like a war than a giant boondoggle to benefit the big contracting companies like Kellogg Brown & Root. I thought it was peculiar that we had Sri Lankans working in our chow hall, Filipinas doing our laundry, and Turks handing out basketballs in the recreation center. It all seemed colonial and corporate. And I definitely found it repulsive that the American KBR employees were making five or ten times my salary.

It was only after I got home that I began to learn about the multibillion-dollar no-bid contracts that companies like KBR received to provide logistics and construction services in Iraq. The debate back home about whether the war was just about capturing Iraqi oil was still simmering when I returned to college in 2005, but as far as I could see, any future oil contracts for American companies would be icing on the cake. The money was already in the bank from the logistical operations before the first boots even hit the ground. And it kept flowing for years, while more Americans died and got critically wounded, and Iraq was torn to shreds in the security vacuum created by Saddam's removal.

I watched the chaos unfolding in Iraq from the safety of Charlottesville, Virginia, where I felt like a bit of an alien. I made friends through working at a running shop and joining the cycling team, but I was older in more ways than one. I didn't know any other veterans. My friends and acquaintances knew that I had served in Iraq and was still serving in the National Guard, but they didn't ask many questions. I might have opened up if they had asked. I might have told them about how much I enjoyed getting to know some of the Iraqi soldiers and how green the northern Iraqi plains were in the spring when we first arrived, before the summer heat scorched away every last bit of color. I might've told them that I never fired my weapon—that some days I wished I had, and other days I was almost more thankful for having never killed than for having survived.

I might've told them about my best friend, who shot and killed a civilian at a checkpoint in a moment of confusion, and how that one story seemed to sum up the entire war for me. And I might've told them about the mass grave site where I worked for a month providing security while forensic pathologists exhumed the remains of Kurds murdered by Saddam's henchmen. I might've told them about how the bodies buried in the dry soil of Iraq for fifteen years had become almost mummified, and how the remaining moisture in their skin filled the air with the unmistakable odor of decaying flesh. Some of the men were in their suits, as if they'd dressed up for the occasion of being thrown into the back of a truck and carted out to the barrens to be shot. The women were swathed in abayas and floral-print dresses. One of them had a baby in her arms. They all had small holes in the backs of their skulls.

As I made my way through college, I thought of Mason and Ruhren often. Both had started college before we deployed and would've gone back to finish after we got home. I tried to live in their memory, pushing myself to study hard and exercise like a madman. If I slowed the pace, I felt as if I were letting them down. Then, in my final year of college, my unit redeployed to Iraq. Although my contract was up, the Army could have ordered me to deploy anyway—a policy called stop-loss allowed that. But I had recently broken my arm, so I got listed as medically non-deployable, which meant I got to stay home and finish school.

It was 2007 and the Iraq "surge" was in full swing. My former unit went to Baghdad to do counter-IED patrols, and my old squad lasted only a couple of weeks before they hit a massive IED that killed two men and severely wounded three more. A few months later, another IED claimed the life of a guy I had served with during all my six years in the Guard, a soft-spoken kid from Norfolk, Virginia, named Jeremiah McNeal.

These deaths and injuries among my former unit devastated me and made it difficult to imagine a future in which I would be free from the war, even if I knew that I would never again carry a rifle in a combat zone. I started thinking about what I could do to channel my guilt, anger, and sadness into something worthwhile. As luck would have it, I happened to meet a magazine editor as all these thoughts were swirling in my head. He offered me an assignment to write about my unit's tour in Iraq. That day, a new chapter in my personal war story began.

* * *

Journalism is often described as a vocation rather than a trade—not a job but a calling. In my case, the call came from the men I served with in Iraq, who came home to a country that thanked them for their service but had little interest in understanding what they had actually done overseas or what they had left behind. The call came from weary Iraqis whom I patted down at the gate to our base—men who couldn't afford to pass up the opportunity to make a few dollars doing day labor for the Americans, even though the identification we issued could get them killed on the other side of the wire. The call came from the hollowed-out expression on a mother's face as our chaplain thanked her for her son's "ultimate sacrifice," from the tremble in her hand as she raised a cigarette to her lips. It came from the realization that my education gave me skills to interrogate the wars in a way that many of my fellow veterans could not.

I had a desire to go back and confront what most of us just wanted to forget. I became a journalist because there were questions I had to ask, and seeking answers seemed a matter of life and death.

How did hundreds of thousands of mostly young American men and women wind up sagging under the weight of body armor and weapons in a country that many of us could not find on a map, learning to hate the very people we were sent to help? Did Americans realize things were not going as planned, that tens of thousands of Iraqis were dying in a civil war that our invasion had unleashed? How was it possible that we charged into the same kind of quagmire that killed fifty-eight thousand American troops and two million civilians in Vietnam? Would we remember this time around, so that we might avoid forcing the same tragedy onto our children?

When I was nearing graduation from college, I knew that I had to return to the Middle East as a journalist to answer these questions. I had absorbed the work of Vietnam veterans Tim O'Brien, Philip Caputo, and Oliver Stone, the Korean War fiction of James Salter, and the World War II writings of James Jones and Paul Fussell. The distance between America's twentieth-century wars and the wars of my generation closed. Iraq and Afghanistan seemed part of a much larger "forever war," to expand on Dexter Filkins's phrase. That war ebbs and sometimes skips a whole generation, but it always returns with lethal ferocity, forming a bloody continuum of imperialism that extends from Wounded Knee to Manila, Managua, Hue, Mosul, and Kandahar.

That first assignment, which I wrote for the *Virginia Quarterly Review*, profiled the grieving parents of Nick Mason and David Ruhren, the two soldiers from my unit who were killed in the Mosul chow hall suicide bombing in December 2004, a few weeks before our unit was due to rotate home. Pulling into the parents' driveways and walking up to their doorsteps was the hardest thing I had ever done—much harder than racking a round in the chamber and heading out on patrol. I knew I would force them to relive the most awful moments of their lives, when other soldiers had come to their doors to deliver news of their sons' deaths. But they welcomed me, unguarded. They did not fight the tears, because four years after the bombing there were no brave faces left to put on.

I also interviewed an older NCO from my unit who had been a father figure to the soldiers who were killed. He had reenlisted in a fit of post-9/11 patriotism after many years as a civilian, stoked by American flag magnets and the repetition of video footage of the Twin Towers collapsing. He joined to get revenge—*Never forget!*—and now his own life had been shattered by guilt and the lingering effects of combat exposure.

With my notebooks full, I sat down to write. This was no term paper, no intellectual exercise. These people had placed their most intimate memories and emotions into my hands and given me permission to try to make sense of it all. I have never forgotten the gratitude I felt for their willingness to simply talk to me or the sense of purpose I felt when they entrusted their stories to me. They showed me how to talk about difficult subjects with openness, humility, and courage—a lesson that has informed my work ever since.

A decade later, I am still making sense of it all. The effort has taken me back to Iraq and to Tahrir Square, Gaza, Kandahar, and over many thousands of miles of American highways. Throughout that time, I've written about the environment, immigration, and politics—fascinating and vital subjects—but the wars always call me back.

I wrote about Obama's troop surge in Afghanistan, following soldiers and marines on patrol and drinking tea with civilians who would not get to go home after a yearlong tour. I traveled to Jalal-Abad to track down the lone survivor of a helicopter attack that left eight children dead—a case of mistaken identity that Hollywood did not dramatize, but that brought the Afghanistan War into sharp focus. In Marjah, I watched marines try to save a girl who'd lost all four limbs and most of her face to an IED they knew was meant for them. When they handed her tiny corpse to her uncle, he had tears in his eyes, and so did the marines.

But they were not Good Samaritans—they were teenagers and twentysomethings who'd been trained to kill and had been doing that job well against an enemy they didn't understand. All they knew was that letting their guards down for one minute might get their friends killed. That was enough to go on in Afghanistan, but they often brought their hypervigilance with them when they came home, and sometimes their loved ones found themselves on the receiving end. One soldier I met in Kandahar carried the violence home to El Paso, Texas, where he killed someone in a fit of rage that may have had its origins in a blood-soaked Afghanistan guard tower. I took all these stories and put them into prose, photographs, and video, hoping these small contributions would, if nothing else, ensure that a record has been made. Most days, that seems like the best that any of us can hope to accomplish.

Of course, I think we ought to challenge ourselves to accomplish much more. Our overwhelming collective ignorance of (and isolation from) our recent wars does not absolve us of responsibility for the damage done in our names. We have a duty to reckon with the costs and consequences, and we have a duty to learn. Failing to meet this obligation will ensure that it was truly all for nothing. By asking hard questions about America's post-9/11 wars—and by examining the experiences of the survivors at home and abroad—I hope we can do more than inform our future decision-making. I hope we can look at ourselves honestly, and in the process come to know ourselves for who we really are: a warlike nation with a habit of visiting destruction on distant strangers for reasons that have everything to do with us and little or nothing to do with them. Looking more closely at ourselves would at least address one half of Sun Tzu's famous admonition—know the enemy and know yourself—and it might address both.

One would have to be a fool to hope that writing about

the folly of the wars and the devastation they've wreaked could prevent the next war, big or small. I suppose I am a fool, then, because I still hold on to a sliver of hope. The questions that burned inside me when I walked up those doorsteps to the Mason and Ruhren households a decade ago remain largely unanswered. Even so, journalism has provided a path out of the tunnel of my own postwar bewilderment. It allows me to help those who have served or sacrificed find meaning, understanding, and, above all, a voice.

CONCLUSION

THE PRICE OF FREE PIZZA

Andrew Bacevich

On a recent Veterans Day, merchants in my corner of New England offered vets an abundance of good deals: free coffee, free doughnuts, free pizza, free car washes, and as much as 30 percent off assorted retail purchases. Here was "thank you for your service" as something more than an empty sentiment.

I got my car washed and took a pass on the rest.

I confess that this gaudy display of generosity—mostly from franchise outlets rather than mom-and-pop stores—annoyed me. Was I witnessing an authentic display of heartfelt gratitude? Or had Veterans Day become yet one more pretext for corporate virtue-signaling?

Or consider this third possibility: in our era of "forever wars," Veterans Day may well combine elements of each. It is both contrived and genuine, cynical yet also sincere, deeply fraudulent and simultaneously expressing an important truth.

Despite such incongruities, or perhaps because of them,

Veterans Day serves an essential civic purpose. The goodies and giveaways that impart a celebratory air help to mask a contradiction lodged at the very heart of the American military system: in a nation insistent upon remaining the dominant power on the planet, only those actively *seeking* to serve actually do so. Meanwhile, the vast majority of citizens remain content to stay on the sidelines—and to distribute gratuities like doughnuts and pizza once a year.

When it comes to providing for what the Constitution refers to as the common defense, no collective obligation exists. On this point, governing authorities and most Americans are of one mind: together they have agreed to dissolve any link between citizenship and national security, thereby waiving the principle of equality on which the republic was ostensibly founded and to which American democracy today is ostensibly devoted. For earlier generations of Americans, war entailed widely shared sacrifice. Certainly, this was true of the conflicts that Americans have enshrined as formative: the Civil War and World War II. Today, however, well-established mechanisms insulate the people from wars waged in their name.

So those who serve do so voluntarily. The motives prompting them to join up vary. Among them are family tradition, ambition, the urge for adventure, the prospect of a steady job with benefits, the possibility of personal betterment, and, yes, perhaps even patriotism. Prior to Vietnam, it was also not uncommon to hear military service described as a way to "make something of oneself" or even to "become a man." In any number of pulp novels and B movies, this transformation figured as an overarching theme: time spent in uniform, especially during wartime, offering a pathway to manhood along with tutelage in the meaning of courage and honor. On this score, to don a uniform was to encounter, emulate, and ultimately exemplify masculine virtue.

I do not know whether the contributors to this volume ever subscribed to that last notion, with all its gendered baggage. I suspect that few if any of them do so today. Yet however much their actual experiences may have differed from what books and movies once led recruits to expect, they did offer a form of edification.

General Sherman's famous dictum that "war is hell" is accurate as far as it goes. Yet though essentially true, it turns out in practice to be insufficient. To participate in war is to submit to an involuntary education, one that demolishes preconceived notions, both superficial and profound, about matters ranging from one's self to the meaning of human existence. War burns away naïveté. In at least some participants, very much including the contributors to this volume, it leaves a residue of wisdom.

"You did not return from hell with empty hands." So wrote a French intellectual to an American journalist who had served as a Soviet agent during the 1930s. Even allowing for Gallic hyperbole, a similar judgment pertains to the writers whose essays appear in *Paths of Dissent*. They have not returned to civilian life with empty hands. In sharing what they experienced in uniform and in charting their individual journeys to dissent, they offer their fellow citizens an invaluable opportunity to learn from and reflect on the last twenty years of disastrous military misadventures.

What we Americans owe vets is not free pizza but the

decency to hear them out and ponder what they have learned. There is value in their testimony. To listen attentively is the least the rest of us can do. It just may be that as citizens we do have an obligation after all.

ACKNOWLEDGMENTS

This project would never have come to fruition without the timely support of the Lannan Foundation. On behalf of Danny Sjursen and myself, I want to thank Lannan, and especially Sarah Knopp, director of Lannan's Cultural Freedom Program, for providing the wherewithal that made *Paths of Dissent* possible. This is not the first instance in which Danny and I have individually benefited from the Lannan Foundation's generosity. It is one of America's underappreciated treasures.

Thanks also to John Wright, my estimable agent; to Sara Bershtel, the esteemed publisher of Metropolitan Books; and especially to Grigory Tovbis, senior editor at Metropolitan, who skillfully transformed a pile of essays into a book in which Danny and I take real pride.

Danny and I owe a special debt to all those who contributed to this collection. We appreciate the patience and good humor of those who worked with us through multiple revisions. We hope that they can join us in finding satisfaction in the result.

I will conclude on a personal note. Danny and I have worked together on this project from conception to completion. It has been a most gratifying partnership. I am honored to call him my friend.

Andrew Bacevich
Walpole, Massachusetts
December 2021

ABOUT THE CONTRIBUTORS

Andrew Bacevich (coeditor) grew up in Indiana, graduated from West Point and Princeton, and served in the Army. Presently the president of the Quincy Institute for Responsible Statecraft, he is the author of many books, among them *The New American Militarism*, *The Limits of Power*, *America's War for the Greater Middle East*, and *After the Apocalypse: America's Role in a World Transformed*.

Daniel A. Sjursen (coeditor) grew up in Staten Island, New York, graduated from West Point and the University of Kansas, served tours in Iraq and Afghanistan, taught history at West Point, and is now an author, activist, and senior fellow at the Center for International Policy. He is the author of two books, *Ghost Riders of Baghdad* and *Patriotic Dissent*, and cohosts the *Fortress on a Hill* podcast.

Gil Barndollar is a senior research fellow at the Catholic University of America's Center for the Study of Statesmanship.

From 2009 to 2016, he served as an infantry officer in the United States Marine Corps. He is working on a book examining America's all-volunteer force, conscription, and future national security threats.

Dan Berschinski grew up in Georgia, graduated from West Point, and served as a rifle platoon leader in Afghanistan's Arghandab River valley in 2009. While leading his men on a patrol, Lieutenant Berschinski stepped on an IED, which severed both his legs above his knees. He spent almost four years at Walter Reed Army Medical Center and became the military's first above-the-knee and hip-disarticulation amputee to be able to walk with prosthetics. Following his medical retirement, he attended graduate school at Stanford University and is now a small business owner in Atlanta.

Joy Damiani, originally from Syracuse, New York, was an enlisted Army public affairs specialist from 2002 to 2008, including two deployments to Baghdad, Iraq, and since 2010 has engaged in public critique of US wars and the military-industrial complex. In addition to contributing to various news and literary publications, Damiani is a songwriter, musician, poet, artist, cohost of the podcast *What the Folk*, and author of a darkly comic military memoir, *If You Ain't Cheatin', You Ain't Tryin': And Other Lessons I Learned in the Army*.

Daniel L. Davis retired from the US Army as a lieutenant colonel after twenty-one years of active service and currently serves as senior fellow at the Defense Priorities think tank. During his career, he deployed into combat zones four times, beginning with Operation Desert Storm in 1991, followed by Iraq in 2009 and Afghanistan in 2005 and 2011. He was awarded the Bronze Star Medal for valor at the Battle of 73 Easting in 1991 and a Bronze Star Medal for service in Afghanistan in 2011.

Jason Dempsey served for twenty-two years as an infantry officer in the US Army. He served in leadership and staff assignments in airborne, Ranger, mechanized, and air assault units, and last served as special assistant to the chairman of the Joint Chiefs of Staff. During his career he deployed to Kuwait, Iraq, and Afghanistan, and he has written extensively on the military's failures in those efforts. He is a graduate of the United States Military Academy at West Point and holds a PhD in political science from Columbia University.

Erik Edstrom was raised in Stoughton, Massachusetts, graduated from West Point in 2007, and then deployed to Afghanistan, where he served as an infantry platoon leader. He graduated from the US Army Ranger School, received the Rippetoe Trophy during the Best Ranger competition, and was selected for the US Special Forces. After leaving the Army as a captain, Erik earned both an MBA and a master of science degree from Oxford University, where he studied climate change. He is the author of *Un-American: A Soldier's Reckoning of Our Longest War.*

Vincent Emanuele served in the United States Marine Corps from 2002 to 2006. After his second combat deployment to Iraq, he refused orders for a third deployment and joined Iraq Veterans Against the War. In 2008, he testified before the United States Congress about rules of engagement, torture, and war crimes. His story has been featured in documentary films such as *We Are Many* and *On the Bridge.* He cofounded Politics Art Roots Culture (PARC), a community cultural center in Michigan City, Indiana.

Gian Gentile is a senior historian at the RAND Corporation. Before joining RAND, he completed thirty-two years of active service in the US Army, including assignments in the United States, Korea, and Europe. His final assignment was as director of West Point's Military History Program. Gentile served two combat tours in Iraq, in 2003 as a brigade executive officer and in 2006 as commander of a cavalry squadron in west Baghdad. A graduate of the Army's School of Advanced Military Studies, he holds a BA from the University of California, Berkeley and a doctorate in history from Stanford.

Matthew P. Hoh is a senior fellow with the Center for International Policy in Washington. In 2009 he resigned his position with the State Department in Afghanistan to protest the Obama administration's escalation of the Afghanistan War. He had previously served in Iraq with a State Department team and as a US Marine officer. He is a 100 percent disabled veteran.

Jonathan W. Hutto Sr., a native of Atlanta, embraced his calling as a human rights organizer while an undergraduate at Howard University in the late 1990s. Just shy of his twenty-seventh birthday in 2004, he enlisted in the US Navy. During his enlistment, Hutto served as the initial catalyst for the Appeal for Redress, which organized over two thousand active-duty, reserve, and National Guard personnel to send protected communications to Congress advocating for an end to the Afghanistan and Iraq Wars. In 2007, the appeal received the Letelier-Moffitt Human Rights Award from the Institute for Policy Studies.

Buddhika Jayamaha was born and raised in Sri Lanka. Upon completing his undergraduate and master's degrees in the United States, he enlisted in the Army as an airborne infantryman. He served in Iraq with the 82nd Airborne Division. After leaving the Army, he earned a PhD in political science from Northwestern University and is now an assistant professor in the Department of Military and Strategic Studies at the US Air Force Academy.

Roy Scranton grew up in a working-class family in Oregon and dropped out of college after his freshman year. In 2002, he enlisted in the US Army and served four years, including a fourteen-month deployment to Iraq. After leaving the Army at the rank of sergeant, he resumed his education, eventually earning a PhD in English at Princeton. Currently an associate professor of English at the University of Notre Dame, he is the author of several books, including *Learning to Die in the Anthropocene: Reflections on the End of a Civilization*, *Total Mobilization: World War II and American Literature*, and the novel *War Porn*.

Kevin Tillman was born and raised in San Jose, California. After the attacks of 9/11, he left the Cleveland Indians minor league baseball system and enlisted in the Army with his brother Pat, an NFL standout. They were stationed together at 2/75 Ranger Battalion and served in Iraq and Afghanistan. On April 22, 2004, Pat was killed in Afghanistan. Kevin was honorably discharged in July 2005 after finishing his enlistment.

Elliott Woods is a writer and acclaimed photojournalist based in Bozeman, Montana. An Iraq War veteran, he subsequently reported extensively from the Middle East and Afghanistan, focusing in particular on telling the stories of war veterans to an indifferent public. His work has received numerous honors, including the 2011 National Magazine Award for Multimedia. He is a graduate of the University of Virginia and a contributing editor at the *Virginia Quarterly Review.*

Paul Yingling was born and raised in Pittsburgh, and enlisted in the US Army at the age of seventeen. He served for most of his twenty-eight-year military career as a field artillery officer, including deployments in the 1991 Gulf War, the 1995 NATO intervention in the former Yugoslavia, and three tours in Iraq between 2003 and 2009. He holds a master's degree in political science from the University of Chicago, and is a graduate of the US Army's School of Advanced Military Studies. He has written and spoken extensively on military adaptation and irregular warfare, and is the author of "A Failure in Generalship."